The Commentators' Machzor Companion

by
Rav Yitzchak Sender

The Commentators' Machzor Companion

❦ ❦ ❦

Insights of the Sages on the High Holiday Prayers

by
Rav Yitzchak Sender

The Commentators' Machzor Companion

Copyright © 1998 **Rabbi Yitzchak Sender**
All rights reserved.

No part of this book may be used
or reproduced in any form without written
permission from the publisher, except for
brief quotations in reviews.

Address of the Author
Rabbi Yitzchak Sender
6620 North Whipple
Chicago, Il. 60645
Tel. (773) 274-8384

Distributed by
Phillip Feldheim, Inc.
200 Airport Executive Park
Nanuet, NY 10954

First Edition, August 1998

Printed in the United States of America

Printing by Laine, Ltd.
Brooklyn, New York

ספר זה מוקדש בהיכל התורה לזכרון עולם
להני תרי צנתרות הזהב

הרב משה ורניק ז"ל
והרב דר. יוסף באבד ז"ל

הונצח ע"י תלמידם
הרב משה אספורמס שיחי'

This sefer is dedicated
in fond memory of

Rabbi Moshe Wernik
and
Rabbi Dr. Yosef Babad

by their devoted student
Rabbi Moshe Esformes

אלון בכות
לזכרה ולע"נ של האשה הצנועה
מוכתרת בעין טובה
מרתביילא
בת
חיים יוסף אליעזר

הונצח על יד נכדיה
Marc and Debbi Geller

לזכרון עולם בהיכל ה'

ר' יעיש בן דוד ע"ה
מרת זהר בת מכלוף ע"ה

ר' אפרים ב"ר יצחק מאיר רימל ע"ה
מרת דבורה בת ר' יוסף מאניס ע"ה

ברכה
מהגאון הגדול, פאר הדור,
מרן ר' שלמה זלמן אויערבאך זצוק"ל
ראש הישיבה "קול תורה" בירושלים
ומחבר ספר "מעדני ארץ" ב"ח ועוד

ב"ה

כבד איתמחי האי גברא יקירא ידידי הרה"ג המופלא והמהולל מוה"ר יצחק אייזיק סנדר שליט"א ונודע לתהלה בספריו היקרים שזכה לחבר על הרבה ענינים חשובים וגדולי תורה נתנו עליהם עדותם ויהללו אותם. אשר על כן גם יקרתו של ספר חשוב זה תעיד על ערכו החשוב וכל מכתב תהלה אך למותר הוא. רק מברך אני את ידידי הרה"ג המחבר שנותן התורה יהא בעזרו וימלא משאלות לבו להיות שבתו כל הימים באהלה של תורה ולהרביץ תורה לרבים מתוך הרחבה ושמחה וגם יפוצו מעינותיו חוצה להג- דיל תורה ולהאדירה כאות נפשו ונפש ידידו ומוקירו.

שלמה זלמן אויערבאך

Table of Contents

Preface I

Selichos

The Seder Selichos 3
Selichos and Prayer: One Mitzva or Two? 17
Selichos at Night 30
The Meaning of Selichos: To Attain a Pure Heart 43
The Ashrei Prayer 51
The Kaddish — יתגדל 64
The Thirteen Attributes of Mercy: י״ג מדות 71

Rosh Hashanah Night

The Chazzan of the High Holy Days: Requirements 89
The Nine Berachos of the Rosh Hashanah Amidah 98
Remember Us For Life 116
The Blessing of Kedushas Hashem 125
The Requirement of המלך הקדוש and המלך המשפט 143
The Rosh Hashanah Kiddush 153
Various Customs of Rosh Hashanah 160

Rosh Hashanah Day

Why No Hallel on Rosh Hashanah? 169
The Order of the Mussaf Amidah Prayers 184
The Akeida and Its Implications For Us 190
למנצח Said Before Sounding the Shofar 211

Sources For the Ten Verses.. 221
The Ten Verses of the מז״ש: An Overview...................... 227
Outline of the Verses of מז״ש 240
Why Are the Kesuvim Verses From Tehillim?.............. 244
There is No One Besides You — מלכיות 249
"ה׳ ימלוך לעולם ועד": Its Place in the מלכיות 255
"ויהי בישורון מלך".. 265
"ותרועת מלך בו"... 273
The Unusual Place of "Shema Yisrael" in Malchiyus ... 283
"מלך ישראל וגואלו" 295
"שאו שערים": One Verse or Four?..................................... 300
The Controversy Over the Pasuk of "וביום שמחתכם"........ 313
The Order of the Verses: מלכיות זכרונות ושופרות................ 323
The Issue of "אדיר המלוכה" 333
Zichronos 343
The Verses of Zichronos 350

Yom Kippur Night

Kol Nidre... 361
"ברוך שם כבוד מלכותו לעולם ועד":
    Said Aloud on Yom Kippur.................... 367

Yom Kippur Day

The Nusach of the Yom Kippur Amidah....................... 387
The Seder of the Avodah 393
The Law of Prostrating Oneself in the Avodah............ 419
The Minchah Torah Reading on Yom Kippur 427
The Sounding of the Shofar 436

Preface

Halacha requires the laws of a holiday to be studied thirty days before that particular holiday. Chazal tell us:

"שואלין ודורשין בהלכות הפסח קודם הפסח שלשים יום".

"Questions are asked and lectures given on the laws of Pesach for thirty days preceding Pesach."

Most commentators maintain that this law is not unique to Pesach, but applies to the other holidays as well. And there is a disagreement among the commentators as to whether or not Rosh Hashanah is included. But in actual fact we know that there is no other holiday for which we begin to prepare ourselves spiritually thirty days in advance as we do for Rosh Hashanah. It is during this period of Elul that we turn all our attention to the process of repentance, *teshuvah,* by sounding the shofar early each morning, adding the recitation of Psalm 27, "לדוד ה' אורי" to our prayers and reciting Selichos. (Indeed, it is the custom of the Sefardim to recite Selichos the whole month of Elul.) Many begin this *teshuvah* process even earlier, in the month of Tammuz, for the acronym of this Hebrew month of תמוז is equivalent to "those who are zealous are quick to repent," זריזים מקדימין ועושין תשובה.

But why do we "sound the alarm" so early rather than wait until just before Rosh Hashanah, the Day of Judgement, to begin our process of *teshuvah*. Why do we devote an entire month to feelings of remorse for past transgressions and resolve to improve in the future? The obvious answer to this question (as we discuss in the chapter on "The Order of the Selichos") is that *teshuvah* must take place in a prescribed order, gradually. It must not be merely a fleeting momentary feeling of remorse. Crocodile tears will not achieve true repentance; that can only be achieved through concentrated, prolonged serious efforts.

The Chofetz Chaim was once asked why he insisted that specific works of mussar should be studied each day. Wouldn't it be sufficient to study the ethical teachings which we find contained in the Gemara? The Chofetz Chaim answered with a parable.

It is known that in Poland roadside inns are situated at appreciable distances from each other; whereas in Siberia the Russians set up inns relatively close to each other. Why? Simply because the climate in Poland is gentler than it is in Siberia, and therefore people need to stop at inns to warm up less frequently and at greater intervals. But in Siberia, where the cold is harsh and the roads frozen and covered with snow most of the year, the

Preface

traveler needs to warm his body and thaw his frozen feet after traveling relatively shorter distances. This is why they set up inns so much closer to each other.

This can be compared to the study of mussar. In earlier generations, when people were on a higher spiritual level and they were steeped in faith, it was possible to learn mussar through the study of Gemara, where words of ethical reproof appear only occasionally and at appreciable intervals. But in our generation, when frigid winds blow and chill our hearts, we need to turn to the inns to warm our freezing bodies every day. Thus it is incumbent on us to warm ourselves every day through the study of specific works of mussar, in order to thaw our frozen hearts.

This, then, is the answer why we need to make extended efforts to do *teshuvah* for a whole month prior to the Day of Judgement. We must thaw out our frozen emotions with a barrage of warm prayers for ourselves, our loved ones and Klal Yisrael, in order to approach the day of Rosh Hashanah in the appropriate spirit.

We can carry the Chofetz Chaim's analogy even further. We know that in order to warm someone who has become frozen, we give him a shot of whiskey. Similarly, to warm us up spiritually, we need prayers. Thus we pray throughout the month of Elul — during the day, late at night, and even before dawn. And to this end we add unique prayers on these days and especially on Rosh Hashanah itself. These include many piyutim, composed by tzaddikim, poets who had a flair for the Hebrew language and great knowledge of the midrashic literature. These piyutim help us thaw out from a long and tedious year of spiritual numbness.

We offer this new volume in the "Commentators'" series to acquaint the reader with the makeup of the High Holy day prayers, which contain these unique additions to the usual yearly prayers. We hope this sefer will enable the reader to gain a deeper understanding of the well thought out structure and purpose of the Rosh Hashanah and Yom Kippur prayers, and to realize that they are not simply a random assortment of psalms and fragments of poems, but rather מלאכת מחשבת — a blueprint for effectively attaining our spiritual goals on these special days.

My prayer is that by studying this sefer one's prayer on Rosh Hashanah will be more meaningful and the reader, his loved ones and Klal Yisrael will be inscribed for a good year, לחיים טובים, a year in which we merit to see the coming of the Moshiach and that the Bais HaMikdash will be rebuilt so that we will merit to offer once again the

Preface

required sacrifices in the prescribed order on Yom Kippur, סדר־העבודה.

Once again, I wish to express my sincere and heartfelt gratitude to all those contributors who have made this publication possible. I am grateful not only for their generosity in material terms, but also the generosity of spirit evident in the gracious manner in which their contributions were given. I also offer my heartfelt thanks to my editor and friend, Mrs. Wendy Dickstein, who has, as always, given of herself above and beyond the call of duty. Her talents and dedication have made this volume what it is. Finally and most importantly, my gratitude to my dear wife, נחמה תחי׳, who has always been most encouraging, patient and understanding of the time and effort required to finish this book. May Hashem bless her and our children and grandchildren, along with Klal Yisrael, that our prayers be received on High for a כתיבה וחתימה טובה and for the imminent coming of the Moshiach, במהרה בימינו אמן.

The Seder Selichos: סדר הסליחות

I
The importance of order

In Elul, the month before Rosh Hashanah, prayers of supplication, called "סדר הסליחות" are recited. These prayers were initially composed of verses taken from the Tanach, *Kisvei HaKodesh*, which allude to the theme of forgiveness, "סליחה". This theme explains why they are called "סליחות". This parallels the three main prayers of the Mussaf of Rosh Hashanah which quotes verses from Tanach alluding to the themes of Kingship, Remembrance, and Shofar — מלכות, זכרונות ושופרות. These sections are therefore referred to as מלכיות, זכרונות ושופרות. Later, however, the Selichos were expanded to include additional liturgical poems, called *piyutim* (פיוטים). These prayers are referred to as the *"order of the prayers of repentance"*, סדר הסליחות, for they follow a definite prescribed order.

The requirement of a specified order, or סדר, also applies to the following Mitzvos:

1) סדר תפלה, The Amidah prayer must begin with *praise*, then *petition* and finally, expressions of *thanksgiving* — שבחות, צרכיו, הודאה.

2) The Sacrificial Offerings of Yom Kippur must follow a specific sequence, which is referred to as "סדר העבודה".

3) The Pesach Seder also follows a prescribed order, which includes the eating of *matzah, maror, Korban Pesach* and retelling the story of the Exodus from Egypt.

In these three instances, if the prescribed order is not followed, then the Mitzva has not been fulfilled. Thus, for the Selichos prayers, which are referred to as the סדר הסליחות:

1) the prescribed order must be followed.

2) failure to follow that order results in non-fulfillment of the Mitzva.

This raises the following questions.

1) What is the actual order required in the Selichos prayers?

2) Why does failure to adhere to that specific order result in non-fulfillment of the Mitzva?

These questions are answered in the sefer "לבוש", סימן תקפ"א. There we are told:

"ואומר קדיש שלם עם תתקבל אע"ג שבכל ימות השנה אין אומרים תתקבל אלא אחר תפלת שמונה עשרה, שכן הוא משמעות לשון 'צלותהון'

The Commentators' Machzor Companion

שפירש 'תפלה' וסתם תפלה ר"ל [רוצה לומר] תפלת י"ח [שמונה עשרה]. שאני סדר הסליחות שנתקנו כולם על סדר התפלה שבכל היום, כי הפסוקים שקודם הסליחות הם כנגד פסוקי דזמרה, והסליחות עם הי"ג מדות שאומרים בין כל אחת ואחת, במקום תפלת י"ח עיקר התפלה הוא י"ג מדות ואחר כך נופלין על פניהם כמו אחר כל התפלות ומסיימין 'ואנחנו לא נדע', לכך אומרים אחריהם קדיש שלם..."

"After the recitation of the *Selichos*, a full Kaddish is said, including the petition that Hashem accept our prayers, תתקבל. Although Kaddish is recited only after the Amidah prayers — for the word 'prayer' mentioned here in the Kaddish refers to the Amidah prayers — yet here the *order* of the Selichos also follows the prescribed order of the everyday Amidah prayers, which is, first praise and then supplication; for we begin with "אשרי", (praise), and then continue with a recitation of the *Thirteen Attributes of Mercy*, which is the essence of the Selichos (petitions), and then we say Tachanun (prayers of supplication). Therefore we justifiably recite here the full Kaddish..."

From this statement we see clearly that Selichos is equated with the Amidah prayers of the day, and therefore it too must follow a specified order, which is why it is called "the Order of Selichos", "סדר הסליחות".

II
Following the correct order of prayers brings forgiveness

The sefer "תנא דבי אליהו", פרק כג is the source for the designation "סדר הסליחות". For there we read the following:

"הי' דוד יודע שעתיד בית המקדש להיות חרב, וקרבנות יהיו בטלים בעוונותיהם של ישראל, והיה דוד מצטער על ישראל במה יהי' להם כפרה לעוונותיהן. אמר לו הקב"ה לדוד: בשעה שהצרות באות על ישראל בעוונותיהן יעמדו בפני יחד באגודה אחת ויתודו על עוונותיהן ויאמרו בפני סדר סליחה ואני אעְנֶה אותם. ובמה גילה אותן הקב"ה זאת.

אמר ר' יוחנן, הקב"ה גילה זאת בפסוק (שמות לד), "ויעבור ה' על פניו ויקרא" מלמד שירד הקב"ה מן הערפל כשליח צבור שנתעטף בטליתו ועובר לפני התיבה וגלה לו למשה סדר סליחה. אמר לו הקב"ה: אם יהי' תלמיד חכם בדור שיש בידו להוציא את ישראל מידי חובתו, אל יזיח דעתו עליו מלהתפלל על ישראל אלא יסתכל בי, שלא היה שום שותף עמי במעשה בראשית וירדתי וגליתי סדר סליחה למשה, כן ממני ילמדו כל באי עולם. וכל מי שיש בידו להוציא את ישראל מידי חובתן והוא מוציא אותן להם שכר טוב...".

"David, knowing that the Bais HaMikdash was to be destroyed and that offerings were to cease, was distressed for Yisrael and asked: When troubles come upon Yisrael in the wake of sin, who will atone for them? The Holy One replied: David, do not be distressed. Long ago, I disclosed to Moshe the *order of prayers* for forgiveness, saying to him: When troubles come upon Yisrael, let them stand before Me as one band and utter in My presence the prayer for forgiveness, and I shall answer them.

When did He reveal this *order of prayers*?

Rav Yochanan said: In the verse, 'when Hashem showed His face and proclaimed the Thirteen Attributes of Mercy' (Exodus 34:6). Rav Yochanan pointed out that this verse proves that the Holy One came down out of His thick cloud like an emissary of the congregation who enfolds himself in his prayer shawl as he takes his place before the Ark, and He disclosed to Moshe the *order of the prayers* for forgiveness. God also said to Moshe: If there be a disciple of the wise who has the ability to relieve Yisrael of its burden of guilt, let him not disdain them; let him keep Me in mind, who had no partner in the work of Creation, yet I did not disdain to come down and reveal the *order of prayer* for forgiveness. Let all inhabitants of My world learn from Me. And I shall give ample reward to him who has the ability to relieve Yisrael of their burden of guilt."

Rav Yosef Dov Soloveitchik sees this Midrash as giving a היתר, or license for Selichos to be said by stressing the need for a specified order in the prayers of forgiveness. For Chazal instituted three daily prayers, and it is forbidden to add to this number of prayers. But, if Selichos follows the format of prayer, תפילה, and is recognized as such, as attested to by the previously quoted "לבוש", then it would seem that we are adding to the number of prayers allowed by our Chazal, and we know that this is strictly prohibited. What, then, is the justification for adding Selichos to the number of acceptable prayers? According to Rav Soloveitchik, that justification is provided in this Midrash, where we are told that in *a time of crisis* for Yisrael, we may approach Hashem using this order of prayers of forgiveness, for it is Hashem Himself who sanctioned this addition.

III
Why this specific order?

We might suggest a reason why we need to be told that the Selichos prayers are to be recited according to a specified order.

The Mishna in Rosh Hashanah 32a tells us:

"סדר ברכות: אומר אבות, וגבורות, וקדושת השם..."

"The order of the Mussaf Shemoneh Esreh is: we first say the blessing of the Avos, then the blessings of strength, and then the blessing called Kedushas Hashem — the Holiness of the Name."

The ריטב״א asks: Why was it necessary for the Tanna to teach us that the *Avos*, the strength and the *Holiness of the Name* must be said in the Mussaf prayer of Rosh Hashanah? For surely these elements are an integral part of *every* Shemoneh Esreh prayer. Why, then, should this prayer be any different? The answer given is that we might view Mussaf of Rosh Hashanah as a prayer said in a time of crisis, תפלה בעת צרה, since we concentrate in this prayer on the three elements of מלכיות, זכרונות ושופרות. Under such circumstances, we might think we need not prolong the introduction before which we petition for our needs. Thus, perhaps we can do away with the *Avos*. The Mishna informs us that we must always follow the prescribed order of prayer, and therefore the section of Avos, as well as the other specified sections, must never be omitted.

We might think that Selichos can be viewed as a prayer said in a moment of crisis, and therefore it need not follow a specified order, and we could begin with the Thirteen Attributes of Mercy, which is a petition for His mercy. But the truth is, since Selichos is considered to have the legal status of Tefillah, it too must follow an exact specified order.

IV

Why is the normal order of repentance reversed?

We might suggest another, homiletical, reason why these prayers for forgiveness are called "סדר סליחות". In order to embark on the road to repentance, one must follow a prescribed order. We have elaborated elsewhere the need for order (see *The Commentators' Haggadah*, pp. 15-19). One can only hope to be successful in any venture if he proceeds carefully, step by step, according to a prescribed order. This is alluded to at the beginning of the Torah, when we are told that Hashem created the world in six days. The work of each day is delineated in great detail. This is to teach us that man must emulate his Creator, and to be creative in his own life he must do so in the manner presented here — slowly and patiently, proceeding in a careful order. We can apply this process to Teshuvah. One must take the "road back" to Hashem slowly and patiently, one step at a time, and in a prescribed order. Thus we are told here, at the beginning of the "Days of Awe", that in order to attain forgiveness for our wrongdoings we must follow a specified order in the prayers of forgiveness — סדר הסליחות — and that true Teshuvah entails meaningful, long-term efforts to repair what has gone wrong, and momentary feelings of remorse are not enough to rectify the situation.

And yet, we might think that the order of the prayers of forgiveness which we have here, the prescribed סדר הסליחות, seems to follow the reverse order of true repentance. For the normal order of Teshuvah would be to first rid ourselves of bad influences — סור מרע — and only then to approach the good — עשה טוב. Yet here we first petition for atonement, with the recitation of the central Selichos prayers, consisting of the Thirteen Attributes of Mercy — "ה' ה' א-ל רחום" — and only then do we confess our sins — וידוי — when we recite the אשמנו. We might have thought that the reverse order would have been more appropriate. And indeed, we follow that reverse order in the prayers of forgiveness which we recite in the Amidah of Yom Kippur. For there we begin with a confession of our guilt, when we say אשמנו, and that is followed by a request for forgiveness, כפרה, with the recitation of the על חטא, when we say: "ועל כולם...סלח לנו, מחל לנו, כפר לנו". This seems to follow the natural order of Teshuvah. How, then, do we explain the reverse order here in the Selichos prayers?

HaRav Yosef Dov Soloveitchik suggests the reason for this particular order. We are offered special compensation at this time of the year, which allows us to depart from the normal order and then approach Teshuvah through the normal order as we come closer to the Days of Awe. Hashem seems to be saying to us:

"גש נא אל האלקים עם כל מה שאתה מסורבל בעוונות האור ייבקע לקראתך ואתה תשוב ותיטהר."

We are to approach Hashem although we are defiled in the mire of sin. We must make the first move, and in time we will reach true Teshuvah, where we will be purified.

Thus, at the beginning of the High Holy Days we are called upon to initiate Teshuvah, with hope and anticipation that by Yom Kippur we will have reached the level that we can approach Hashem in the normal order of first confessing our sins, in the וידוי, and then we will be able to petition Him for forgiveness and atonement, סליחה.

And so the order here is reversed on purpose, to teach us how we are to approach Hashem, "באשר הוא שם".

This concept is alluded to by the *Sfas Emes,* in his commentary to the Haggadah. There he points out that we first say "קדש", and then "ורחץ". However, before we advance towards the Mitzva of reciting the story of the Exodus, we must first do Teshuvah. This is accomplished when we purify our hearts and minds symbolically with the washing of the hands, ורחץ. Only then can we approach the holy service of the night, קדש. But this implies that the appropriate order should have been ורחץ and then קדש. Why is this order reversed? The *Sfas Emes* suggests that the night of Pesach is unique, in that we do not have to follow the normal order. The reason for this is that when Bnai Yisrael were slaves in Egypt they had reached such a low spiritual level that the normal order by which they could have attained Teshuvah was suspended and Hashem, by His Mercy, first granted us the holiness of the night, קדש, and only then did He enable us to cleanse and uplift ourselves spiritually, ורחץ. And even now, on this night of Pesach throughout the ages, we are able to approach the Almighty at the level at which we find ourselves, and in this way we can ask Him first for His forgiveness and that we may be cleansed from our spiritual impurities, so that eventually we will be able to return to the normal order of Teshuvah which is required of us.

V

Return to the normal order on Yom Kippur

With this in mind, we can now appreciate the aspect of *order* which is common to the Selichos prayers, סדר הסליחות, as well as to those other Mitzvos which call for a specified order. These include:

1) סדר תפלה, the order of prayers. Since the סדר הסליחות, as described by the לבוש, is to be viewed as תפלה, it therefore requires a specified order, as do the regular daily prayers.

2) עבודת יום כפור, the service of sacrifice on the day of Yom Kippur. The purpose of the Yom Kippur service is to attain atonement, and for it to be accepted as properly performed, a specific order must be followed. So, too, are the supplicatory prayers of Selichos for the purpose of atonement, and they, too, may be viewed as עבודה. This means that to be accepted, they must follow a specified order.

3) Yet although the daily prayers and the Yom Kippur service call for a normal order — first confession, וידוי, in the prayer of אשמנו, and then a petition for forgiveness, in the prayer of על חטא — in the Selichos prayers, we are granted a special dispensation, just as we are in the Pesach

Seder, so that we need not follow the normal order. Instead, we are allowed to approach Hashem just as we are, באשר הוא שם, with the hope that by the time we reach Yom Kippur, we will have attained the spiritual level through our efforts at repentance, when we can return to the normal order of prayer.

This concept applies in another instance, where the role of סדר, prescribed order, is decisive. This is in relation to the law of sanctifying the land of Eretz Yisrael, קדושת ארץ ישראל. The verse which decribes this law cites two prerequisites which must be present before the land can become holy. We find this description in the Rambam's *Hilchos Terumah,* perek א, halacha א-ב.

1) First of all, the land must be conquered by all of Yisrael joining in the conquest — כיבוש רבים.

2) And secondly, Eretz Yisrael proper, which includes the territories within the boundaries which were promised to our forefathers, must be conquered first, and only then can we annex new territories beyond the borders of Eretz Yisrael proper. (See my sefer "אהל רבקה", כיבוש רבים ותנאיו)

The lesson which is derived here also teaches us that in order to attain holiness, קדושה, going from חיל אל חיל (one spiritual level to a higher one) is only possible if one does it in the proper sequence and order. One must not reach out to "territories" beyond the place where one finds himself at any particular time. This means that gradual progress, both spiritual and material, is the true secret of success.

Selichos and Prayer — One Mitzva or Two?

I

The reader for Selichos

leads all the prayers of the day

The Rema (רמ״א) in או״ח סימן תקפא סעיף א states:

"ויש מקומות שנוהגים שהמתפלל סליחות מתפלל כל היום."

"There are places where it is customary for the one who serves as reader for the Selichos prayers also to serve as the *shaliach tzibbur*, the reader, for all the prayers of that day."

The Magen Avraham (שם, סק״ז) explains the source of this custom to be the halachic concept that one who begins a Mitzva must be the one to complete that Mitzva:

"דכל המתחיל במצוה אומרים לו גמור."

The Gra, in his commentary "ביאור הגר״א", gives the source of this halacha as "ירושלמי סוף פ״ק דר״ה", which states:

"המתחיל במצוה אומרים לו מרוק - פי׳ גמור."

"To one who begins a Mitzva we say to him, complete the Mitzva."

From this we see that the Gra also accepts the approach of the Magen Avraham.

The "בנין שלמה", Rav Shlomo HaKohen of Vilna, (חלק א, סימן לז) asks the following question:

"תמוה לי דמהו ענין זה לענין להמתחיל במצוה, דהתם דעוסק במצוה אחת צריך לגמור, אבל הכא המצוה שהתחיל כבר גמרה, ומה ענין סליחות לתפלה? ועוד דאף בתפלה גופא אטו מי שמתפלל שחרית צריך להתפלל מוסף..."

"What does the matter of Selichos have to do with the concept of 'one who starts a Mitzva has to complete it'? For this principle was stated regarding one who has started a Mitzva, and therefore it is required that he complete it, (for otherwise it would appear that one who initiated the Mitzva 'deserted' his obligation and thus in a sense 'cheapened' the Mitzva by not completing it himself). However, concerning two distinct Mitzvos which are independent of each other and are considered to be two different Mitzvos, the above principle of "המתחיל במצות" does not apply. Thus, since the Selichos are a separate entity and have no direct relation to the subsequent morning Amidah prayer, the above principle does not apply. Secondly, even if there was a common denominator between the two, we never find that the reader for the Shacharis prayer is also called upon to act as reader for the

Mussaf prayer. And in fact the halacha calls for a different person to serve as reader, in order that the service be performed by many participants, "ברוב עם הדרת המלך".

This makes it difficult for us to accept the rationale of the Magen Avraham. Therefore the "בנין שלמה" offers his own approach to the halacha that one who acts as reader of the Selichos acts as reader of all the prayers of the day. Rav Shlomo HaKohen contends that when we divide the various duties of the daily service, we find that the one who removed the ashes from the Altar, תרומת הדשן, was also assigned the task of placing the two logs on the sacrificial pyre, "שני גזירי עצים". This was an additional bonus offered to the one who removed the ashes, for this service was not viewed as an important one and was done in the early morning. To entice a person to accept this task of תרומת הדשן, an added incentive was offered (see יומא כב,א). Similarly, in order to entice a person to accept the task of reader of the Selichos, an incentive was offered, namely being able to serve as reader for the rest of the prayers of the day. An incentive was needed for the following reasons.

1) The Selichos prayers are not looked upon with the same awe as is the Amidah prayer. Therefore the promise of being able to serve as chazzan for those supposedly more

exalted prayers was an attractive incentive for the reader of Selichos.

2) Since Selichos was recited in the middle of the night, the reader was offered a compensation for having to get up so early.

3) Acting as reader for the Selichos required great effort, since the reader did not merely read aloud the concluding verses of each prayer but instead recited all of the prayers in their entirety, while the rest of the congregation listened. For such tiring effort a "reward" was called for.

And so, the בנין שלמה concluded, the custom cited here by the Rema was followed only in earlier times, where the Reader was the one who did all the "work". Today, however, when everyone reads Selichos for himself, all the Reader does is recite the concluding words of each paragraph. Thus, no reward or incentive is called for and so this law does not apply today.

II
Selichos: an introduction to the day's prayers

In defense of this rationale of the Magen Avraham, HaRav Yosef Dov Soloveitchik, ז״ל, (see עמ' ו' חוברת ,"מסורה", כב) offers the following insight. The three daily Amidah prayers are separate entities and have no connection to each other. Thus the one who serves as שליח צבור, reader, for שחרית has no obligation to do so for מוסף. Each Amidah is to be considered a unique prayer, unrelated to any other. And so, if one were negligent and missed the Morning Prayer, for example, he is still obligated to recite Minchah and Ma'ariv later in the day. However, regarding Selichos, if one were to recite these prayers and then sleep the rest of the day, consequently missing the שחרית and מנחה prayers, not only has the person not fulfilled his obligation of *tefillah* for that day, but he also has not fulfilled his obligation of reciting the סליחות either. The reason for this is that the סליחות serves as a הקדמה, an introduction to the other prayers of the day. Therefore, if he did not pray at all on that day, even if he recited the prayers of Selichos, he is not given credit for having recited them. Thus, contends Rav Soloveitchik, the Magen Avraham is indeed correct to apply here the principle that if one begins a Mitzva he is obligated to complete it, "המתחיל במצוה אומרים לו גמור". For the prayers of Selichos are considered to be only an introduction to the day's Amidah prayers. And this is the reason we call upon the reader of the Selichos prayers to serve as reader for all the day's Amidah prayers, in order that he will complete his obligation — finish the Mitzva which he has begun with his early morning recitation of Selichos.

Another line of reasoning is to be found in the sefer סימן ב ו חלק ,"וזמנים מועדים" by Rav Moshe Sternbuch, who suggests that we require the reader of the Selichos to serve as reader of the other prayers of the day for another reason altogether. The רמ"א tells us that the person we select as שליח צבור for סליחות must be someone with outstanding character traits. He must be well-versed in Torah and an examplary individual. If we should then choose an ordinary person to act as chazzan for the daily prayers, this would insult the prestige of the weekday prayers, for there we do not require the reader to have the special talents called for in one who serves as reader for the Selichos prayers. And so that we do not lower the prestige of the weekday prayers, we insist that the reader of the Selichos, who is an exceptional individual, also serve as chazzan for the rest of the day's prayers.

III
Is Selichos "prayer at a time of crisis"?

To defend the position of the Magen Avraham, we might suggest the following. There is a well known difference of opinion between the Rambam and the Ramban regarding whether or not prayer originates "from the Torah", מן התורה, or is only "ordained by the Rabbis", מדרבנן. The Rambam maintains that tefillah comes directly from the Torah (see הלכות תפלה פרק א הלכה א); whereas the Ramban believes it is decreed by the Rabbis. However, the Ramban does admit that there is such a thing as tefillah from the Torah, and this is prayer in a time of crisis, "תפלה בעת צרה" (see *The Commentators' Gift of Torah*, pp.335-337). We might suggest that Selichos falls into this category. As we have already discussed (see "The Order of the Selichos") Selichos follows the format of tefillah and is therefore seen as halachically ordained tefillah. In addition, we consider it to be prayer at a time of crisis because we stand before the Almighty at a critical moment and in a precarious situation, when we are about to be judged by the King of kings. Indeed, we might extend this definition to include all the Amidah prayers recited during these days of Selichos. For the quickly approaching Day of Judgement requires us to beg for forgiveness as we approach the Heavenly Court on Rosh Hashanah and Yom Kippur. This theme of urgently begging forgiveness is common to all the Amidah prayers at this time, and it gives them the shared characteristic, along with the Selichos prayers, of being prayers at a time of crisis, תפלה בעת צרה. This connection, then, explains why the reader of Selichos, who is viewed as one who begins a Mitzva, is also required to act as chazzan for the Amidah prayers for the rest of the day. For he must complete the Mitzva he has begun, which views all the day's prayers as prayers recited in time of crisis.

And certainly on Rosh Hashanah and Yom Kippur we can consider all the prayers of the day as תפלה בעת צרה. Why, then, do we not call upon the chazzan of the Morning prayer, בעל שחרית, to serve as the reader also for Mussaf, בעל מוסף? The answer can be explained as follows. Rashi explains what is meant by saying that one who begins a Mitzva must complete it — that if he does not complete the Mitzva it remains as a burden upon him, and therefore another is summoned to complete the Mitzva and remove the burden from his shoulders. Regarding the prayers on Rosh Hashanah, they are so long and complex and require so much effort on the part of the reader, that one can understand why the reader of the Morning prayer may not have the strength to serve as reader for Mussaf, too. Thus, instead of viewing him as deserting his obligation, we can understand his difficulties and excuse him from the overwhelming burden. And furthermore, although a בעל שחרית must know the prayers, a בעל מוסף requires even greater expertise, for this prayer includes the difficult sections of מלכיות זכרונות and שופרות. Therefore, it is understandable that a new and more experienced reader is called for when it comes time to recite the Mussaf prayer.

IV
Two sources for letting one who begins a Mitzva finish it

We have seen that the מג"א understands the halacha which requires the chazzan of Selichos to serve also as the chazzan of the rest of the day's prayers to be based on the principle of "המתחיל במצוה וכו'". And he gives its source as the ירושלמי פ"ק דמגילה, which clearly articulates this principle. The גר"א, on the other hand, cites an additional source for the same halacha cited here by the רמ"א. Here are the statements of the רמ"א and the ביאור הגר"א:

(רמ"א): "ויש מקומות שנוהגים שהמתפלל סליחות מתפלל כל היום".

(ביאור הגר"א): "ויש מקומות: ירושלמי מגילה סוף פ"ק מי שהתחיל במצוה וכו' והביאו תוס' בחולין כט,א, ד"ה ומירק כו'. כל היום: ברכות מב,א."

The words of the גר"א raise several questions:

1) If indeed there are two sources for this halacha, why did he elaborate them in two separate footnotes, rather than combine them into one footnote?

2) And if, by making a separate note of the second source, the intention of the גר"א was to allude to something else altogether, what exactly did he intend to allude to?

In answer to these questions we might suggest the following. In pointing out the Mishna in ברכות מב,א we might say, based on the halacha mentioned there, that the one who makes the blessing over the wine that follows Bircas HaMazon also recited the blessing over the burning of spices. (It was the custom in those days to burn spices after a meal, in order to give off a sweet fragrance and thus obligate those present to recite a separate blessing of "בורא עצי בשמים").

From this it seems that the one who *begins* with the blessing over wine is being instructed to *complete the Mitzva* by reciting the second blessing, even though the two are not in any way related, but are two separate berachos. Thus what the גר"א must have been alluding to here by quoting this Gemara was an answer to the question posed by the בנין שלמה regarding the Selichos and the daily prayers, which are also two unrelated Mitzvos. That question was: how does the Magen Avraham apply the principle of המתחיל במצוה when *two* Mitzvos are involved, since this principle would seem to be applicable in the case of a single Mitzva?

The גר"א, by citing the example, contends that this principle is indeed applicable in the case of two separate Mitzvos as well. But even if this is so, we are still confronted with the question that if the principle of המתחיל במצוה applies to two separate Mitzvos, why does the בעל שחרית not also serve as the chazzan for מוסף?

Therefore the גר"א must have had something else in mind when he pointed out the Gemara in ברכות. The Magen Avraham here in סימן תקפא comments that the chazzan of Selichos, who is obligated to serve as reader all day, takes precedence in that position over even those who would normally be designated as reader, such as one who had a Yahrzeit, one who was a mourner, etc. The reason for this is based on the concept of המתחיל במצוה.

The Magen Avraham cites proof for this position from another of his opinions, in the name of the Tur (see מג"א,

(סימן קע"ד, ס"ק יז). There the מחצית השקל explains the rationale behind the Magen Avraham's position by saying that the Tur maintains that if the spices are already upon the table when the Grace After Meals is being recited, then the one who leads the bentsching must also make the blessing over the spices, even if there is someone more distinguished now present, who would ordinarily be called upon to make the blessing over the spices.

In light of this comment of the Tur, we can make a distinction between Selichos and the daily prayers, on the one hand, and between שחרית and מוסף of Shabbos and Yom Tov on the other. This distinction is the following: when we recite שחרית, the prayer of מוסף is not yet "present", rather it will follow later. Therefore, we do not now apply the principle of המתחיל במצוה, for even if this principle were to be applied to two separate Mitzvos, they must both be present at the same time in order for it to be applicable. However, in the case of Selichos and the daily prayers, they are not to be viewed as separate Mitzvos, but are all seen as part of the Mitzva of prayers recited at a time of crisis, תפלה בעת צרה, as we have previously discussed. Thus we may apply the principle of המתחיל במצוה here.

And so, we may extend the thinking here to include the following. The principle derived from the Gemara in

ברכות is that if a person merits to do a Mitzva, he is entitled to complete the subsequent Mitzvos which arise from it, although there may be people present who might be more distinguished or more appropriate to complete those subsequent Mitzvos. And this is the reason the גר"א made a separate notation, to point out, as did the Magen Avraham, that even when we now have present at the daily prayer service those who should legally serve as chazzan — such as a mourner or one who has yahrzeit, yet the privilege to serve as chazzan belongs to the one who served as reader for the early morning Selichos.

To conclude, we might reiterate why the גר"א made here two separate comments.

1) He emphasized the ירושלמי מגילה to allude to the law of המתחיל במצוה.

2) By directing our attention to the Gemara in ברכות, the גר"א emphasizes that this law of המתחיל במצוה supercedes all ordinary considerations, so that the privilege to act now is governed by that principle.

It is worthwhile to note that there is a dissenting opinion cited in the *Mishna Berurah* (see סימן תקפ"א ס"ק יד) which disputes the claim of the Magen Avraham and contends that a *mourner* takes precedence over the reader of Selichos.

Selichos At Night

I
Just before daybreak: באשמורת הבקר

Most commentators believe that the best time to recite Selichos is just before daybreak, באשמורת הבקר. The Gemara in Berachos 3a explains that the night is divided into three (or four) periods, each consisting of three (or four) hours. Each period is referred to as a watch, "משמר". This means that אשמורת הבקר is the third watch, which occurs just before daybreak. The reason this period was chosen is based on a statement in the Zohar, Parashas Chai Sarah (עמ' קלב,ב), which says:

"שמשעות הבוקר מתעוררים חסדים בעולם, כפי שנאמר יומם יצוה ה' חסדו. ואילו משעת מנחה עד חצות הלילה מתעוררים מדות הדין. ולכן בענין חורבן בית המקדש נאמר: אוי לנו כי פנה יום כי ינטו צללי ערב, פנה היום שהוא מדת החסד, ומעת שנטו צללי ערב התעוררו הגבורות והדינים בעולם עד שגרמו לחורבן. אולם משעת חצות לילה מתעוררים שוב החסדים ומדת הרחמים.

ולכן נעים זמירות ישראל, דוד המלך, אמר: חצות לילה אקום להודות לך, שהיה קם בשירות ותשבחות ומזמורי תהילים להשי"ת, וכן אמר: ובלילה שירה עמי."

The Commentators' Machzor Companion

"The mercy of Hashem (חסד) endures during the day, as in the passage (Ps. 32:3): 'The mercy of Hashem endures the whole day.' However, from the period of Minchah (afternoon) till midnight, 'the shadows of the evening are stretched out', at which time there rages the attribute of stringency (דין), at that very hour was the Sanctuary destroyed and the Holy Temple burnt down.

However, from midnight on, the attribute of mercy reappears, and thus King David arose at midnight to chant songs and hymns, as it is written, 'and in the night His song is with me'. (Ps. 52: 9)."

Thus the proper time to petition for mercy (חסד, רחמים) is after midnight, before daybreak.

Some maintain that midnight, חצות, is the proper time to recite Selichos, and indeed many do recite it at midnight on the first night, motzei Shabbos. Others allow Selichos to be recited even during the first watch, that is, right after Ma'ariv. Recently, many synagogues have introduced an early Selichos service (at ten p.m.). This new innovation is justified since many Jewish neighborhoods have changed and it is now dangerous to be found in the streets before daybreak. Thus we can consider it a case of פיקוח נפש. Yet another *heter* we can employ in allowing an early Selichos is to accommodate those who would not otherwise awaken at the break of dawn, באשמורת הבקר, to say Selichos.

The common practice in the yeshivos of today is to recite Selichos just before the morning prayers, תפלת שחרית. The rationale for this is that if the students were forced to arise at midnight in order to say Selichos at daybreak, they would lose a good night's sleep and consequently they would not be able to learn properly the next day. Others, however, decry this practice and consider it a mistake. (See "נוראת הרב", חלק ו' עמ' 240, who writes as follows):

"Although nowadays it is customary to recite Selichos in the morning, before Shacharis, there is no precedent for this practice. It is wrong, for Selichos should be said at night and concluded at night or at daybreak."

The Rambam rules:

"ונהגו לקום בלילה בעשרה ימים אלו ולהתפלל בבתי כנסיות בדברי תחנונים עד שיאור היום" — פרק ג' מהלכות תשובה הלכה ד'

"It is customary to awaken *at night* during the ten days between Rosh Hashanah and Yom Kippur and to pray in the synagogue with words of supplication until daybreak."

Even reciting Selichos after Ma'ariv or the first part of the evening met with opposition (See "יחוה דעת" מהרב עובדיה יוסף, ח"א סימן מח):

"וכן כתב רבינו האר"י בספר שער הכוונות בזו הלשון: ודע שבחצות הלילה הראשון אין לומר כלל שום סליחות, ולא להזכיר שום י"ג מדות."

"Our master, the Ari, wrote that in no way should one recite the Selichos during the first part of the evening."

However, based on a responsa of HaRav Moshe Feinstein, זצ"ל, (see שו"ת אגרות משה, חלק או"ח ב', סימן קה) many have found a *heter* to recite Selichos in the early evening:

"שאם אי אפשר לצבור לומר סליחות אחר חצות, יש להתיר להם דרך הוראת שעה לומר סליחות קודם חצות הלילה, אין מקור לדברים אלו [לומר סליחות אחר חצות] מהגמ' רק מהאחרונים על פי ספרי הקבלה ומסתבר שאין בזה ענין איסור, אלא שאין מועלים בכח י"ג מדות שיש הבטחה שאין שבים ריקם, אלא כסתם תפלה, ולכן כדי שלא יתבטלו מלומר סליחות לגמרי, טוב יותר לומר סליחות בתחילת הלילה."

"Since we don't find a source from the Gemara regarding the exact time Selichos should be said, therefore in order that Selichos be said at all, we can allow it to be said in the early evening."

II
After midnight: אחרי חצות

Thus, as the quoted Zohar explains, it seems preferable to recite Selichos after midnight. HaRav Yosef Dov Soloveitchik, though, suggests another reason why midnight was chosen as the most opportune time. (See "נוראת הרב", עמ' 242-244). Nighttime is reserved for Torah and not for tefillah, and accordingly, Chazal have spoken in glowing terms about studying Torah at night. The Rambam, in *Hilchos Talmud Torah*, פרק ג' הלכה יג tells us:

"אף על פי שמצוה ללמוד ביום ובלילה אין אדם לומד רוב חכמתו אלא בלילה. לפיכך מי שרוצה לזכות בכתר תורה יזהר בכל לילותיו ולא יאבד ממנו אפילו אחד מהם בשינה ואכילה ושתיה אלא בתלמוד תורה.

אמרו חכמים אין רנה של תורה אלא בלילה, שנאמר קומי רוני בלילה לראש אשמרות (איכה ב, יט).

וכל העוסק בתורה בלילה חוט של חסד נמשך עליו ביום, שנאמר, יומם יצוה עליו חסדו ובלילה שירה עמי תפלה לא-ל חי."

"Although it is obligatory to study Torah both by day and at night, man cannot acquire wisdom unless he studies at night. Whoever wants to be adorned with the crown of Torah should be careful at night and should not waste even a single night with sleeping, eating, feasting or conversing.

He should rather utilize the night solely for the study of Torah.

Our Rabbis taught that hearing the song of Torah has added significance only when it is recited at night; as it is written: 'Arise and sing at night'.

One who religiously studies Torah at night, will have the grace of Hashem bestowed on him. As it is written: 'In the daytime Hashem bestows His lovingkindness, and at night I engage in song and prayer to Hashem Who gave me life.' "

There are many sayings of our Sages, מאמרי חז״ל, which emphatically state that the nighttime should be devoted to the study of Torah. Similarly, the Book of Psalms is not recited at night before midnight. This is why we do not recite Selichos until after midnight. For Selichos is a compilation of verses from Psalms and thus may be recited only after midnight. For the nighttime is reserved for Torah study and not prayer. This is what Chazal meant when they stated:

"לא איברי לילא אלא לגירסא" — עירובין סח,א

"The night was created only for study."

III
Reciting Selichos early

Whether or not to say Selichos early is not, in fact, a recent issue. רבי משה ניגרין, who was a contemporary of Rav Yosef Karo, the Bais Yosef, discussed this matter in the sefer "ראה ב"ישורון" — מאסף תורני, חלק ג' "ר"מ" "ראש אשמורת" (ניגרין וספרו ראש אשמורת", מהרב יצחק סץ, עמ' תקי"ג). There in his preface, the author records the various groups of people who wanted to change the time of reciting Selichos from the pre-dawn period to the early evening or the early morning. But he rejects all such attempts by contending that ראש אשמורת is the halachically ordained time for Selichos, and there are a number of other considerations related to the recitation of Selichos which explain why this particular time was chosen.

To those who prefer the early evening, the author counters that one is not always free at that time to engage in this most important act of prayer. One may have either prior business commitments or guests who come to visit and engage him in idle conversation. Reciting Selichos now, while the unfinished business or the idle conversation still lingers in one's mind, is not conducive to the deliberate concentration and immersion in the meaning of the prayers which is absolutely required. In addition, one is often exhausted after a hard day's work or after eating a heavy evening meal. If one were to recite Selichos in the early evening and then retire to bed, this would not be in the spirit of what Selichos was intended to achieve — reflection and the resolve to improve one's spiritual state. For after Selichos one should approach the morning prayers feeling like a new person ready for true repentance. And there is also the danger that one will oversleep and miss saying *Kriyas Shema* at the proper time.

"אי לזאת מאלו הסבות לא מצאנו מקום למנהג הכת הזאת אשר ראו לפרוק עול הסליחות מעליהם ולצאת ידי חובתם מהן בתחלת הלילה, כי הנה בתחלת הלילה עדיין דעתם מעורבבת עליהם מעניני היום ואינם כ"כ פנויים ותאוות המאכל והמשתה לא נחו ולא שקטו כי הבשר והמאכל עדיין הוא בין שיניהם בעת היותם מתנפלים ומתחנני'...וגם עדיין לא נח חושיו מרוב מוחשיו בתחלת הלילה כי עדיין רואה מה שיטרידהו ושומע מה שיפסיקהו מקול המיית האנשים ונשים ושיחת הילדים אשר עדיין הם נעורים...שבתחלת הלילה עדיין לא נתפרדו איש מעל אחיו...שלאחר שהשלימו בסדר זה חוזרים לבתיהם ומרבים בשינה קודם קריאת שמע ותפלה. וכבר מיחו הגאונים הרבה בענין זה, אם מפני שמא יאנס בשינה זו ויקרא ק"ש שלא עם הצבור או בעונתה ונמצאת תקנתו קלקלתו...אחד מן הדברים הנכבדים שבאותה מנהג [אמירת סליחות] כדי לעמוד בתפלה מתוך דברי סליחה..."

And to those who would say Selichos after sunrise prior to the start of the morning prayers, the objection here is that those who follow this practice usually abbreviate the Selichos, leaving out many moving and important Selichos prayers.

"אנשי הכת אשר ראו לאומרם בתפלת שחרית בדברים מעטים וראשי אמרים שנים שלשה גרגרים כי גם אלה למבין אינם נכוחים. אם מצד היותם נאמרים שלא בזמניהם...ואם מצד אחר כי במקום שאמרו להאריך אינו רשאי לקצר..."

See (244 'עמ ששי חלק), "הרב נוראת", where we read as follows:

"Originally Selichos was recited for hours at a time. Nowadays the first Selichos takes about forty-five minutes to an hour. In ancient times, they had many more verses of Selichos. There was much more activity and beauty. Over time, Selichos has been abbreviated, and nowadays we have only a few fragments left of the original Selichos introduced by the Gaonim."

IV
The relation of Selichos to the daily Tamid sacrifice

There is a beautiful insight which suggests why the night was chosen as the appropriate time for reciting Selichos and how we are justified in expanding on the day's three standard prayers when we know that Chazal were strongly opposed to adding new prayers.

This is explained in the essay "עיונים בסליחות" מר' חיים צבי פנט, מוריה תשמ"ו גליון א/ב.

Near the end of the Selichos recited on erev Rosh Hashanah (סליחה מד) we find a detailed description of all the services that took place in the Bais HaMikdash prior to the service of the daily offering, the קרבן תמיד של שחר. In every step leading up to the description of the morning service, each particular step is accompanied with the petition that this service should find favor in the eyes of Hashem and should be considered as if we actually performed the daily sacrifice in the Bais HaMikdash. However, once the poet reaches the point of describing the daily sacrifice, he describes the actual process of the offering but no longer includes the petition that the service be accepted.

Here is the description of the duties performed before the offering of the Daily Tamid sacrifice. The petition for acceptance is:

"תפלה תקח תחנה תבחר, תמור ניחוח תמיד השחר."

"__Accept our prayer__ and select our supplication, in place of the sweet scent of the morning's Tamid offering."

"שקול לעומדים שמך לשבח, כאלו זכו תרום מזבח."

"__Account those__ who stand forth to praise Your Name, as if they had won the privilege of removing the ashes from the Altar."

"רצה עבודתם במקדש שביתם, כבית עולמים לעושי חביתם."

"__Be favorable__ to their service in their Temple in Exile, as You are to their *chavittim* makers in the Eternal Temple."

"קשב מקראות וחינון סדרים כעין אברים ועכול פדרים."

"__Be attentive__ to their ordered verses and supplications, as you were to the limbs and fats consumed on the pyre of the Altar."

"צרוף שטוח פני טפוח, כמעלה אפר על גב תפוח."

"Regard the hands that are spread out in prayer before Heaven, as the heaping of ashes in a mound on the Altar."

This outline of the early morning service, which is performed before daybreak, באשמרות הבקר, and its accompanying petitions for Hashem to accept our service as if it were performed in the actual Bais HaMikdash, is based on the following statement of the Gemara in Berachos 26b: "תפלות כנגד תמידים תקנום"

"The prayers were instituted to replace the daily sacrifices."

This reflects a statement of Chazal on a pasuk in Hosea 14:3:

"ונשלמה פרים שפתינו. אמר ר' אבהו: מי משלם אותם פרים שהיינו מקריבים לפניך, שפתים שאנו מתפללים לפניך."

"Concerning the verse, 'let us render bulls for the offering of our lips', Rav Avuha said, with what can we compensate for the sacrifice of bulls that we offered before You? With our lips with which we offer our prayers before You."

Consequently, we can assume that the Selichos prayers are also petitions to Hashem that He accept them as if we offered the daily sacrifice. And so we may conclude:

1) The license to add the Selichos prayers is that we do so in lieu of the daily sacrifices that were performed before the Tamid at daybreak. This means that just as our daily prayers are offered in place of the sacrifices of the day, so too may we offer the Selichos prayers in place of the pre-dawn Tamid sacrifice.

2) Just as this service was performed at night, before the offering of the daily Tamid, so too the proper time for reciting Selichos, which is a substitute for that sacrifice, is באשמרות הבקר, just before dawn. Thus Selichos should be said at night.

The Meaning of Selichos

I
To attain a pure heart

In the sefer "קונטרס עצות לזכות בדין בימים הנוראים", the author quotes his rebbe, Rav Dov Tzvi Karelenstein, שליט״א, who offers an insight into one of the crucial Selichos prayers.

Rav Karelenstein explains why in one of the Selichos (סליחה כד) which we recite on the day before Rosh Hashanah, we say the following:

"שבטי פליטי ישראל הכונו בלב נבר

תם החזיקו ותחן הפיקו נשקו בר

את ה' בהמצאו לדרשו חיל יגבר."

"Tribes of the survivors of Yisrael, prepare yourselves with cleansed hearts!

Cling wholeheartedly [to Hashem's Mitzvos], bring forth supplications, strive for purity of heart.

May strength be increased to seek Hashem

When He allows Himself to be found."

We are being told here that we must make an effort to enter Rosh Hashanah day with a pure heart. This is the meaning of the verse which says: "הכונו בלב נבר", "Prepare yourselves with cleansed hearts". This is the source for the Meiri's statement, in his (מאמר ב, פרק א) "חיבור התשובה":

"ובדרש אמרו ז"ל על ענין היותו קרוב, שראוי לכל להשתדל קודם ראש השנה בהפצר בתפלות, ובהערת תשובות כדי שיכנס בראש השנה בטהרת הלב וכו'".

The Meiri explains that we must strive before Rosh Hashanah with <u>constant prayer</u> to arouse a <u>sense of repentance</u> so that we may arrive at the day of Rosh Hashanah with a pure heart.

The way to achieve this is through increased prayer. This is the meaning of the words we say here in our Selichos prayer: "תחן הפיקו נשקו בר", "Bring forth prayers to attain a pure heart." For it is only by offering prayer sincerely that one's heart becomes pure. And so the Meiri writes (ibid. מאמר ב, פרק ב):

"המנהג בהרבה מקומות להקדים ולהרבות בתפלה מראש חודש אלול ולהעיר השחר <u>בסליחות</u> כדי שיהיו מחשבותיהם זכות ונקיות בהגיע היום, יצא חודש אלול בטהרה, ונכנס תשרי בקדושה וכו'".

"It is the custom in many places to increase the saying of prayers from Rosh Chodesh Elul, and to arouse the early morning with the recitation of Selichos. The purpose of this is to assure that our hearts are purified by

Judgement Day, and that we take leave of the month of Elul in purity and enter Tishrei in a state of holiness..."

In describing the status of the Ten Days of Repentance between Rosh Hashanah and Yom Kippur the Rambam, in הלכות תשובה פרק ב, הלכה ו, writes as follows:

"אף על פי שהתשובה והצעקה יפה לעולם, בעשרה הימים שבין ראש השנה ויום הכפורים היא יפה ביותר ומתקבלת היא מיד שנאמר דרשו ה' בהמצאו."

"Even though repentance and calling out to Hashem are desirable at all times, during the ten days between Rosh Hashanah and Yom Kippur, they are even more desirable and will be accepted immediately, as Isaiah 55:6 states: "Seek Hashem when He is to be found".

Thus we see that the prescription here for the Ten Days of Repentance to nullify the decrees issued on Rosh Hashanah is "תשובה וצעקה", "a sense of remorse and a cry for mercy". This, then, is the meaning of the Selichos prayer here, which tells us to bring forth supplications *before* Rosh Hashanah, the time when prayer alone can be beneficial in attaining Divine mercy. For if one comes to Rosh Hashanah with a pure heart, which is the result of sincere prayer, then he will bring upon himself a favorable decree. After that, however, during the Ten Days of Repentance, prayer alone is not enough, "חיל יגבר". Rather, one must make an additional effort, "וצעקה", and cry out for mercy. Thus we are advised on the eve of Rosh Hashanah to take advantage of the opportunity of "תחן הפיקר", to make the most of the gift of prayer when it alone will be effective, and not to wait for the time when it will have to be accompanied by additional efforts, צעקה.

II
Praying with deep emotion

The following story might suggest a homiletic explanation of this prayer, "לדרשו חיל יגבר", "May strength be increased to seek Hashem".

Once a chassid dressed in traditional garb appeared in the courtyard of the holy Rebbe of Chorkov. He was distraught and told the gabbai: "I must see the Rebbe immediately, it is a great emergency."

When he was ushered into the Rebbe's chambers, he was asked to explain what was the great emergency that brought him there.

The chassid answered, "I have a son of draft age, who has been called up to take his physical exam. If he passes he will be inducted into the Royal Austrian army. We Jews know all too well what that means....Please, Rebbe, pray that he does not pass his physical and that he will be released from serving in the army."

The Rebbe heard the man's petition, closed his eyes, and asked him to repeat it. Once again the man made his request, just as before. When he was finished the Rebbe asked him to repeat his request yet again. Again the man made the same request. The Rebbe asked him to repeat it a fourth and a fifth time. Although the man was puzzled, he did as he was told, spelling out his request exactly as he had done before.

Suddenly the Rebbe jumped out of his seat and began to berate the chassid.

"You ingrate, you selfish man! We Jews are afforded a safe haven here in Austria, we enjoy equal rights and have the opportunity to earn a decent living. We are protected by the government without having to pay additional taxes for that protection. We are recipients of the benevolence of our Royal Majesty, and you seek to escape from the sacred duty of serving in his army. Get out, you ungrateful man, and let your son serve in the army and thereby show our gratitude to the government."

With these words the Rebbe sent away the chassid, who was confused and disappointed, though grateful to have escaped with his life. Everyone who heard of this incident was puzzled and could not understand what had happened. Why had the Rebbe asked the chassid to repeat his request so many times? Why did he scold the man and have him thrown out?

A few weeks later, it all became clear. The Rebbe received an official letter from the Austrian government, accompanied with a small box containing a medal of honor. The letter read as follows: "The Austrian government, on behalf of His Royal Highness, presents this medal of honor to the Rabbi of Chorkov for his outstanding patriotism. You should know that the man who appeared before you several weeks ago, appealing to the Rabbi to pray that his son be freed from military service, was a spy sent by us. Information reaching us subsequently proved false — that the Rabbi was disloyal to the Austrian government and was harboring young men in his courtyard, fugitives who sought to escape serving in the army. When our spy returned, he reported on the Rabbi's great loyalty and appreciation of the Austrian government. Therefore we present you with this medal to commemorate your patriotism."

When the Jews of the city heard that there had been a spy in their midst they were aghast. Their beloved Rebbe could have been jailed or even worse. How had he known that the "chassid" was really a spy? "It must have been *ruach hakodesh,* the Holy Spirit!" they all agreed.

The Rebbe then turned to his chassidim and told them: "I detected that this man was a fraud not because of *ruach hakodesh,* but rather as the result of a simple conclusion on my part. When I asked him to repeat his request a second time, he repeated it exactly as he had done the first time. And when I asked him again and again, he showed no change of emotion but repeated his request as coldly as if he had rehearsed it many times. From this I understood that he was an imposter; for if one needs something desperately, each time he repeats his petition, he feels greater and greater emotion."

From this we can learn that when we beseech Hashem on these days (nights) when we recite Selichos, we should pray with an increased outpouring of heartfelt emotion. Otherwise, this is an indication that our prayers are not sincere and we are saying them by rote. For only if we put this kind of effort into our prayers can we rightfully claim that we did all we could to arouse Hashem's mercy. And furthermore, when we come to the final prayer of the day of Yom Kippur, Neilah, when the gates of repentance are about to close, if we remain unchanged and stand before the Almighty the same as we were throughout this period of repentance, then this is an indication that we have failed to take advantage of this most opportune moment to shake the gates of heaven with our prayer, "דרשו את ה' בהמצאו".

And so this is why we say here in the Selichos prayer on the eve of Rosh Hashanah, "לדרשו חיל יגבר", to show that when we seek out Hashem with our petitions, we must intensify our efforts with each subsequent prayer. For it is only when we focus our concentration and our emotion on what we are saying that we will reach Hashem, "ה' בהמצאו", and only then will He allow Himself to be "found", and He will then answer our prayers with a favorable response.

Ashrei — אשרי

I
Why do we begin with Ashrei?

We begin the סדר הסליחות with the prayer of אשרי, Psalm 145. There are several reasons for this:

1) In order to be able to recite Kaddish we must first recite chapters of Kisvei HaKodesh, of which Ashrei is a part. Therefore, in the Minchah prayer we say Ashrei and then Kaddish. Even in the Ma'ariv prayer, according to the נוסח ספרד, the congregation begins by reciting Psalm 134 (שיר המעלות, הנה ברכו את ה' כל עבדי ה') and other selections from Tehillim before the recitation of Kaddish, for the same reason, namely, that Kaddish must be preceded by a quotation from Tanach.

2) As we have previously mentioned, Selichos follows the *order* of the regular prayers which call for *praise and supplication*. Thus we begin here as we do in the Morning Prayers, with Ashrei (See *The Commentators' Siddur*).

3) In order to fulfill the requirement set down by Chazal in Mesechtas Berachos 31a, as follows: "אין עומדים להתפלל אלא מתוך שמחה של מצוה...מתוך דברי שבח ותנחומים."

"One should only stand up to pray while still rejoicing in the performance of a mitzva...with words of praise and consolation."

We might suggest here that by beginning Selichos with Ashrei, we are being taught an important approach to prayer in general and to the Days of Awe in particular (see *The Commentators' Siddur*, pp 159-62).

Ashrei serves as the opening of the Psukei D'Zimra. We can understand why this particular psalm was chosen to open the prayers, based on the following considerations. The uniqueness of Ashrei is twofold:

1) Its verses are arranged in an alphabetical acrostic.

2) It contains the phrase "פותח את ידיך" ("He opens His Hands") which acknowledges Hashem as the Provider for all living creatures.

These two factors have far-reaching implications.

The Besht (Ba'al Shem Tov) attempts to define the meaning and influence of prayer. How, he asks, can prayer change the Will of God? For He is not like a human being who might be persuaded to change his mind as a result of someone's petitioning him. The answer he gives is that since the decree is handed down in the form of letters, one's petition may cause a change in the arrangement of those letters to give them a new meaning completely different from what was originally intended.

To illustrate this approach we might examine an insight of the Bais HaLevi, in his comments on the pasuk quoted in Hosea which describes how an evil decree which is followed by sincere repentance can be transformed into a completely opposite decree of good tidings. The pasuk here tells us:

"במקום אשר יאמר להם לא עמי אתם יאמר להם בני אל חי."

"And it shall come to pass that instead of saying to them, 'You are not my people', it shall be said to them '[you are] the children of the living God'."

The Bais HaLevi explains that at first Hashem reprimands Bnai Yisrael and rejects them as His nation. However, after they sincerely repent and return to following His ways, the words take on new significance and may be understood in a very different light, "לא עמי אתם", "You are not My nation," but you are even closer to Me — "you are My children", "בני אל חי". Thus an evil decree, which would have meant the rejection of the Jewish people as Hashem's chosen nation, has been transformed into a positive bond of greater closeness between them.

The Kabbalists tell us that in the Ashrei, the phrase "פותח את ידיך", which contains the word "ידיך", "Your Hand", is to be understood as "יודיך", "Your yud". In kabbalistic terminology, "yud" signifies "thought". The idea here is that through concentrated and sincerely directed thought, one who prays can become a new and different person; and so we might say that the original decree was not intended for this "new" person.

Thus, the Ashrei placed here (and in the Psukei D'Zimra) at the threshold of our prayers, gives us a moment to stand back and reflect on the great power which prayer has to nullify an evil decree, providing that the person for whom this evil decree was intended transforms himself into a new person through sincere repentance. Through prayer, one can be assured that his needs will be met by an all-seeing and ever-merciful God. And so, the Ashrei challenges us to concentrate and have faith in this transforming power of prayer.

II
Praising Hashem

"דור לדור ישבח מעשיך, וגבורתיך יגידו"

"Each generation will praise Your deeds to the next, and of Your mighty deeds will they tell".

This psalm articulates the praise which Moshe Rabbenu uttered to Hashem in Devarim 10:17:

"כי ה' אל-היכם הוא אל-הי הא-להים ואדני אדנים, הא-ל הגדול הגבור והנורא אשר לא ישא פנים ולא יקח שחד."

"For the Lord your God is the God of gods and the Lord of lords, the great God, the mighty and the awesome, Who regards not persons, nor takes reward."

These words of praise: "הגדול, הגבור, והנורא", are the same words which constitute the praise uttered at the outset of the Amidah prayer. And these same words of praise are found here in the psalm:

"גדול ה' ומהולל מאד וגו', "

"דור לדור ישבח מעשיך, וגבורתיך יגידו."

"ועזוז נוראותיך יאמרו וגו'."

"Hashem is *great* and exceedingly lauded."

"Each generation will praise Your deeds to the next, and of Your *mighty* deeds will they tell."

"And of Your *awesome* power they will speak."

Chazal comment on these words of praise uttered by Moshe Rabbenu (יומא סט,ב):

"דאמר רב יהושע בן לוי: למה נקרא שמן אנשי כנסת הגדולה, שהחזירו עטרה ליושנה, אתא משה אמר: הא-ל הגדול הגבור והנורא (דברים י:יז). אתא ירמיה ואמר: נוכרים מקרקרין בהיכלו, איה נוראותיו, לא אמר 'נורא'. אתא דניאל ואמר: נכרים משתעבדים בבניו איה גבורותיו, לא אמר 'גבור', אתא אינהו [אנשי כנסת הגדולה] ואמרו: אדרבה זו היא גבורת גבורתו, שכובש את רצונו שנותן ארך אפים לרשעים. ואלו הן נוראותיו, שאילמלא מוראו של הקב"ה האיך אומה אחת יכולה להתקיים בין האומות."

"For Rav Yehoshua ben Levi said: Why were they called the Men of the Great Synod? Because they restored the crown of the Divine Attributes to its ancient crown. For Moshe had come and said: 'The great God, the Mighty and the Awsome.' Then Yirmiyahu came and said: 'Aliens are revelling in His Temple. Where, then, are His Awsome deeds?' Hence he omitted from his prayer the attribute of 'the Awsome'.

Daniel came and said: 'Aliens are enslaving His sons. Where are His mighty deeds?' Hence he omitted from his prayer the attribute of 'the Mighty'. But they (the Men of the Great Synod) came and said: 'On the contrary, therein lie His mighty deeds, that He suppresses His wrath, that He extends patience to the wicked. Therein lie His awful powers. But for fear of Him, how could one single nation [Yisrael] persist among many nations?'."

Based on this Gemara the Brisker Rav, הגרי"ז הלוי, explained the purpose of the prayer, "'אתה גבור לעולם ה", "You are *eternally* mighty, Hashem", recited at the beginning of the "גבורות". It serves to offset those attributes of "גבור" and "נורא" which Yirmeyahu and Daniel had sought to remove from our praise of the Almighty. Thus we say here in the Amidah prayer, "'אתה גבור לעולם ה", and these words acknowledge that Hashem is, and always has been, the all-powerful, awesome One, even in those moments when one might question His power, as did Daniel. Thus we emphasize that these attributes *always* have been present and always will be.

III
Two kinds of Divine powers

The above-mentioned Gemara, however, leads us to ask the following questions:

1) How can we say that the attribute of "גבורה" was temporarily removed by the prophet Yirmeyahu, when in our prayer here King David attests to the eternal nature of גבורה?

"דור לדור ישבח מעשיך וגבורתיך יגידו."

"Each (and *every*) generation attests to Your mighty deeds."

2) In the commentary עיון יעקב to the sefer עין יעקב the following question is raised. Why do we refer to those who restored the glory of the Divine Attributes as the "אנשי כנסת הגדולה", the "Men of the *Great* Synod", with its emphasis on the attribute of "greatness", גדול; for that attribute was never abolished, but rather only the attributes of "powerful" and "awesome", גבור and נורא, were interfered with by the prophets Yirmeyahu and Daniel. Why, then, not call them "the Men of the *Powerful* Synod", אנשי כנסת הגבורה, in reference to their role in reinstating the attribute of גבורה?

3) How could Yirmeyahu and Daniel remove what was established in the Torah by Moshe Rabbenu, who was certainly a greater prophet than they? The Gemara touches upon this question, when it asks:

"ורבנן [ירמיה ודניאל] היכי סמכי אדעתייהו ועקרה מה דאמר משה?"

"How could the earlier Rabbis (Yirmeyahu and Daniel) abolish something established by Moshe?"

And the following answer is given:

"אמר ר' אלעזר: מתוך שיודעים בהקב"ה שאמיתי הוא לפיכך לא כזבו לו."

"R' Elazar said: Since they knew that the Holy One, Blessed be He, insists on truth, they would not ascribe things to Him that did not seem so."

To answer this and the rest of the above questions, we might suggest that there are two kinds of גבורות ה', Divine powers. One is revealed through the normal course of nature, מתוך דרך הטבע. An example of this is rain, which clearly represents Divine blessing and the manifestation of Hashem's might within the laws of nature. And so, appropriately, we refer in our prayers to the giving of rain as "גבורות הגשמים". But there is another kind of גבורה, represented by that Divine power which operates beyond the laws of nature, למעלה מדרך הטבע. This includes all those miracles which Hashem performed on behalf of the Jewish people, such as the Splitting of the Red Sea. We might say that the גבורות within natural law never were and never will be suspended; whereas those גבורות which operate beyond natural law may be suspended whenever Bnai Yisrael do not deserve that such miracles be performed for them.

If this is so, then we can see that the attribute of "גבורה" was never removed from our prayer; rather what was removed was the secondary meaning of this concept — the power which operates above natural law. Thus, when we say in our prayers, "ה-אל הגדול הגבור והנורא", the impact of the term "הגבור" is somewhat weakened, since half its meaning has been removed. Thus what the אנשי כנסת הגדולה achieved was to restore the full meaning of גבורה, when they tell us "אתה גבור לעולם", that Hashem's might is everlasting, and He can effect miracles whenever He wishes, both within and above natural law.

This means that Yirmeyahu and Daniel did not succeed in completely suspending the Divine Attributes established by Moshe Rabbenu, for, as we have seen, גבורה, which they, too, agree alludes to miracles within natural law, were never suspended. And so we might say that the words of King David, "דור לדור וגו' וגבורתך יגידו", refers to those Divine powers within the laws of nature which were never suspended. Therefore, what the אנשי כנסת הגדולה accomplished was to magnify and extend the meaning of גבורה to include miracles which occur beyond the laws of nature. And so we can justifiably refer to them as the אנשי כנסת הגדולה, for the meaning of הגדול here is "to magnify"; and thus they are the Synod which magnified the meaning of the concepts of גבור and נורא. Once this has been established, we can understand the particular emphasis of the words of the prayer "אתה גבור לעולם מחיה מתים וכו'", which is: "You are *forever powerful*, *even* in the realm of powers beyond the laws of nature, such as resurrecting the dead."

IV
Hidden and open miracles

The following insight of HaRav Meir Tzvi Bergman, שליט"א, seems to contradict the position we have just presented. In his sefer "שערי אורה על התורה", ח"א פ' ויחי he points out that in the Ashrei prayer we find the phrase "דור ודור" mentioned twice.

"דור לדור ישבח מעשיך וגבורתך יגידו.
מלכותך מלכות כל עולמים וממשלתך בכל דור ודר."

Here one may notice that in the first instance both words ("דור לדור") are written in full "מלא", with a vav; whereas in the second instance, although the first word "דור" is written מלא with a vav, the second word, "דר" is written "חסר" (incompletely), without a vav. What is the reason for this difference?

He answers that Hashem's מלכות, His sovereignty over the world, is recognized and acknowledged whether or not the generation is deserving of it, "מלא", whether they live according to the principles of the Torah, or whether it is lacking, "חסר", whether they do not live according to those principles. In this latter case, God's Sovereignty can not be so easily detected in the world. Yet all acknowledge that His reign is eternal. However, when it comes to praising the might of Hashem for performing open miracles beyond the laws of nature, this can only occur at a time when the generation is "מלא", deserving of such Divine intervention.

Thus we can see that praise is expressed only in a generation which deserves that open miracles be performed for them. But this seems to contradict our previous statement, that when open miracles are not detected, we offer no praise for them; whereas hidden miracles, which occur *within* the laws of nature, are always being performed for us and thus praise for them must continually be offered.

But there is really no contradiction here, for the halacha states that praise in the form of Hallel (שירה) is offered only for those miracles which are openly revealed — נסים גלוים. Hidden miracles, on the other hand, although they too transcend the laws of nature, do not call for the recitation of Hallel. And so we may understand these words of King David in the following way. "דור לדור" — only in a generation which witnesses open miracles, — "ישבח"

"מעשך, do we sing Hashem's praises in the form of Hallel (שבח). However, from this we can deduce that for hidden miracles, even though shirah is not said, we must nevertheless still praise Hashem,"וגבורתך יגידו", for His mighty deeds (those hidden miracles). When viewed in this way, there is no contradiction with our previous statement.

Kaddish: יתגדל

I
Selichos begins with Kaddish

After Ashrei, the chazzan recites Kaddish. As previously discussed, Ashrei, which belongs to the Kisvei HaKodesh, opens the way for the recitation of Kaddish.

The following story teaches us what our mindset should be as we approach the Selichos prayers. In the year 1840 in Russia, no Jews were permitted to live in the city of St. Petersburg. Those Jews who nevertheless found themselves in that city had to be granted special permission by the Czar and his government to remain there. The only shul allowed to hold services was one known as the "Soldiers' Shul", since it was attended by Jewish soldiers of the Russian Army who happened to be stationed in St. Petersburg. Once the Czar called for a delegation of leading rabbis and Jewish lay leaders to meet with him there to discuss issues relating to the Jewish community in Russia.

This meeting was to take place just before Yom Kippur, and so the delegates were forced to remain in the city and daven at the Soldiers' Shul on Yom Kippur. When it came time for Neilah, the closing prayer of the holiest day of the year, the delegates decided that the most distinguished rav there present — Rav Itzikel of Volozhin (some say it was the Tzemach Tzedek) — should have the honor of leading the congregation in this prayer. However, the shul's "regulars" approached the august rabbis and requested that one of the common soldiers be granted this honor. The reason they gave was that this soldier had brought great glory to Hashem's holy Name by withstanding repeated attempts to get him to renounce Judaism. He had been tortured so badly that his whole body was covered with scars and bruises from the many beatings he had sustained. He was repeatedly prevailed upon to take off his shirt and show the rabbis his bruises, and though he modestly declined again and again, when he finally agreed, the rabbis were horrified at what they saw. They all concurred that this righteous individual should certainly be the one to serve as chazzan for Neilah, and as it turned out, the way he davened taught everyone a great lesson about the self sacrifice with which a person should approach the Almighty in prayer on this holiest of days.

For when the soldier took his place before the congregation, before he began to pray, he made the following heartfelt plea.

"Ribbono Shel Olam, at this most critical moment of this most critical day there are three things which a person usually requests of You. They are בני, חיי, ומזוני, blessings for the welfare of his children, long life, and parnassah. However, as far as we soldiers are concerned, these requests have no significance for us, given our particular lot in life. For, first of all, we are not married and therefore we do not have any children to pray for; secondly, we do not request long life, since our situation is so difficult we do not wish to live long and would rather pray for our lives to end as quickly as possible, if that were permissible; and finally, we need no parnassah, since our needs are minimal — a few crumbs and a uniform — and these are provided by the Czar and his army. Thus we have no reason to pray for these things. And so, there is just one thing left to pray for..."

And then, with great sincerity and in a heartbroken voice he began to pray: "יתגדל ויתקדש שמה רבא", "May His Great Name be exalted and sanctified."

From this we can learn that when we begin the seder of Selichos, our prayers should not be centered on our personal needs, but rather we should look forward to the day when all nations will come to recognize the sovereignty of the one true God and His glory will be restored in this world. Thus we begin the Selichos with a recitation of Kaddish, which guides us in the direction we must follow — how and what to pray for — in these most crucial prayers which carry us into the Days of Awe.

II
Another reason for concluding with Kaddish

The complete Kaddish is recited here, for Selichos constitutes a "seder tefillah" which requires that it be concluded with קדיש שלם. We can suggest yet another reason why it is appropriate to conclude Selichos with קדיש שלם, based on the following insight of the משך חכמה.

In Bereishis 48:22 we read:

"ואני נתתי לך שכם אחד על אחיך אשר לקחתי מיד האמרי בחרבי ובקשתי"

"And I have given to you one portion more than to your brothers, that I took from the hands of Emori with my sword and with my bow."

The Targum Onkeles translates the words, "חרבי" "וקשתי", "sword and bow" to mean prayer and supplication, "בצלותי ובבעותי". The משך חכמה explains what the Targum

Onkeles was alluding to here when he translated "חרבי ובקשתי", to mean prayer and supplication, "בצלותי ובבעותי".

"צלותי — הוא סדר תפילה הקבוע, כמו שאמר, שבח והתפילה וההודאה מעכבין (תוספתא מנחות:ו). ובעותי — הוא בקשה, אשר אמרו, אם רצה אדם לחדש בתפילתו מעין כל ברכה שואל אדם צרכיו. והנה הנפקא מינה [בין תפלה לבקשה] כי סדר תפלה, שזו עבודה קבועה, אין הכוונה מעכב, ואם כיוון לבו באבות סגי, ובכוונה מועטת סגי. ולא כן בחידוש, שמבקש אדם צרכיו מחדש, בעי כוונה יתירה...

והנה חרב הוא בעצמו מזיק, שברזל שיש לו חדוד ממית בכל שהוא...

אבל הקשת בעצמו אינו מזיק, רק כוח המורה. ותלוי לפי כוח ורחוק המורה בקשת. לזה קרא לתפילה בשם חרבי — שהיא אף בלא כוונה מרובה,

ובעותי בשם קשתי — שהיא כמו קשת שהיא עד שמשים נפשו בכפו..."

"Prayer refers to the established order of tefillah, as we find in the daily Shemoneh Esreh. Supplications refer to personal requests that a person may add, either in the Shemoneh Esreh or as an extra tefillah.

There is a fundamental difference between a tefillah which is required daily and one which is said as a voluntary prayer, נדבה. The daily required prayer may be said even without כוונה, special concentration on the meaning of the words. As long as one has in mind, at the very least, the meaning of the words of the first beracha (Avos), he fulfills his obligation. The words themselves, particularly when said together with the congregation, have their own independent power to accomplish their task without the special intent of the one praying.

The power of voluntary tefillah, however, depends upon the special intent and concentration of the one praying. Halachically, one must add some personal request whenever he wants to say a voluntary tefillah (תפילת נדבה).

Therefore, the Torah uses the example of a sword to represent the required daily tefillos. Just as the blade of a sharpened sword has the power to cut even without being especially directed to do so by the one wielding it, so too does a required tefillah have the power to be effective even without the special intent of the one offering the prayer.

The bow and arrow, however, can do no damage without being wielded by someone who can shoot with intent and concentration at a specific target. Thus, the supplicatory voluntary tefillah is represented as being a bow in the hands of Yaakov Aveinu, who, like a master marksman, has the ability to direct it to attain the results he desires."

The common practice, when we recite the Selichos prayers, is to put more effort of concentration into the seder tefillos, such as Ashrei, Shema Koleinu, the Thirteen Attributes, etc.; whereas the additional prayers, the piyutim, are usually recited with the hope that we will be able to read the words correctly. But we see from our previous discussion that the opposite should be the case. When we recite Selichos, which are after all voluntary prayers, it should be incumbent upon us to say them with a greater degree of concentration and a measure of heartfelt devotion than we do the standard obligatory prayers. We must therefore practice these piyutim and learn the meanings of the difficult words and phrases even before we recite them, so that we will be able to say them with the appropriate intention and concentration. Only then will these prayers be meaningful to us and have the desired effect of reaching their destination, just as the well-aimed arrow reaches its target. If we do this, we will then be able to say wholeheartedly, "תתקבל צלותהון ובעותהון". And this is the reason we are required to recite a full Kaddish after we recite Selichos, for it challenges us to concentrate on all the separate verses which compose the order of the Selichos prayers, and with a careful recitation of Kaddish we declare that we have indeed met that challenge.

The Thirteen Attributes of Mercy: י״ג מדות

I
A prescription for Divine forgiveness

The central prayer of Selichos is the recitation of the *Thirteen Attributes of Mercy*, "י״ג מדות", which begins with the words: "ה' ה' א-ל רחום וחנון"

"Hashem, Hashem, God, Compassionate and Gracious..." This is a unique prayer which was taught to Moshe Rabbenu by Hashem after Bnai Yisrael had sinned with the Golden Calf. Klal Yisrael is assured that this prayer will always be answered and will bring them forgiveness. Thus we are told in Mesechtas Rosh Hashanah 17b:

"אמר רב יהודה: ברית כרותה לי״ג מדות שאינן חוזרות ריקם, שנאמר, הנה אנכי כורת ברית."

"Rav Yehudah said: A covenant has been made with the Thirteen Attributes, which promises that they will not be turned away empty-handed, as it says: 'Behold, I have made a covenant.'"

Tosafos Yom Tov maintains (see his comments on the Mishna in Nedarim 3:11) that a covenant was made regarding each "Attribute" (מדה), and thus we have thirteen covenants. The Gemara also tells us, just prior to the above statement, that Hashem emphasized the efficacy of this prayer to Moshe Rabbenu.

"ויעבור ה' על פניו ויקרא - אמר רב יוחנן, אלמלא מקרא כתוב אי אפשר לאומרו מלמד שנתעטף הקב"ה כשליח צבור, והראה לו למשה סדר תפלה. אמר לו, כל זמן שישראל חוטאין, יעשו לפני בסדר הזה, ואני מוחל להם."

"Hashem passed before him [Moshe Rabbenu] and proclaimed [Shemos 34:6]. Rav Yochanan said, 'If the scriptural verse had not been written, it would be impossible to say it. This teaches us that the Holy One, Blessed be He, wrapped himself [in a tallis] like a leader of prayer and showed him the order of the prayer.' He then said to him, 'Whenever Bnai Yisrael sin before me, let them perform this procedure and I will forgive them.'"

According to Chazal, we are being given here a prescription for attaining Divine Forgiveness. We are told to emulate what Hashem Himself is doing. He wraps Himself in a tallis like a prayer leader and he shows Moshe Rabbenu the order of prayer.

But these words of Chazal lead us to raise the following questions:

The Commentators' Machzor Companion 73

1) It appears that all one must do to attain forgiveness is recite the Thirteen Attributes of Mercy, the "order of prayer". However, this prescription seems rather simplistic. And indeed, it has been pointed out by some commentators that even though many have poured out their hearts to Hashem with this prayer, they still have not attained forgiveness.

2) The גרי"ז הלוי, in his commentary to the Torah (Parashas V'Eschanan) points out that based on the description given here — that Hashem appeared before Moshe like a prayer leader wrapped in a tallis — the assurance of forgiveness granted by the Thirteen Attributes of Mercy applies to a congregation and not to an individual. But why, we might ask, is it effective only for a congregation and not for an individual?

3) The בית יוסף, in סימן תקסח, asks why the recitation of the Thirteen Attributes of Mercy requires a minyan, a quorum of ten men? For a minyan is usually called for only in the case of a דבר שבקדושה, such as Kaddish, Kedushah, Borchu. The י"ג מדות do not seem to belong to this category of "holy utterances". Why, then, is a minyan required for its recitation?

The בית יוסף himself answers this question by saying that the י"ג מדות is referred to here as "תפלה", prayer; and so, just as the Amidah, which is described as תפלה, prayer, requires a minyan, so, too, does this prayer.

4) The י"ג מדות is recited on the three pilgrimage festivals, the שלש רגלים, at the time the Torah is taken out of the ark. This raises the question, what place does a prayer for forgiveness have on a festival, when we are not allowed to petition Hashem for forgiveness?

II
Deeds, not words alone, bring forgiveness

To answer our first question, many commentators maintain that in order for our petition for forgiveness to be answered, not only must we recite the Thirteen Attributes, but we must also *emulate* these Divine Attributes.

"מה הוא רחום אף אתה רחום."

"Just as He is Merciful, should you be merciful; as He is forgiving, so should you be forgiving to those who have done you wrong."

For only when Klal Yisrael can be identified as a merciful people, can they hope to receive forgiveness from Above. This is explained in the sefer "צרור המור", in the commentary to this pasuk.

"ופירושו ידוע, שהרי אנו רואים הרבה פעמים בעוונותינו, שאנו מעוטפים בטלית, ואין אנו נענין. אבל הרצון, כל זמן שישראל עושין סדר הזה שאני עושה -- לרחם, לחנן דלים, ולהאריך אפים, ולעשות חסד אלו עם אלו, ולעבור מידותיהן, כאומרם כל המעביר על מידותיו וכו', אז הם מובטחים, שאינן חוזרות ריקם. אבל אם הם אכזרים ועושי רשעה, כל שכן בהזכרת יג מדות הם נתפסין וזהו, "וחנותי את אשר אחון' -- מי שראוי לחנן ולרחם עליו. ולכן הוצרך לומר, ויעבור ה', כאילו הוא מעצמו עבר לפניו ללמדו כיצד יעשה וכיצד יקרא..."

Another commentator, the אלשיך הק', takes a similar approach in his sefer (תורת משה, (במדבר יד,יז), where he writes as follows:

"ושמעתי בשם ספר לבנת הספיר שדקדק באומרו 'עשו לפני' ולא אמר 'אמרו לפני' כי בזה תשובה אל קצת נענים על ידי הסדר הזה. שהוא כי מה שנדר הוא יתברך שאינם חוזרת ריקם הוא בעשותנו אנחנו המדות ההם מה הוא א-ל עושה חסד ורחום וחנון כן אנחנו. וכן על דרך זה בשאר. אך באמירה ובלי מעשה לא יהי' כן..."

"From the fact that Hashem said, '*Do* before Me', and did not say, '*Say* before Me', these attributes, we are being told that mere words alone will not gain us atonement. Only through deeds that emulate Hashem, such as being merciful, etc., can we be assured of Hashem's covenant with us. This answers the question why many are not answered after saying this prayer [alone]."

Thus, actions rather than words are required here, those actions which reflect one's ability to emulate Hashem's Attributes of Mercy. And this explains why the assurance that this will bring atonement was given only to a congregation and not to an individual. This is explained by the "משך חכמה" with the following insight.

The continued existence of the Jewish people as a nation, a צבור, depends on upholding its social and moral standards. What is of greatest importance is not the observance of the ceremonial Mitzvos for their own sake, but rather the relationship of kindness and compassion between man and his fellow. Thus, Hashem pointed out to Moshe Rabbenu, "אם ישראל חוטאין", "if the nation of Yisrael sins" it will lose its identity as a collective Jewish entity. If this should happen, then they must emulate Hashem's attributes of mercy, and they will attain forgiveness and survive as a nation, a צבור. For a nation is judged on its merits, on how successfully it emulates the Divine Attributes of mercy and lovingkindness which Hashem embodies. An individual, on the other hand, achieves forgiveness if he identifies himself with the nation. And as for the other sins, confession and repentance, וידוי ותשובה, are called for.

וז"ל המשך חכמה -- בשלח, יד,ד"ה והמים להם חומה:

The Commentators' Machzor Companion 77

"בהתבונן בדרכי התורה נראה כי במצוות מעשיות כמו מחלוקת לשון הרע, רכילות, גזל, אין בו מלקות...אולם זה דוקא ביחיד העושה, אבל אם הצבור נשחתין, בזה מצאנו להיפך בירושלמי דפאה... דורו של דוד כולם צדיקים היו, ועל ידי שהיו בהם דלטורין [בעלי לשון הרע] היו נופלים במלחמה...אבל דורו של אחאב, עובדי עבודה זרה היו, ועל ידי שלא היו בהם דלטורין היו יורדים במלחמה ומנצחים...

וגדולה מזו אמרו (יומא ט,א), שבמקדש ראשון היו עובדי עבודה זרה, עריות, ובמקדש שני היו עוסקים בתורה ובמצוות וגמילות חסדים, ומפני מה חרב? מפני שנאת חנם...ושם שאלו, מה הם גדולים? תנו עיניכם בבירה [בית המקדש] שחזרה לראשונים ולא חזרה לאחרונים, הרי דאם הצבור נשחתים במידות, גרוע יותר מאם נשחתין במצוות... ולכן מצאנו שעל העגל שהיה החטא בעבודה זרה, מחל הקב"ה להם ונתרצה להם, אבל על מרגלים שהיה לשון הרע וכפיות טובה לא מחל להם ונגזור, "במדבר הזה יתמו'..."

"When we examine the ways of the Torah, we discover that certain active Mitzvos and transgressions, such as idolatry, bloodshed and incest carry various punishments, ranging from whipping to the death penalty. On the other hand, there are Mitzvos which pertain between man and his fellow, such as lashon hara, slander, stealing, causing arguments, etc., which do not receive even lashes.

However, this is true only when the individual violates these Mitzvos of etiquette; but when the *tzibbur*, the society as a whole, violates these Mitzvos, the opposite effect occurs. The Yerushalmi in Peah tells us: The generation of King David, although it was completely righteous, fell in battle because there was internal strife, jealousy and lashon hara. The generation of Achab, however, although they worshipped idols, emerged victorious from battle because there was no internal strife.

Moreover, we are told in Mesechtas Yoma 9a that during the period of the First Temple the people engaged in idol worship and incest, and therefore the Temple was destroyed. However, the destruction of the Second Temple was due only to the sin of baseless hatred.

Which is a greater sin, asks the Gemara? And it answers based on the fact that the First Temple was quickly restored; whereas the Second Temple still remains in ruins. This is proof that the sin against one's fellow man is greater."

With this in mind, we can understand why the covenantal promise of the Thirteen Attributes of Mercy applies to a congregation, a צבור, rather than to an individual, and why the congregation has a greater responsibility to adhere to certain Mitzvos than does an individual. Thus, we can now answer all our previous questions.

1) We receive forgiveness, not by simply repeating these words but by emulating Hashem's characteristics, such as mercy, lovingkindness, etc. This means that if our prayers are not answered, it is not because we did not pray in a heartfelt enough manner, but because we failed to put into action the character traits enunciated here.

2) The covenantal promise of the Thirteen Attributes applies only to a צבור, for the way to rectify the wrongs of a צבור is to follow the prescription laid down here in the יג מידות.

3) Even though the יג מידות is not considered a דבר שבקדושה, a צבור is required to recite the Thirteen Attributes of Mercy for two reasons: firstly, because the יג מידות refer only to a צבור, and secondly, because they have a greater responsibility for correcting their behavior.

As for the question how we are allowed to recite the יג מידות on Yom Tov, since we are not permitted to petition Hashem on this day, the answer is that rather than petitioning Him for forgiveness, we are really reminding ourselves, by our recitation on Yom Tov, that the way to gain that forgiveness is to emulate His Attributes.

The reason we bring this to our attention on Yom Tov can be traced to what is written in the פרשת המועדים in Parashas Emor. There, before the Torah begins to enumerate the festivals, we find a description of the Mitzva of *peah*, פאה — leaving the corners of one's field for the poor to glean whatever produce has been left there. Rashi here (in ויקרא כג, כב) asks the following question. Why was this Mitzva of peah placed in the middle of the parasha of the festivals? Perhaps the answer lies in the idea that when we are about to celebrate a holiday with fine clothes and festive food and drink, we should not forget those in need. For this reason we recite the יג מדות on Yom Tov, to remind us how important it is to emulate Hashem's Attributes of lovingkindness and mercy, particularly on these days of celebration.

III

Why the 13 Attributes must be said in their proper order

However, a problem remains, related to the stipulation that the יג מדות must occur in a prescribed order. For, if all that is needed is for us to recite the Thirteen Attributes, then it is quite understandable why they must be said in the order in which they were written in the Torah. But if we must emulate these attributes, how do we account for the need for סדר, a particular specified order, here?

The sefer "בינת יששכר" (עמ' מו) addresses this question and suggests an answer by posing another question. It would seem that the order here should be אמת ורב חסד, for initially Hashem judges with אמת, according to the strict letter of the law, and only afterwards does He apply חסד, lovingkindness, and forgives us. Why, then, do we first say רב חסד ואמת, placing lovingkindness before strict justice? Why must we first say that Hashem is kind enough to forgive us (with חסד) for wrongdoing in our relationship with Him, and only then He is good enough to help us. This implies that חסד alludes to forgiveness, whereas אמת is related to the fact that He still helps us in whatever we request from Him. In this way, we are called upon to emulate His ways. For when one who has wronged us requests our help, we must first forgive him with חסד, and then we must not hesitate to fulfill that person's needs, which is an embodiment of אמת. For when we help one who is in need, even though he may have wronged us in the past, we succeed in emulating Hashem's attribute of truth, אמת. This, then, explains the order prescribed here.

To answer the question why there is a need for proper order, "סדר", we may adapt the following insight of HaRav Moshe Leib Sachor, זצ"ל, in his sefer "אבני שהם", חלק ב, עמ' קלז, where he points out the discrepancy between the middos of רחום and חנון. In the Torah we have Hashem's attribute of compassion, רחום, listed first, and only then do we find the attribute of graciousness, חנון. However, in Sefer Tehillim, 112:4, graciousness, חנון, comes before compassion, רחום. The reason for this, HaRav Sachor suggests, is that in the יג מדות human beings are called upon to emulate Hashem, and it is natural for a human being to feel compassionate and then, as a result of that, he acts graciously. Therefore, here in the Torah when it is man who is called upon to act, he must first be compassionate and then gracious, in accordance with human nature. However, Hashem's graciousness is not dependent upon compassion. This is why in Sefer Tehillim, where Hashem's attributes are enumerated, חנון is mentioned first and then רחום.

Thus, if human graciousness arises from compassion, we must make sure that our gracious acts spring from a true feeling of compassion rather than from any other self-serving considerations. The need for סדר here, thus teaches us that we must first train ourselves in positive middos, and these will in turn lead us to demonstrate further positive character traits. From this process we learn that even in emulating Hashem's attributes, there is a need for following a prescribed order.

IV
How to count the 13 Attributes

Other commentators maintain that we are required only to recite the יג מדות. They attempt to prove this by analyzing the constitution of the Thirteen Attributes. There is a wide difference of opinion over how to count the Thirteen Attributes.

1) Rabbenu Tam, cited in the Tosafos in Mesechtas Rosh Hashanah, 13b (ד"ה יג מדות) believes that the first two names of Hashem (ה',ה') here are an integral part of the Thirteen Attributes. The first of these Divine names (ה') alludes to His mercy *prior* to human sin. For even though man has not yet sinned, Hashem knows that he will sin and He is prepared to forgive him. (See Rashi on this Gemara.) The second name of Hashem (ה') refers to Hashem's mercy *after* man has sinned.

2) Other commentators contend that only the second mention of Hashem's name is to be counted as one of the Divine Attributes of Mercy.

3) The Ari HaKadosh, on the other hand, does not count the first two names of Hashem (ה',ה') at all, but rather begins with the word "א-ל".

4) Yet others do not count "א-ל" either, but begin to count only from the word "רחום".

The famous commentator, the Nodah B'Yehudah, in his classic sefer "אהבת ציון" (דרוש ד') brings the following proof that the first two names of Hashem are not to be counted among the 13 Attributes. It is well known that Hashem's Ineffable Name, the שם מפורש, can be uttered only in the Bais HaMikdash. Therefore, if "ה', ה'" alludes to the Thirteen Attributes, then it would have to be said with the שם מפורש. How, then, could this be said outside the Bais HaMikdash? And if we were to contend that it was only recited in the Bais HaMikdash, what happened after its destruction, how could we recite it then? And if we were to suggest that instead of the שם מפורש, we used the four-letter Name of Hashem, this could not be the case, for the שם מפורש alludes to the God of Mercy, whereas the four-letter Name of Hashem alludes to the Master of the Universe. Therefore, we must conclude that the 13 Attributes begin with the word "א-ל".

Thus we can appreciate the statement we make just prior to the recitation of the יג מדות, that: "א-ל הורית לנו לומר שלש עשרה",

"O God, You taught us to *recite* the Thirteen [Attributes of Mercy]."

We can understand this statement in the following way. We begin here with the word "א-ל" and not with "ה', ה'", for "You have taught us to *recite* these words", and we cannot recite the Ineffable Name of Hashem outside the confines of the Bais HaMikdash.

A similar approach is taken by the "הפלאה", (see פנים יפות תשא ד"ה שם בר"ה) who brings proof on behalf of those who contend that the intention of the 13 Attributes is not to emulate Hashem but rather to recite the proper order of Divine attributes. For if we were being called upon to emulate His attributes, how could we possibly emulate the attribute of א-ל? Or how could we say "אל אתה אף א-ל הוא מה"? For we clearly state in Bamidbar 23:19 that "God is not a man, and a man is not God," "לא איש א-ל".

And so we must conclude that since we begin the 13 Attributes with the word "א-ל", this must imply that we need not emulate these attributes but need only recite them. With this in mind, we can understand that when we say: "א-ל הורית לנו לומר שלש עשרה", we know from the word

"א-ל" that we are required to recite these attributes, "לומר", and not to emulate them.

This is the argument of those who maintain that when one recites the יג מדות, forgiveness will be forthcoming. Our recitation, however, must be with absolute concentration and pure intention, כוונה. This explains the imagery of Hashem "wrapping Himself in a tallis", for when a person prays, he must shut out all the distracting influences of the world. Only then can one hope to realize the full benefits of this unique prayer.

Yet this still leaves the question unanswered of how many have said the prayer and were not answered. But we could perhaps resolve this problem by pointing out that this prayer is essentially that of a congregation, a צבור. And so, even though the individual, יחיד, may not have been answered, yet the צבור, despite whatever it may have suffered, did indeed attain forgiveness, in the sense that despite everything, it has managed to remain intact as a congregation.

The Chazzan for the High Holy Days: Requirements

I

A person of great stature

The Rema (רמ"א) in Hilchos Rosh Hashanah, סימן תקפ"א סעיף א, writes as follows:

"וידקדקו לחזור אחר שליח צבור היותר הגון והיותר גדול בתורה ובמעשים שאפשר למצוא שיתפלל סליחות וימים נוראים ושיהא בן שלשים שנים גם שיהא נשוי..."

"We should be particular to search for the most fitting prayer leader it is possible to find to serve on the High Holy days, one who is most distinguished in Torah scholarship and good deeds, at least thirty years of age and married..."

This is in light of what the Rambam stipulates in Hilchos Tefillah 8:11:

"אין ממנין שליח צבור, אלא גדול שבצבור בחכמתו ובמעשיו. ואם היה זקן — הרי זה משובח..."

"Only a person of great stature within the community in both wisdom and deed should be appointed as leader of the congregation. If he is an older man, it is very praiseworthy..."

Thus we see that appointment of a person as prayer leader with outstanding ability and recognition in scholarship and good deeds is required *all year round*. Why, then, did the Rema find it necessary to point out the need for these qualities on Rosh Hashanah in particular?

An answer to this question might be suggested in light of the comments of the לחם משנה to the above Rambam. The לחם משנה contends that these qualities enumerated here by the Rambam refer only to the appointment of a *permanent chazzan,* שליח צבור קבוע. However, when it comes to a chazzan who serves on a temporary basis, שליח צבור עראי, these qualities can be waived. And so we might say that the Rema here is telling us that if one comes to serve as the prayer leader on the High Holy days, even temporarily, then all of the above-mentioned qualities are required and essential.

Others suggest that the reason the Rema felt compelled to list the requirements of a chazzan on Rosh Hashanah, even though we might think they would be the same as those called for in a chazzan the rest of the year, is that this helps us draw a distinction between one who is merely competent and one who is *highly competent*. All year what is required is a chazzan who is merely competent; in other words, he must be recognized as a talmid chacham, a man of good deeds, but this does not mean that he must be the most outstanding in these qualities. On Rosh Hashanah, however, we must seek out the best and most qualified person available. This is alluded to in the words of the Rema when he says: "וידקדקו", "we must be *most particular*", which implies that we must actively search for the most competent candidate available.

A plausible answer to the above question might be that there is a basic difference between "all year round" and on the High Holy days. This difference is alluded to in the words of the Rambam here in Hilchos Tefillah (op. cit.): "אין ממנין אלא גדול שבצבור"

"Only a person of great stature within the community... should be appointed as leader of the congregation." In other words, we need not seek out someone outside the members of the community. One who is considered in the eyes of the worshippers to be a scholar, a man of good deeds, is suited to act as chazzan all year round. However, on the High Holy days, one must search beyond the immediate community for the best candidate available to serve as chazzan. This approach is also alluded to in the words of the Rema, where he says: "וידקדקו לחזור",

"We should be particular to *search*", and this implies that we must search even beyond the immediate community.

Based on the following insight, we might suggest yet another reason why the Rema emphasized the qualities a chazzan for the High Holy days must possess, even though these might seem to be the same as those required for a chazzan during the rest of the year.

The Rambam in Hilchos Sanhedrin, after describing the position of Nasi, president of the Sanhedrin, and Av Bais Din, the head of the Rabbinical Court, describes the elaborate seating arrangements of the seventy elders. But there appears to be a discrepancy in this description. He says:

"ושאר השבעים יושבין לפניו כפי שניהם וכפי מעלתם. כל הגדול מחבירו בחכמה יהי' קרוב לנשיא משמאלו יותר מחבירו..."

"The other seventy elders sit before the Nasi according to age and ability. One who is greater than his colleagues in wisdom sits closer to the Nasi's left..."

From here it seems that the factor determining who sits closest to the Nasi is age — "כפי שניהם". And yet, from the words of the Rambam the determining factor seems to be scholarship — "wisdom", "כל הגדול מחבירו בחכמה". In order to reconcile this discrepancy, the כסף משנה comments on the word "בחכמה" as follows: "שזהו כשהם שוים בשנים", "and that is when both are of the same age". And the sefer "סדר משנה" (by HaGaon Rav Chaim Yonah Tumim) explains the meaning of the כסף משנה, that he was alluding to the apparent discrepancy here. And indeed, there are two requirements here: the first, wisdom; and the second, age.

Thus if one is the same age as his colleague but superior in scholarship, he takes precedence. However, if both are equal in scholarship but one is older, he takes precedence. And in the case that one is much older than another, he will take precedence over his younger colleague, even if the younger colleague is only a little superior in scholarship, but the difference is not great.

Thus we see that age can sometimes take precedence over scholarship. And so we might suggest that this is the reason the Rema delineated the qualities needed by a chazzan for the High Holy days, to emphasize the importance of scholarship and good deeds in choosing a chazzan. For had he merely stipulated that a chazzan must be at least thirty years old, which is not a requirement all year round, we might mistakenly think that age was the determining factor in choosing a chazzan for the High Holy days.

The rationale behind this thinking might be that an older person who has experienced the trials and tribulations of life can best serve as the one to petition for life on Rosh Hashanah. However, the Rema emphasizes that in truth it is scholarship and good deeds which are the determining factors. And so, even though it may be true that if two candidates are equal in scholarship, the one who is older takes precedence, however, if one candidate is superior to the other in learning, even if he is younger, then the one who is a scholar will take precedence.

II

He must be married

One of the requirements of a chazzan for Rosh Hashanah and Yom Kippur is that he be married. The commentators point out the source for this in the fact that the Kohen Gadol who served on Yom Kippur had to be married. This is based on the pasuk of "וכפר בעדו ובעד ביתו", "And he shall atone for himself and for his household". Chazal explain this by saying, "ביתו זו אשתו", that the Kohen Gadol atoned not only for himself but also for his wife. Therefore a chazzan, who serves us in a sense just as a Kohen Gadol did in the Bais Hamikdash, must also be married. This analogy which compares the שליח צבור to a

כהן גדול is challenged by many. And even if we accept the comparison, we are confronted with the question, isn't it only applicable to Yom Kippur, where the Kohen Gadol played a dominant role in the service of the day? On Rosh Hashanah, however, the Kohen Gadol played no special role. Why, then, must a chazzan for Rosh Hashanah be married, based on this comparison?

To answer this question and the previous one of why the Rema delineated the requirements of a chazzan for the High Holy days, we may quote the following insight of HaRav Yosef Dov Soleveitchik:

"אלמלא מקרא כתוב אי אפשר לאומרו." בשעה ששליח הצבור עומד לפני העמוד עטוף בטליתו ואומר את הסליחות שלפני יום-כפור...הוא ממלא כביכול את מקומו של רבש"ע. בעמדו לפני העמוד בעת אמירת הסליחות הריהו בעצם נציגם של שניים: הוא שליחו של הציבור, כי הרי בראש השנה וביום-כפור הוא מתייצב ואומר "הנני העני ממעש...באתי לבקש רחמים וכו'" או "היה עם פיפיות עמך בית ישראל", תפילות שהוא אומר בשם הציבור כולו. מצד שני מקיים שליח-הצבור מעין שליחות של הקב"ה..."

There is indeed a distinction between the role of a chazzan all year round and on the High Holy days, Rav Soloveitchik contends. All year round the role of the chazzan is to *present* the petitions and prayers of the congregation before the Holy One, blessed be He; whereas on the High Holy days his role assumes a new dimension.

Apart from presenting the petitions of Klal Yisrael before Hashem, he *teaches and directs* the congregation how to petition and in what manner to recite the Selichos prayers. For when he recites the י"ג מדות, he is calling upon the Klal to recite this petition. We might even say, based on Chazal's words, "מלמד שנתעטף הקב"ה כשליח צבור", that Hashem in a sense assumed the role of שליח צבור and subsequently directed the שליח צבור to assume the role that Hashem had played at that moment, when he taught Bnai Yisrael the secret of attaining forgiveness.

Thus, if the chazzan stands in the place of Hashem Himself, as it were, and teaches us how to pray for forgiveness, then he must be a very special person of high moral stature. With this in mind, we might suggest why he must also be married, based on the following verse in Parashas Bereishis:

"על כן יעזוב איש את אביו ואת אמו ודבק באשתו",

"Hashem commanded man to leave his parents and cleave to his wife."

The question asked here related to the timing of this pasuk is this. Hashem is speaking to Adam HaRishon, who had no parents. How then is He commanding him to leave his parents? The answer must be that this pasuk was directed to subsequent generations. For Sefer Bereishis does not merely record how Hashem created a new world, but how He also called upon man to emulate Him. Just as he is a Creator, so, too, should man be a creator. And just as Hashem is perfect, so, too, should man strive for perfection. Unmarried men lack perfection, and therefore the command was given for man to marry. Thus if a human being is to stand in place of Hashem, Who is perfect, he must reach a state of perfection as close as he is capable of, and this requires that he be married.

Consequently, since the chazzan of the High Holy days plays a more important and meaningful role than the chazzan of the rest of the year, he is therefore required to be married. This more important and more meaningful role, where the chazzan is called upon to "step into the shoes of the Almighty", as it were, requires the chazzan to have greater qualifications than he would need during the rest of the year, and that is why the Rema found it essential to enumerate them here.

The Nine Berachos of the Rosh Hashanah Amidah

I
Seven berachos or nine?

The Mishna in *Berachos* 28b tells us that the weekly Amidah prayer consists of eighteen benedictions; and therefore we refer to this prayer as the *Shemoneh Esreh*. On Shabbos and Yom Tov, however, only seven blessings are said. These consist of the first and last three of the regular weekday prayers: אבות, גבורות, קדושת השם, עבודה, הודאה, ברכת כהנים, שים שלום and the middle beracha of קדושת היום, which describes the holiness of that particular day. On Rosh Hashanah, in addition to these seven Yom Tov berachos, we add three more, those of מלכיות, זכרונות ושופרות. Thus we now have a total of nine berachos.

Most commentators maintain that we recite all nine berachos only in the Mussaf prayer, and that accords with our practice today. In the other prayers of the day — Ma'ariv, Shacharis and Minchah — only seven berachos are recited. However, some opinions, in particular that of the בעל המאור, hold that all nine berachos should be said in all the Amidah prayers of the day.

There is also another difference between the Amidah prayers of Yom Tov and Rosh Hashanah in relation to the following halacha. The Mishna in Rosh Hashanah states:

"כשם ששליח צבור חייב כך כל יחיד ויחיד. רבן גמליאל אומר, שליח צבור מוציא את הרבים ידי חובתן."

"Just as the chazzan himself recites the Shemoneh Esreh silently before reciting it aloud for the benefit of the congregation, so, too, the individual does not rely on the recitation of the chazzan to discharge his own obligation of prayer.

Rabban Gamliel says the chazzan discharges the congregation's obligation."

The Gemara in Rosh Hashanah 35a concludes that the halacha all year follows the opinion of the first Tanna that each individual should pray on his own and not rely on the chazzan. However, regarding the Mussaf prayer of Rosh Hashanah one may discharge his obligation by listening to the שליח צבור, even if he is able to pray on his own. Rashi explains the rationale behind this relaxation of the law on Rosh Hashanah to be that since the prayers are long, not everyone can complete them on their own. This is especially true considering that in earlier times people prayed not from a Siddur, but by heart. (See Rashi in ד"ה א,לה). There we read as follows:

"אלא משום דאווּשי: שהרי כאן תשע וארוכות ומטעות דאין הכל בקיאין בהן."

And the Rambam in Hilchos Tefillah 8:10 writes:

"מפני שהן ברכות ארוכות ואין רוב היודעים אותן יכולין לכוין דעתם כשליח צבור."

How the chazzan "discharges the congregation's obligation" is a matter of dispute among the Rishonim.

1) Some maintain that the chazzan fulfills the congregation's obligation with only the extra three berachos of מלכיות, זכרונות ושופרות, but he cannot discharge their obligation with the seven berachos which are normally recited on Shabbos and Yom Tov, that is, the first and last three berachos and the קדושת היום. The entire congregation must recite on their own the תפילת שבע, the seven berachos, during the silent prayer of Mussaf, תפלה בלחש.

2) Others contend that all nine berachos must be said by the congregation, for this constitutes the essential Rosh Hashanah Amidah prayer. There is no special Amidah on this day of "שבע ברכות". And although the halacha states that the chazzan discharges the obligation of the congregation, this applies only to those who are unable to recite all nine berachos on their own.

3) There is another opinion, which is that the congregation need not say the silent prayer at all, and what is required is that they listen to the chazzan's repetition, חזרת הש"ץ.

The Rishonim also disagree as to whether or not the shofar is to be sounded during the silent prayer, תפלה בלחש.

1) Some hold that we are not to sound the shofar when reciting the silent prayers.

2) Others call for the shofar to be sounded during the recitation of the silent prayers.

On the surface, we might say that there is an inter-relationship between all these positions.

One opinion holds that the nine berachos were recited only at Mussaf and therefore the shofar is to be sounded then. This means that the shofar is sounded only when all nine berachos are read. This implies that only seven berachos were said in the silent prayer, and therefore the sounding of the shofar is not called for.

However, those who believe that the shofar should be sounded in the silent prayer base their opinion on the fact that:

1) In the silent prayer all nine berachos were said and therefore we sound the shofar to accompany them, even in

the silent prayer. Indeed, Rav Chaim Brisker maintains that today, when all agree that all nine berachos are to be recited in the silent prayer, it follows that we should sound the shofar.

2) Only seven berachos were said in the silent prayer. However, in all the prayers repeated by the chazzan throughout the day nine berachos were said. But the shofar was only sounded during the Mussaf prayer, which indicates that sounding the shofar is to be viewed as a separate Mitzva, and it can be sounded even when only seven berachos are recited in the silent Mussaf prayer. This was done in order not to make a difference between the Mussaf prayer said silently and the Mussaf prayer recited by the chazzan.

II
The opinion of the בעל המאור

The בעל המאור, in דף יב מדפי הרי״ף, maintains that the nine berachos of מלכיות זכרונות ושופרות should be recited in each of the Amidah prayers — Maariv, Shacharis, Mussaf and Minchah — even though the shofar is sounded only in the Mussaf prayer. He writes as follows:

The Commentators' Machzor Companion

"ואני אומר כי משרש ההלכה אין בר"ה שבע ברכות אלא תשע הן לעולם בין בערבית בין בשחרית בין במוסף בין במנחה כמו שתראה בפרק תפלת השחר: הני שמונה עשרה כנגד מי, הני שבעה דשבתא כנגד מי, הני תשע ברכות דראש השנה כנגד מי. נראה לנו מכאן שאין אנו לחלוק בתשע ברכות בכל תפלות היום כמו שאין לך לחלוק בשמונה עשרה של חול ובשבע של שבת ואף על פי שאין תוקעין אלא במוסף כדתנן העובר לפני התיבה ביום טוב של ראש השנה השני מתקיע, הא לענין ברכות זה וזה שוין..."

The בעל המאור cites here two proofs that all nine berachos were recited during all the prayers of the day.

1) The Gemara in Berachos 29a asks the question, "From where do we know that on Shabbos day there are seven berachos and on Rosh Hashanah nine berachos?" From this the בעל המאור concludes that just as on Shabbos the seven berachos are said throughout the day in all the Amidah prayers, so are the nine berachos to be said on Rosh Hashanah in all the day's Amidah prayers.

2) The Mishna in Rosh Hashanah 32b states:

"העובר לפני התיבה ביום טוב של ראש השנה השני מתקיע..."

The shofar is sounded during the repetition of the second chazzan, the one who leads the Mussaf prayer. Thus we can conclude that since the Mishna only mentioned the requirement of sounding the shofar at Mussaf and did not also include in the requirements of

Mussaf the recitation of the nine berachos, we can conclude that in this regard the number of blessings recited in all the Amidah prayers of the day was nine.

The בעל המאור, however, concluded:

"אלא שמנהג הוא בידינו מאבותינו שאין מתפללין תשע אלא במוספין ובשאר תפלות מתפללין שבע ומנהג אבות תורה היא ואין לשנות."

"We have a tradition handed down by our forefathers that the nine berachos are to be said only in the Mussaf prayers, and in all the other prayers of the day only seven berachos are to be said. The custom of our fathers is deemed as 'Torah' itself and therefore we cannot change that custom."

One page earlier (11a of the pages of the Rif) the following statement is made:

"ואל תתמה על מה שאמרנו שנשתנו המנהגות בדורות האחרונים מדורות הראשונים. כי אני זוכר כי ראיתי בילדותי כל הצבור מתפללין במוספין 'שבע' וש"ץ לבדו היה מתפלל 'תשע' והי' תלוין מנהגם במנהגי ישיבות הגאונים, כי כן מצאו כתוב בספריהם, וכן תמצא בהלכות ה"ר יצחק בן גיאת. ועכשיו חזרו הכל להיות מתפללין תשע ברכות."

"One should not wonder at that which we have said that the customs of the later generations have changed from earlier generations. For I distinctly remember when I was a child I witnessed that the congregation would only recite the 'seven' berachos in the silent blessings, whereas today we all recite the 'nine' in the silent prayers."

Thus, maintains the בעל המאור, just as the number of berachos said in the silent prayer changed in the course of time, so did the custom to recite nine berachos also change; and although the earlier generations said the nine berachos in all the day's prayers, today we say them only in the Mussaf prayers.

III
The position of the Ramban

The Ramban disagrees with all the contentions of the בעל המאור. Regarding the question whether מלכיות זכרונות ושופרות are to be said in all the prayers of the day, the Ramban writes as follows:

"אמר הכתוב מה נעביד ליה למר דלא ליסרי רוקיה שהוא בא לחלוק על דברי כל הגאונים ועל מנהג כל ישראל בלא ראיה ולא סמך."

He attacks the position of the בעל המאור, for it goes against the customs and the teachings of the gaonim and is not based on solid proofs from the Gemara and tradition. He dismisses the various proofs cited by the בעל המאור in the following manner:

"שאמרו, אמרו לפני מלכיות וזכרונות כדי שיעלה זכרונם לפני לטובה — ובמה בשופר אלמא אין מזכירין אותן אלא כשתוקעין וא״כ בערבית שחרית ומנחה נתקע..."

Chazal tell us, contends the Ramban, that the *malchius,* etc., are to be said in conjunction with the sounding of the shofar. Thus, if they are to be said at all the prayers of the day it should follow that the shofar should have been sounded at all the prayers of the day. But since we do not sound the shofar except at Mussaf, this proves positively that the nine berachos were not recited at all the prayers of the day.

The proof offered by the בעל המאור from the Mishna of "העובר לפני התיבה", also can be readily dismissed:

"וזו היא ששנינו, סדר ברכות אומר אבות גבורות וקדושת השם וכו' זכרונות ותקע, שופרות ותקע אלמא אין סדרן של ברכות הללו אלא בזמן שתוקעין מדלא קתני ובשעת התקיעות תקעו. ולפיכך נמי שנינו, השני מתקיע לאו למימרא דלענין ברכות זה וזה שוין, אלא מפני שלא תקנום במוספין אלא בשביל התקיעות לפיכך אמרו, השני מתקיע וכו', ומש״ה מקרי הני ברכות תקיעתא."

"This, then, is the meaning of the Mishna that teaches the order of the Mussaf prayers: *Avos, Gevuros, Kedushas Hashem,* etc., the remembrances, and the *shofaros,* and then we sound the shofar. Thus we see that the order of the berachos was only said at the time we sound the shofar. Consequently, when the Mishna states: 'we sound the shofar in Mussaf' one cannot conclude that in relation to the berachos of Kingship (*malchius*), etc., both the Shacharis and the Mussaf prayers are the same, in that all nine berachos are recited at each of these prayers. For what is being said here is that the shofar is sounded at the Mussaf prayers, and it is self-evident that the sounding of the shofar is accompanied by the pasukim of *malchius*, etc., for, as we have said, only when we sound the shofar do we read these additional prayers."

The Ramban contends that we can prove that only in the Mussaf prayers were the additional verses of מלכיות זכרונות ושופרות recited by looking at what was stated in the Yerushalmi *Shavuos*, Chapter 1, where we read the following:

"ר' יעקב בשם ר' יסא: העובר לפני התיבה ביום טוב של ראש השנה בשחרית, בית שמאי אומרים ח' ובית הלל אומרים ז'. במוסף בית שמאי אומרים י' ובית הלל ט'."

"Rav Yaakov in the name of Rav Assi states that for the reader in the Shacharis prayers, Bais Shammai contends we say eight berachos [the first and last three berachos each of the standard Amidah prayer, in addition to the berachos of Yom Tov and those of the specific holiday]. Bais Hillel says, seven, [for we combine the beracha of Yom Tov and Rosh Hashanah into one]. In the Mussaf prayer, Bais Hillel says we say nine berachos [the first and last three berachos each, the *'holiness of the day'* coupled with the *malchius, remembrances* and *shofaros.*] Bais Shammai says, ten, for according to him the *'holiness of the day'* of Rosh Hashanah called for a separate beracha, and thus we have ten berachos in the Mussaf prayer."

This provides positive proof, maintains the Ramban, that the מלכיות זכרונות ושופרות were recited only at the Mussaf prayers on the day of Rosh Hashanah.

As for how many berachos are to be said in the תפלה בלחש, the silent prayer, the Ramban writes as follows:

"וכיון שפסק הלכה כרבן גמליאל בשל ראש השנה בלבד נמצאו פטורין מט' וחייבין בז' כשאר יום טוב שהרי חובת היום חייבים הם בה כשאר ימים טובים..."

The Gemara explains that even the chachamim who disagree with Rabban Gamliel and do not normally permit the chazzan to discharge the obligation of one who is proficient in reading the prayers for himself (a בקי), they nevertheless concede that on Rosh Hashanah, the chazzan (ש"ץ) discharges the obligation even of the בקי, one who is proficient in reading.

The rationale here is that although the chazzan can discharge the obligation even of the בקי, this is only in relation to the unique prayers of Rosh Hashanah, such as the מלכיות זכרונות ושופרות. However, regarding the usual berachos of Yom Tov, the seven (including the קדושת היום), the chazzan does not discharge the obligation of the congregation, and each individual must recite these seven berachos for himself.

Thus we can conclude that the Ramban distinguished two separate prayers here in the Mussaf, two different motifs which constitute Mussaf.

1) The seven berachos, which constitutes the standard Mussaf of all the Yom Tov prayers. These are viewed as an obligation of the day of Yom Tov, חובת היום.

2) The unique prayer of Rosh Hashanah, which consists of the additional three blessings of מלכיות זכרונות ושופרות. Therefore the prayers of חובת היום which are recited on all the holidays, must be read by each individual even on Rosh Hashanah, as it is read on all holidays. However, the nine berachos (which allude to the three additional berachos of Rosh Hashanah) do not have to be said in the silent prayer and can be listened to when the chazzan recites them in his repetition of the Amidah prayer.

IV
The opinion of the רא״ש

The רא״ש agrees with the Ramban that only in the Mussaf prayer do we add the מלכיות זכרונות ושופרות; however he disagrees regarding the number of berachos recited by the congregation in the silent prayer, תפלה בלחש, and maintains that all nine berachos must be said. He writes as follows:

"לא הבנתי דברים הללו שנאמרו למשה מסיני, דכיון שתיקנו תשע ברכות לאומרן במוסף של ראש השנה הן כמו שבע של שבתות וימים טובים. וכשם שאי אפשר לדלג מאותן שבע, כך אי אפשר לדלג מן התשע, דברכות מעכבות זו את זו. ושליח צבור פוטר את הציבור מכולן דאוושי אלא שהציבור מתפללין כדי שיסדיר תפילתו. וצריכים להתפלל כולם דאם יתפללו שבע יהי' ברכה לבטלה..."

The רא״ש here cites the source of the various customs as to whether seven or nine berachos should be said. He quotes רבי יצחק אבן גיאות, who cites the custom followed by רב האי גאון and others that only seven berachos were said. And רבי יצחק אבן גיאות cites sources which maintain that all nine berachos should be said.

He writes:

"ואנו קבלנו מחכמים גדולים בעלי הוראה ואנשי מעשה שקבלו אף הם מחכמים שלפניהם, וכגון רבינו שמואל הלוי שקבל מהרב ר' חנוך וזקנים

שבדורו, הלכה למעשה שאין מתפללין בתפלת המוספין של ראש השנה כלל ז' אלא ט' וכן מורין ועושין."

The רא״ש directs his attack cited here in the first paragraph to this statement of the Ramban, that indeed it makes no sense to say that seven berachos were ever said but rather the Rosh Hashanah prayers call for nine berachos to be recited, both in the silent prayer and in the chazzan's repetition of the Amidah.

V

Reconciling the opinions of the Rishonim

We might attempt to clarify the various positions of the Rishonim cited here by first posing the following question. Are the nine berachos of the Amidah prayers that include מלכיות זכרונות ושופרות to be viewed as "מטבע הברכות", the "coinage" of the berachos? In other words, does everything said here in the Amidah prayer belong to the Rosh Hashanah prayers? Or are we to view these additional prayers of מלכיות זכרונות ושופרות not as an integral part of the Rosh Hashanah prayers, but rather in the same light as we view the "יעלה ויבוא" of the Rosh Chodesh prayer, as a "מעין המאורע" passage that alludes to *the occasion of the day* and therefore is inserted in the Amidah prayer?

We might say that the בעל המאור considers all nine berachos to be an integral part of the Amidah prayer, "מטבע הברכות", and since these nine are viewed as the proper format of the Rosh Hashanah Amidah prayer, they should be recited throughout the day in all the prayers — Maariv, Shacharis, and Minchah, as well as Mussaf. Yet the בעל המאור concedes that since the common practice was to recite the nine berachos only in the Mussaf prayer, we must follow that practice.

The רא״ש, however, disagrees and maintains that only at Mussaf are we to view the additional prayers of מלכיות זכרונות ושופרות as being "מטבע הברכות". His opinion coincides with the approach of the מאירי which dismisses the proof of the בעל המאור from the Gemara in Berachos, that as the seven berachos of Shabbos allude to all the Amidah prayers of the day, so too, the nine berachos of Rosh Hashanah allude to all the Amidah prayers of Rosh Hashanah. The מאירי believes that this is not necessarily the case, and he bases this doubt on the words of the גדולי זקנינו, "for even the seven berachos of Shabbos are exclusive to the Mussaf Shabbos prayers, and the only reason the other prayers also contain only seven berachos is because of a statement of our Rabbis quoted in Mesechtas Berachos 7a, that it was the Rabbis who did not trouble us to recite the whole of the weekday prayers, out of respect for the Shabbos". And this

The Commentators' Machzor Companion

is also the reason why on Rosh Hashanah we recite all nine berachos only in the Mussaf prayer. And since, maintains the רא"ש, the nine berachos in the Mussaf prayer are to be viewed as "מטבע הברכות", then even in the silent prayer recited by everyone, all nine berachos must be said in the תפלה בלחש.

The Ramban, however, contends that the nine berachos are to be viewed as additional prayers, "כעין המאורע", which represent the occasion of the day. However, they are to be added only to those prayers in which the shofar is sounded, that is, Mussaf. Perhaps the Ramban's source is based on the following consideration. In the Gemara of Berachos, in answer to the question, "to what do the nine berachos of Rosh Hashanah correspond?" the Gemara answers: to the nine berachos of Hashem's Name (אזכרות) mentioned in the prayer of Hannah which we find in the First Book of Shmuel 2:10 (עלץ לבי בה'). This prayer serves as the Haftorah of the first day of Rosh Hashanah. And since Hannah's prayer for a child was answered on Rosh Hashanah (Chazal tell us that on Rosh Hashanah it was decreed that Hannah would bear a child) we recite in our Amidah prayer nine berachos, corresponding to the nine times Hannah mentioned Hashem's name in her prayer.

The Yerushalmi Berachos adds to this answer of why we add nine berachos on Rosh Hashanah, that since the prayer concludes with the words: "ה' ידין את אפסי ארץ", "May Hashem judge to the ends of the earth", which refers to the Day of Judgement, we therefore allude to this prayer of Hannah on Rosh Hashanah and mention her nine אזכרות when we recite the nine berachos, which correspond to the nine berachos to be found in the Mussaf Amidah related to the Day of Judgement.

The other prayers of the day do not require nine berachos, and consequently in the silent prayer, where the shofar is not sounded, we need not say all nine, but only the seven which are required by the day, חובת היום, since they represent the *Yom Tov* of Rosh Hashanah.

Furthermore, we might suggest that the Ramban dismisses the proof from the Gemara of Berachos, that nine berachos were recited for the purpose of that statement, not so much to tell us how many berachos are to be recited, but rather to correct a misconception. Because we sounded the shofar just before the Amidah prayer without reciting the accompanying sections of מלכיות זכרונות ושופרות, one might get the impression that sounding the shofar in conjunction with this particular recitation need not be within the context of the Amidah prayer but could be done independently. To dispel this possible misconception, we are told that nine berachos are to be recited, including the מלכיות זכרונות ושופרות, and it is here that the shofar is to be sounded. However, this pertains only to the chazzan's repetition, and the individual need only recite the seven berachos, and by listening to the chazzan's repetition of the Amidah he fulfills his obligation in relation to both the Yom Tov aspect of Rosh Hashanah and the unique Rosh Hashanah day prayers.

Remember us for Life: זכרנו לחיים

I
How can we petition in the first part of the Amidah?

In the ten days between Rosh Hashanah and Yom Kippur we add the following plea in the Avos section of the Amidah prayer:

"זכרנו לחיים, מלך חפץ בחיים, וכתבנו בספר החיים, למענך אלוקים חיים."

"Remember us for life, O King Who desires life, and inscribe us in the Book of Life, for Your sake, O living God."

This raises an immediate question. How are we allowed to insert petitions in the very first part of the Amidah, which is exclusively reserved for expressions of praise? For aren't we explicitly told by Chazal that the halacha forbids petition in this early part of our Amidah?

"אמר רב יהודה: לעולם אל ישאל אדם צרכיו לא בשלש ראשונות ולא בשלש אחרונות אלא באמצעיות, דאמר רב חנינא: ראשונות דומה לעבד שמסדר שבח לפני רבו. אמצעיות דומה לעבד שמבקש פרס מרבו. אחרונות דומה לעבד שקבל פרס מרבו ונפטר והולך לו."

"Said Rav Yehudah: A person should never ask for his needs, neither in the first three berachos [of the Amidah] nor in the last three, but only in the middle section, for Rav Chanina taught: The first three blessings have the character of a servant extolling his master's praises; the middle blessings have the character of a servant begging his master for his needs; the last three blessings have the character of a servant who, having his needs fulfilled by his master, leaves his master's presence and departs." — Berachos 34a

Regarding this addition of "זכרנו", we find a difference of opinion among the Rishonim. Most follow the Shulchan Aruch, and maintain that if one omits this special plea he need not repeat the Amidah; yet the Baalei Tosafos in Berachos 34a (ד"ה אמצעיות) are of the opinion that if one fails to mention it he must recite the Amidah prayer again.

וז"ל: "והיכא שטעה בג' ראשונות...או לא הזכיר בין ר"ה ליוה"כ בברכת אבות זכרנו...חוזר לראשונה..."

What, then, is the basis for these different opinions?

II

Petition here is allowed but not obligatory

This question of how we are permitted to insert a petition here in the first section, שבחות, of the Amidah is touched upon by the Rishonim. The Ritba writes as follows (ר"ה לב,א):

"מתני' סדר ברכות אומר אבות וגבורות וכו'. פי' קתני הא [אבות וגבורות] לאשמעינן שאין משנין בהם כלום, אע"פ שמוסיפין בשאר התפלה. וא"כ זה שנהגו לומר זכרנו ומי כמוך וכו' הוא טעות, שהרי אמרו, לא ישאל אדם צרכיו לא בג' ראשונות ולא בג' אחרונות: אבל במסכת סופרים נמצא סעד למנהגינו, שכך אמרי' שם [פרק יט, הלכה ח], כשם שחתימתן של ר"ה ויוה"כ משונה משאר ימים, כך תפלתן משונה. ואין אומרים זכרנו ומי כמוך בג' ראשונות אלא בשני ימים טובים של ר"ה ויה"כ. ואפילו בהם בקושי התירו...

ולפי זה יש לי לומר לפי שיטתנו דמתני' קתני מה שאומרים בחיוב, ולומר דאומר ג' ראשונות ושלשה אחרונות כדרכו ואינו צריך יותר, שאין זכרנו ומי כמוך מעכבין, ולפי שהיו נוהגין לאומרן הוצרך התנא לומר כך, ומ"מ מודה תנא שאם בא לאומרן אין מוחין בו...ופשוט הוא שאם לא אמר שאין מחזירין אותו..."

"The Ritba asks: It would seem that the need for the Mishna 32a to tell me that the prayer of Avos must be mentioned in the Mussaf Amidah prayer is superfluous, for it is obvious that this section accompanies all the Amidah prayers. Therefore, we must say that the Tanna came to inform me that although additions are made in the middle section of the Amidah prayer, none should be made in the Avos section, and it should be said as it always is. Thus, it is a mistake to add the petitions "זכרנו" and "מי כמוך" and they should not be included here.

Yet we do find in Mesechtas Sofrim a justification for adding these prayers. However, it should be noted that the addition of "זכרנו" is not obligatory and the failure to mention it does not call for one to repeat the prayers."

In the "תשובות הגאונים החדשות" (see "תשובות הגאונים החדשות" הוצאת אופק, תשנ"ה, תשובה ד') the following answer to our question is given (attributed to רב צמח גאון):

"שלא אמר רב יהודה אין שואלין, אלא לא ישאל אדם, ביחיד שיש לו צורך כגון חולה או צורך פרנסה, שהן צרכי יחיד, אבל צרכי צבור כגון זכרנו לחיים, וכל ישראל צריכים לו, שואלים. ולא קשה על דרב יהודה. וכל שכן שבין ראש השנה ליום הכפורים ושעה צריכה לכך."

"Rav Yehudah's ruling not to petition in the first three [blessings of the Amidah] applies only when the needs of an individual are addressed. However, the needs of the many, for example, the petition of "זכרנו לחיים", especially during the High Holy day period, is certainly allowed and is viewed as *the need of the hour*."

From these two approaches we can see that "זכרנו" is viewed as a petition which normally belongs elsewhere, but because of special considerations was allowed to be inserted here in the section of praises. However, the Tur offers a different view. In אור"ח, סימן קיב he justifies the inclusion of the petition of "זכרנו" by pointing out that because the entire Jewish community here is petitioning for life, this is the clearest indication possible of our dependence on the Almighty, and it is therefore to be viewed as the greatest expression of praise one could give.

וז"ל: "ועם מה שהעבד מסדר שבחו של רבו יכול לשאול צרכי צבור שזה שבח וכבוד לרב שרבים צריכים לו..."

Thus we see that we are to view the petition of the "זכרנו" as שבחות, part of the opening section of praise rather than as a petition.

With this in mind, we might now attempt to explain the rationale underlying the various opinions regarding the question whether or not one must repeat the Amidah prayer if "זכרנו" was inadvertently omitted. The Shulchan Aruch and the Rishonim, who maintain one need not repeat the Amidah, base their opinion on the assumption that "זכרנו" is to be viewed as a petition, צרכיו, which is sanctioned during the Ten Days of Repentance between Rosh Hashanah and Yom Kippur. Therefore it is only *permitted* to be added, but since it is not an obligation ordained by our Sages, its omission does not require a repetition of the Amidah. However, Tosafos in Berachos maintains that one must repeat the Amidah if "זכרנו" is omitted, and this opinion is based on the fact that "זכרנו" is now an integral part of the praise, שבחות, section of the Amidah, and therefore any omission of praise requires that the Amidah be repeated.

Although the Tur maintains that "זכרנו" is to be viewed as an integral part of שבחות, the opening section of praise in the Amidah prayer, yet its omission does not require that the entire Amidah be repeated. This is possible, since this additional "praise" was not originally ordained by those who composed the nusach of the שבחות section of the Amidah, but it was only a later addition; therefore we need not be overly stringent in demanding the repetition of the Amidah if this added blessing is inadvertently omitted.

III
Petition not for our sake but for His glory

The justification for considering זכרנו to be part of the opening section of שבחות is based on the following considerations. In the blessing of זכרנו we ask to be "remembered for life", "זכרנו לחיים". Later on we expand this request to include that we be remembered for a *good* life: "וכתוב לחיים טובים". How do we account for the change? The classic answer is that our petitions should be gradual, and we progress from the more general request "for life" to the more specific and ambitious request "for a good life".

The משך חכמה, at the beginning of the Parashah of V'Zos HaBeracha (Devarim 33:3) suggests that we are not petitioning here for life for our own sake, but rather for His sake, since we remind Him that "the dead are unable to praise Hashem" and therefore if we, His chosen congregation, are not given the gift of life, who then will sing praises to His name? From this perspective, we can see how זכרנו does not constitute a personal request but is rather a petition on behalf of Hashem Himself that Klal Yisrael be granted life in order that they are able to continue praising Hashem. This is why "a good life" is not mentioned in this section of שבחות, for all that is required here in order to praise Hashem is simply life itself. Later on, however, when we speak of the quality of life on a personal level, there we add the request for the blessing, not only of life, but of a good life.

This explanation of the משך חכמה enables us to suggest a possible answer to our previous question as to how petition is allowed here in the שבחות section of the Amidah, even though it is normally prohibited. For we can now see that we are not making a personal request, but rather it is Klal Yisrael as a whole who petition Hashem that His praise should never cease from the world. This is in keeping with the theme of this section of praise, and its intent is to keep that theme eternally alive. And we must remember that it is only personal request which is not permitted in this first section of the Amidah, whereas communal petition is allowed.

Based on this approach, we could perhaps understand the rationale behind the custom (though it is not widespread) that the congregation responds aloud to the phrase, "וכתוב לחיים טובים וכו'"; whereas they do not repeat aloud the phrase, "זכרנו לחיים מלך חפץ בחיים". (See the sefer "נפש הרב" עמ' רד, who cites this custom and offers the explanation that since we have already petitioned for a *good life* here in the silent prayer, it would not be logical to now simply ask for *life*.) As we have pointed out, "זכרנו לחיים" is not considered a personal petition (צרכיו) but rather an integral part of שבחות, praise of Hashem, whereas "וכתוב לחיים טובים", which is said later, is viewed as part of the thanksgiving section, הודאה, of the Amidah. Thus, we can apply the view of the Avudraham, who explains why the "מודים" is repeated by the congregation and the other sections of the Amidah are not. He suggests that this is because מודים is an expression of thanksgiving to Hashem, and this should be done personally, rather than through an intermediary, such as the שליח צבור. Therefore all are required to say "מודים" for themselves. And we might apply this thinking here too and say that since the "וכתוב לחיים" is part of the thanksgiving section, it also requires our personal participation; and this is the reason everyone repeats this phrase. The "זכרנו", on the other hand, is viewed as part of the praise section of the Amidah, and therefore we are never called upon to repeat aloud and in unison any of the praises, but rather we rely on the chazzan to do this on our behalf. Therefore we follow this practice regarding the "זכרנו לחיים", and we allow the שליח צבור alone to recite this blessing on our behalf.

The Blessing of *Kedushas Hashem*

I
Relation to the theme of Hashem's Holiness?

The third blessing of the Amidah prayer focuses on the Holiness of Hashem and His Name — the קדושת השם. The following prayers are included in this section:

1) "אתה קדוש ושמך קדוש..."

2) "לדור ודור המליכו לא-ל, כי הוא לבדו מרום וקדוש" (נוסח ספרד)

3) "ובכן יתקדש שמך ה' אלקינו על ישראל עמך..."(נוסח ספרד)

4) "ובכן תן פחדך..."

5) "ובכן תן כבוד ה' לעמך"

6) "ובכן צדיקים..."

7) "ותמלוך אתה...מהרה לבדך... "

8) "קדוש אתה ונורא שמך...ברוך אתה ה' המלך הקדוש"

The Tur asks (in אור"ח סימן תקפב): "תמהתי מעולם למה אין אומרים 'ובכן תן פחדך' כל עשרת ימי תשובה, דמאי שנא זה התוספת שבברכת קדושת השם ממה שמוסיפין באבות וגבורות וכו'."

"I have always wondered why we do not include the recitation of the 'ובכן תן פחדך' in the prayers throughout the

Ten Days of Repentance, why is it different than the special insertations we make in the previous sections of Avos (זכרנו לחיים) and the Gevuros (מי כמוך) which are said throughout the Ten Days of Repentance?"

We are further puzzled by the insertion of the prayer of "ובכן תן פחדך" in the section of קדושת השם. The addition of ובכן יתקדש שמך is quite understandable, for here we also articulate the theme of קדושת השם — the holiness of His Name. But what is the relevance of the prayer "ובכן תן פחדך" to this theme of קדושת השם, the sanctification of Hashem's Name?

Indeed, the same question can be asked regarding the other prayers of this section as well: "ובכן תן כבוד, ובכן צדיקים, ותמלוך עלינו". How are they related to the theme of קדושת השם?

Even more puzzling is the question raised by the commentators (see the Tur, ibid.): how are we able to insert a petition here: "ובכן תן פחדך", when we know that the halacha forbids petitions in the first three berachos of the Shemoneh Esreh (See ברכות לד: "לא ישאל אדם צרכיו לא בג' ראשונות ולא בג' אחרונות.")

These additional prayers of "ובכן" are added both in the Rosh Hashanah and in the Yom Kippur prayers. The justification for adding these prayers on both these

The Commentators' Machzor Companion

occasions is that they are part of the special prayers of קדושת השם for the Days of Awe. Yet the Rambam, in his "סדר תפלות כל השנה", "Order of the Prayers for the Whole Year", cited at the end of "ספר אהבה", writes as follows:

"מנהג פשוט שמברכין ברכה שלישית בנוסח זה שבשני ימים של ראש השנה בכל תפלה ותפלה מארבע התפלות...וכן נהגו מקצת לברך אותה באותו הנוסח בכל תפלה ותפלה מחמש תפלות של יום הכפורים..."

"It is the common practice that the third blessing of the Rosh Hashanah blessings is said in this manner throughout all the prayers of the day....And it is the custom of *some* to follow this format in all the five Amidah prayers of Yom Kippur."

II

On Rosh Hashanah we follow Rav Yochanan

Rav Meir Simcha of Dvinsk in his sefer "חדושי ר' מאיר שמחה על הש"ס", חלק א עמ' רלו addresses the question of how we justify the inclusion of the prayer of "ובכן תן פחדך" in the קדושת השם by pointing to the Gemara in Rosh Hashanah 32a, which states:

"וכשקידשו בית דין את השנה באושא ירד ר' יוחנן בן ברוקא לפני רבן שמעון בן גמליאל ועשה כר' יוחנן בן נורי. אמר לו רבן שמעון: לא היו נוהגין

כן ביבנה. ליום השני ירד ר' חנינא בנו של ר' יוסי הגלילי ועשה כר' עקיבא. אמר רבן שמעון בן גמליאל: כך היו נוהגין ביבנה."

We have mentioned the argument between ר' יוחנן בן נורי and ר' עקיבא as to where we join the מלכיות. Rav Yochanan is of the opinion that we are to join the blessing of מלכיות with the קדושת השם; whereas Rabbi Akiva believes that we join the מלכיות with the קדושת היום. In the city of אושא they followed the custom of Rav Yochanan, even though the halacha follows the opinion of Rabbi Akiva. Thus, according to Rav Yochanan, the recitation of "ובכן תן פחדך" was not to be viewed as an integral part of קדושת השם, but rather it was considered part of the מלכיות. In other words, according to Rabbi Akiva, "ובכן תן פחדך" was not said at this point, for it has no relevance to the מלכיות. It was only said here according to the opinion of Rav Yochanan Ben Nuri. Even though we do not follow the prescription of Rav Yochanan, yet since in אושא they followed his way of thinking, this nusach remained part of our own nusach and is read by us in the קדושת השם.

"וממה שנהגו באושא כר' יוחנן בן נורי לכלול מלכיות עם קדושת השם מזה נשאר נוסח ובכן תן פחדך ותמלוך וכו', שתמה הטור (סימן תקפ"ב) על הוספה זו. ומטעם זו כתב הרמב"ם בסדור התפלה שנהגו לאומרו בראש השנה. ויש מקומות שאומרים ביוהכ"פ, הרי דעיקר נתקן לאומרו בראש השנה, ודוק."

The Commentators' Machzor Companion

Based on the approach of Rav Meir Simcha that this formulation, which includes "ובכן תן פחדך" should be said in the קדושת השם, Rav Chavel (see הדרום, מד, עמ' 4) points out that we can now simply answer the question raised by the Tur as to why we do not include these prayers in the Amidah prayers of the Ten Days of Repentance, by saying that only on Rosh Hashanah did we adopt the nusach of Rav Yochanan ben Nuri, which assumes that these prayers allude to מלכיות, and they have no relevance to the Ten Days of Repentance, and, according to some, not even to the day of Yom Kippur.

"ולפי דרכי הגאון הנ"ל הלא יש לנו תירוץ מספיק, דהוספת ובכן תן פחדך אינה דומה לזכרנו ושאר הוספת כלל, כמבואר דעיקרו נתקן לאומרו בראש השנה, והבו דלא לוסיף עלה, ומנהג ישראל שלא לאומרו בעשרת ימי תשובה תורה שלימה היא."

III

The Kedushah and the Malchiyos go hand in hand

This approach of Rav Meir Simcha is touched upon by other commentators. (See ספר "נתיב בינה" כרך ה' עמ' 59 and "מעינות" ימים, reprinted in "עיוני תפלה" מאת יוסף היינימן עמ' 56

"מקור הברכות", R' Zev Ya'avetz, in his sefer (נוראים ב' עמ' 548 עמ' 27-29 writes:

"ואם נשאל אם כן מה ענייננו לברכה שלישית, נשיב כי הוא סדר מלכיות דר' יוחנן בן נורי, ואף כי אנו נוהגים כרבי עקיבא שנהגו ביהודה, בכל זאת חביב היה על אבותינו גם מנהג רבי יוחנן בן נורי, שנהגו בו בגליל. ומהיות קדושה ומלכות הבאים כאחד, ונאים ביותר לראש השנה ויום הכפורים — הניחו אותו במקומו, ולא עוד אלא שקימו אותו בכל התפלות של ראש השנה ויום כפורים..."

"The relevance of "ובכן תן פחדך" is that it is considered to be the מלכיות of Rav Yochanan ben Nuri. And although the halacha follows the opinion of Rabbi Akiva, because this nusach of "ובכן תן פחדך" was held in such high esteem by those in the Gallilee, it was left intact. And since the קדושה and the מלכיות go hand in hand, it was added to all of the Amidah prayers of Rosh Hashanah and Yom Kippur."

And if one were to ask how "ובכן תן פחדך" relates to מלכיות, the answer that Rav Zev Ya'avetz offers is that indeed the מלכיות is alluded to here in the concluding beracha of "המלך הקדוש", and the "ובכן תן פחדך" serves merely as a פתיחה, an introduction, to the מלכיות:

"ומשבאנו לכך אין לנו אלא להתבונן בענין עלינו...ועל כן נקוה לך שהן פתיחה למלכיות הנכללות לנו, כדעת ר' עקיבא, עם קדושת היום שבמוספי ראש השנה, ולכוון אותן אל ובכן תן פחדך, ובכן תן כבוד, ובכן

צדיקים. ולהבחין כי רוח אחד להם, ששניהם הם תפלות לגלוי כבודו ומלכותו של הקב"ה על כל באי עולם.

ואחרית דבריה של זו (ובכן)	אחרית דבריה של זו (עלינו)
1) 'ותמלוך אתה ה'	1) 'ותמלוך עליהם מהרה לעולם ועד'
2) 'לבדך'	2) 'כי המלכות שלך היא'
3) 'ככתוב בדברי קדשך	3) ככתוב בתורתך
ימלוך ה' לעולם'	ה' ימלוך לעולם' וגו'

ונמצא שתי ההקדמות שוות, כי גם 'עלינו ועל כן נקוה' גם 'ובכן ובכן ובכן' שתיהם פתיחות לסדר מלכיות, ואם כן כמעט ודאי גמור הוא בעיניו שגם ,ובכן תן' פתיחת סדר מלכיות היא כמו עלינו."

"If one examines the structure of the prayers of Aleinu and "ובכן תן", one sees clearly the parallel between the two. Both proclaim that the "Kingdom" is Hashem's and His reign is eternal. Thus, just as the Aleinu prayer serves as an introduction to the subsequent pasukim of מלכיות, so we may say that the "ובכן תן פחדך" serves as an introduction to the מלכיות contained here (המלך הקדוש)."

If this is the case, then it would seem that indeed the ובכן תן פחדך was not said, according to Rabbi Akiva, for the same concepts are found in the קדושת היום as in the ובכן תן פחדך, which functions as an introduction to the subsequent pasukim of מלכיות.

IV
How many verses from Tanach do we need?

If indeed the "ובכן תן פחדך" serves as the מלכיות of ר' יוחנן בן נורי, we will find ourselves bothered by the following questions:

1) The halacha calls for the section of the מלכיות to contain three quotations each from the Tanach — the Torah, Prophets and Writings. Yet here in the section of the "ובכן תן פחדך" it would seem we have only one quotation from Tanach — from the Writings — Psalm 107:42, where we read:

"ככתוב בדברי קדשך...ימלך ה' לעולם אל-היך ציון לדר ודר הללו-יה".

2) If this section of "ובכן תן פחדך" fulfills the requirements of מלכיות, then the additions of זכרונות, מלכיות ושופרות are only called for when we sound the shofar — in the Mussaf prayer. Why, then, is this prayer of "ובכן" added to the other prayers of the day, the מעריב שחרית ומנחה, when the shofar is not sounded?

3) On Yom Kippur day, there is no requirement of מלכיות. Why, then, does the קדושת השם in the Yom Kippur prayers contain these words of "ובכן תן פחדך וכו'"?

Answering these questions is not too difficult. In reply to the question where are the three pasukim from Tanach mentioned in the מלכיות, there are a number of possible solutions.

1) Since the section of "ובכן תן פחדך" was inserted here only out of consideration for the nusach of Rav Yochanan, we deliberately omit the required number of pasukim in order to call to our attention that this is not the actual position of the מלכיות. For had we enumerated all the required pasukim, we might have thought that we are indeed fulfilling the requirement of מלכיות at this point.

2) We have here only a single quotation from the Tanach, but no additional pasukim are required here, since the number required for מלכיות will be mentioned later in the מלכיות of the Aleinu of Rabbi Akiva. It is therefore not necessary to draw out the pasukim here.

3) We follow the halacha which calls for three quotations each from the Tanach, yet the Mishna also states that even three verses from all of them is sufficient to fulfill the requirement.

"רבי יוחנן בן נורי אומר: אם אמר שלש מכלן יצא".

"R' Yochanan ben Nuri says: If one recited just three verses from all of them, one has discharged his obligation."

And in this section we find one pasuk each from Tanach as follows:

From the Writings: "ימלך ה' לעולם וגו'"

From the Prophets: "ויגבה ה' צב-אות במשפט וגו'" (ישעיה ה:טו)

From the Torah: "שמע ישראל" said in the Kedushah (ibid. נתיב בינה).

And we might ask whether "ובכן תן פחדך" is considered מלכיות at all. If it is not, why, then, include it in the prayers of the rest of the day that do not require the recitation of מלכיות?

According to the opinion of the בעל המאור that the מלכיות was recited in all the prayers of the day, we would have no problem here.

We have already mentioned the rationale of Rav Zev Ya'avetz regarding this issue:

"ומהיות קדושה ומלכות שני דברים הבאים כאחד ונאים יותר לראש השנה ויום הכפורים — הניחו אותו במקומו, ולא עוד אלא שקיימו אותו בכל התפלות של ראש השנה ויום הכפורים."

Since the theme of Kedushah and Malchius go hand in hand, it was therefore joined here in the קדושת השם. And this is the reason it was included in the Yom Kippur prayers as well.

V
תקיעותא דרב ורב המנונא סבא

The Mishna in Rosh Hashanah speaks only of the requirement of the מלכיות זכרונות ושופרות, and explains that they had to be mentioned as part of the Mussaf prayer. And they also had to be accompanied by ten pasukim from Tanach alluding to these three themes.

"אין פוחתין מעשרה מלכיות מעשרה זכרונות מעשרה שופרות. רבי יוחנן בן נורי אומר אם אמר שלש שלש מכלן, יצא."

"They recite no fewer than ten verses relating to Kingship, ten relating to Remembrance, and ten relating to Shofar. Rav Yochanan ben Nuri says: If he recited three verses from each of them, he has discharged his obligation." (Rosh Hashanah, Chapter 4, Mishna 6).

In the other sections of Mussaf, as we have them in the תפלה בלחש, the silent Amidah prayer, this is not discussed anywhere in the Mishna nor even in the Gemara. Thus the question arises, what is the source for the inclusion of these prayers in the Amidah?

The commentators point to the ירושלמי ראש השנה, פרק א, הלכה ג as the source. There we read as follows:

"דתני בתקיעותא דרב: זה היום תחילת מעשיך זכרון ליום ראשון כי חוק לישראל הוא משפט לאלוקי יעקב. ועל המדינות בו יאמר אי זו לחרב ואי זו לשלום אי זו לרעב ואי זו לשובע. ובריות בו יפקדו לחיים ולמות."

In the arrangement of the prayers by Rav our additional prayers are mentioned and it is Rav who authored or included these prayers. This above quotation of "זה היום תחילת מעשיך וכו'" serves as an introduction to the order of the section of זכרונות as we have it today. Thus, what we have here in the תקיעותא דבי רב is a format which we follow throughout the Mussaf prayers of מלכיות זכרונות ושופרות, and this includes:

1) an introductory prayer to each section

2) nine quotations from Tanach that relate to the particular theme.

3) a concluding beracha which includes the ten pasukim from the Torah (except for the מלכיות, where the tenth pasuk is mentioned just prior to the ending section of the beracha, which is a petition); the מעין החתימה petition just before the concluding beracha; and the beracha itself. We will later discuss why מלכיות is different from זכרונות or שופרות in this respect.

Thus Mussaf conforms to the following format:

1) Introduction

Aleinu in the מלכיות
אתה זוכר in the זכרונות
אתה נגלית in the שופרות

2) The quotations from Kisvei Hakodesh (in the מלכיות זכרונות ושופרות)

ככתוב בתורתך — תורה
ובדברי קדשך כתוב לאמר — כתובים
ועל ידי עבדיך — נביאים

3) And the concluding beracha of petition:
In the מלכיות — "או"א מלוך על כל העולם"
In the זכרונות — "או"א זכרינו בזכרון טוב לפניך"
In the שופרות — "או"א תקע בשופר גדול לחרותנו"

The piyutim included in the חזרת הש"ץ, the chazzan's repetition of the Amidah prayer, were additions made by later poets, פייטנים. According to our previous discussion, it would seem that the section of (פחדך) "ובכן ובכן ובכן" serves as the מלכיות of ר' יוחנן בן נורי, and according to Rabbi Akiva the section of Aleinu, as set down in the prayers of Rav, תקיעותא דבי רב, serves as the introduction, פתיחה to the מלכיות.

To prove this contention that "ובכן" serves as the מלכיות according to Rav Yochanan ben Nuri, the following Zohar in Parashas Beshallach is cited.

"אמר רבי ייסא אשכחנא ברזא דא בתקיעותא דרב המנונא סבא תלת ובכן ובכן ובכן, לקבלי להני תלת."

"Said Rav Yossi: We find in the prayers set down by Rav Hamnunah Sava that the prayers of "ובכן ובכן ובכן" – (ובכן יתגדל שמך, פחדך, כבוד) parallel the three attributes mentioned here (in the Shirah)."

The allusion to the "three attributes" in the Shirah refers to the Zohar mentioned just prior to Rav Yossi's statement which alludes to the attributes of *chesed, gevurah* and *tiferes*. (Kindness, strength and splendor.) Each section is followed by the sounding of the shofar, and is thus called "תקיעותא".

The three expressions in our prayer of "ובכן" parallel these three attributes in the following way.

"ובכן יתגדל שמך" alludes to Avraham Aveinu, who *magnified the name* of Hashem in the world and represents the attribute of lovingkindness. We attest to this when we say, "חסד לאברהם".

"ובכן תן פחדך" alludes to Yitzchak Aveinu, who epitomizes the attribute of גבורה. We speak of him as "פחד יצחק".

Finally, "ובכן תן כבוד" alludes to Yaakov Aveinu, who is described as "תפארת".

The Commentators' Machzor Companion

The Zohar explains that these expressions of ובכן were inserted in our prayers "תקיעותא דרב המנונא סבא", and, as previously discussed, it seems that the תקיעותא דרב also omitted these expressions of ובכן, for the Aleinu prayer rather than "ובכן" serves as the opening prayer for the מלכיות. Thus, we must assume that רב המנונא סבא is of the same opinion as ר' יוחנן בן נורי, and both contend that ובכן serves as the introductory prayer of the מלכיות.

It is difficult to understand, though, the reason why the תקיעותא דרב omitted such an appropriate prayer for this day when formulating the מלכיות prayer for Rosh Hashanah.

VI
Different reasons for "ובכן"

To resolve this difficulty, we might suggest that the expressions of "ובכן" really have nothing to do with the מלכיות of Rav Yochanan ben Nuri; but rather they are an integral part of the קדושת השם. Such a conclusion is based on the following considerations.

The word "ובכן" is given a number of different explanations. Some say it alludes to the statement of Queen Esther: "ובכן אבוא אל המלך", when she contemplated the crucial moment when she would stand before King Ashueros and her life would hang in the balance. When we repeat this expression, "ובכן", we should be reminded that we, too, now stand in the presence of the King of kings on this day of Judgement and our lives hang in the balance.

We might further suggest that "ובכן" also serves to connect these sections to the קדושת השם. The source for these three expressions of "ובכן" is to be found in the Zohar (פרשת בשלח, אות קע״ד), where we read the following:

"אמר רבי ייסא, אשכחנא ברזא דא בתקיעותא דרב בבבל, תלת ובכן ובכן ובכן לקבלי הני תלת."

"Said Rebbe Yossi: These three expressions of ובכן (found in the Rosh Hashanah prayers) correspond to the three mentioned here."

The "three mentioned here" allude to three pasukim quoted from "ויסע, ויבא, ויט" of בשלח, יט-כא:

"ויסע מלאך הא-להים ההלך לפני מחנה ישראל וילך מאחריהם. ויסע עמוד הענן מפניהם ויעמד מאחריהם.
ויבא בין מחנה מצרים ובין מחנה ישראל ויהי הענן והחשך ויאר את הלילה ולא קרב זה אל זה כל הלילה.
ויט משה את ידו על הים ויולך ה' את הים ברוח קדים עזה כל הלילה וישם את הים לחרבה ויבקעו המים."

Each of these verses contain exactly 72 letters, and 72 three-letter Names of Hashem are formed by taking one consecutive letter from each verse in a special sequence. The first verse of ויסע is to be read forwards; the second backwards; the third forwards, and so on, as illustrated in the following tables. (See Rashi in Mesechtas Succah 45a, ד"ה "אני והו").

From this we can see that according to the Zohar the three expressions of "ובכן" recited on Rosh Hashanah in the Amidah prayers correspond to the Divine Name of 72 letters, which is spelled out in the three pasukim of "ויסע", ויבא, ויט". And indeed, these letters, which spell out "ובכן", add up to 72 (ב=2, כ=20, ן=50).

Consequently, from this Zohar we have the following:

1) The source of the use of "ובכן" in our Rosh Hashanah prayer.

2) Since these three expressions correspond to the three-letter Divine Name of 72, they justifiably belong here in this section of קדושת השם.

3) It was Rav who established the nusach of "ובכן" and included it in his formulation of the prayer of Rosh Hashanah, thereby proving that "ובכן" was not said to fulfill the requirement of מלכיות, according to Rav Yochanan ben

Nuri, since according to Rav the מלכיות commences with the Aleinu, as we previously explained, and therefore "ובכן" serves as an allusion to the קדושת השם and rightfully belongs in this section of the prayer, which constitutes קדושת השם.

The Requirement of המלך הקדוש and המלך המשפט

I
"The Holy King"

The Gemara in Berachos 12b states:

"ואמר רבה בר חיננה סבא משמיה דרב: כל השנה כולה אדם מתפלל הא-ל הקדוש, מלך אוהב צדקה ומשפט, חוץ מעשרה ימים שבין ראש השנה ויום כפורים שמתפלל המלך הקדוש והמלך המשפט. ורבי אלעזר אמר אפילו אמר האל הקדוש יצא שנאמר, ויגבה ה' צבאות במשפט והא-ל הקדוש נקדש בצדקה', אימתי ויגבה ה' צבאות במשפט — אלו עשרה ימים שמראש השנה ועד יום הכפורים, וקאמר, הא-ל הקדוש.' מאי הוה עלה, אמר רב יוסף: הא-ל הקדוש ומלך אוהב צדקה ומשפט. רבה אמר: המלך הקדוש והמלך המשפט. והלכתא כרבה."

"Rabbah ben Chinena the Elder also said in the name of Rav: Throughout the year one says in the Amidah prayer, 'The Holy God' and 'King Who loves righteousness and judgement', except on the ten days between the New Year and the Day of Atonement, when he says: 'The Holy King' and 'the King of Judgement'. R' Eleazar says: Even during these days, if he said, 'the Holy God', he has performed his obligation, since it says: 'But the Lord of Hosts is exalted through justice, and the holy God is sanctified through righteousness.' When is the Lord of Hosts exalted through justice? In these ten days from the New Year to the Day of Atonement, and nonetheless it says, 'the Holy God.'

What do we decide? R' Yosef said: 'the Holy God', 'the King Who loves righteousness and judgement'. Rabbah said: 'the Holy King' and 'the King of judgement'. The law is as laid down by Rabbah."

This Gemara raises the following questions.

1) The רא״ש asks: we have an established rule that whenever there is disagreement between Rav Yosef and Rabbah, the halacha is established according to the opinion of Rabbah. Why, then, was it necessary for the Gemara to state that the halacha has been established according to the opinion of Rabbah when it should be obvious?

2) Although the halacha states that "המלך המשפט" is the appropriate ending of the beracha during the period between Rosh Hashanah and Yom Kippur, yet we find that some commentators maintain that one who concluded in the regular manner of "מלך אוהב צדקה ומשפט" is not obligated to repeat the Amidah prayer, since he did in fact here mention God's sovereignty (מלך) in conjunction with the concept of justice (משפט). However, others maintain that one must repeat the entire Amidah, since he has failed to

recite the beracha appropriately as required by the halacha during this ten-day period. What is the basis for the various opinions regarding this question?

3) There is a halachic question asked regarding someone who mistakenly says "המלך המשפט" in his Amidah during the year. Is he required to repeat his Amidah, or do we recognize in this instance this ending of the beracha as acceptable?

II
The idea of kingship: explicit or implicit?

To answer these questions we must first clarify the following issues:

1) What is the basis of the difference of opinion here among Rabbah bar Chinena, Rav Eleazar and Rabbah?

2) How are we to view "המלך הקדוש"? Is it enough to allude to the theme of sovereignty without having to recite the actual words, or is it the *coinage*, the "מטבע הברכה", which is of primary importance? Or perhaps what is required here is "מעין המאורע", the need to mention during this ten day period the concept of judgement by the King of kings, and any formulation which alludes to this idea would be acceptable. We can ask the same question about

the phrase "המלך המשפט". Are the actual words of primary importance, or is the concept the most significant consideration?

Tosafos in Berachos 12b ("והלכתא" ד"ה) states clearly that "המלך הקדוש" and "המלך המשפט" are to be viewed as ממטבע הברכה, the only acceptable way to word the berachos during this ten day period. Tosafos reads as follows:

"דכל המשנה ממטבע שטבעו חכמים אינו יוצא ידי חובתן."

The Rambam, too, is of the same opinion, as expressed in פרק י' מהלכות תפלה הלכה יג':
"טעה וחתם בעשתי-עשרה, מלך אוהב צדקה ומשפט', חוזר לתחילת הברכה."

"If he erred and he concluded the eleventh blessing (of the Amidah Prayer), מלך אוהב צדקה ומשפט', he should return to the beginning of the blessing..."

From this we see that although the key word, "מלך", was mentioned here, because the whole phrase, "המלך המשפט", was not said, one must repeat the entire prayer, for he changed the accepted phraseology, "משנה ממטבע הברכה".

However, this does not mean that רבה בר חיננא, who maintains that "הא-ל הקדוש" does not suffice, but one must rather say "המלך הקדוש", believes that "המלך הקדוש" is considered ממטבע הברכה. For we could say that the basis of this argument is that רבה בר חיננא ור' אליעזר are of the opinion that all we need here is a "הזכרה של מלכות" to spell out the key word "מלך". Thus רבה בר חיננה maintains that "מלך" must be mentioned explicitly and no substitute phrase will suffice, even though it alludes to the idea of kingship. ר' אליעזר, however, believes that "הא-ל הקדוש" is sufficient, since this phrase also alludes to the idea of kingship.

Rabbah disagrees with both of them and maintains that what is required here is ממטבע הברכה, which is "המלך הקדוש" and "המלך המשפט", and anything else is unacceptable. And so, because the statement is made here "והלכתא כרבה", the Ba'alei Tosafos in Berachos and the Rambam maintain that what is required here is ממטבע הברכהת,

1) therefore "מלך אוהב צדקה ומשפט" does not suffice, even though it does contain the word "מלך".

2) if "המלך הקדוש" is said during the year, it is also not acceptable, for as "המלך הקדוש" is the מטבע הברכה during the Ten Days of Repentance, "הא-ל הקדוש" is the מטבע הברכה all year round and only this statement is acceptable.

The ראב"ד adds here the insight that the phrase "לא יצא" is not to be taken literally as "one has not fulfilled the obligation", but rather it should be understood to mean that one has not totally completed the requirement, yet in some sense it has been met. In examining the text here, however, it would be difficult to explain the thinking of the ראב״ד. For if ר' אליעזר maintains that with "הא-ל הקדוש" one is "יצא", whereas רבה בר חיננה disagrees, and says "לא יצא", one has not fulfilled his obligation, what he means here is that one has not in any way fulfilled the requirement and he must repeat the prayer. What, then, does the ראב״ד mean here when he says that "לא יצא" means "not in the best prescribed manner"?

The ראב״ד, though, is of the opinion that all that is required here is an allusion, הזכרה, to the idea of kingship, and if one were to say "מלך אוהב צדקה ומשפט" he has fulfilled the requirement. He writes as follows:

וז״ל "כתב הראב״ד יש מי שאומר שאינו חוזר לראש, ומה שכתוב בגמרא ,לא יצא' לומר שלא יצא ידי חובת ברכה כתקנה...״

To answer this question, we might suggest the following.

Rabbah states, at the end of the Gemara, that what is required is the recitation of "המלך הקדוש -- המלך המשפט", and therefore one has not fulfilled the requirement, "לא יצא", if he did not recite this specific formulation. Thus the ראב״ד contends that we are to understand this "לא יצא" to mean that only if one has failed totally to allude to the concept of kingship has he failed to fulfill this requirement. However, if he said "מלך אוהב צדקה ומשפט", he is יצא, since he did mention the concept of kingship in these words, for Rabbah believes that what is required here is a mention, a הזכרה, of kingship. He believes, though, that saying "הא-ל הקדוש" does not suffice, for this does not explicitly mention kingship. In this regard,"המלך המשפט" is preferable, but it, too, is not decisive. According to the ראב"ד this is the opinion of Rabbah. However, רבה בר חיננה disagrees and maintains that "המלך הקדוש" is the מטבע הברכה and no other formulation fulfills the requirement. Thus if רבה argues against רבה בר חיננה who quoted רב, then the question of the רא"ש is answered, for only when רבה argues against רב יוסף is the halacha as he contends. Here, though, he is arguing against רב, and so one might think that the halacha follows the opinion of רב. This is the reason we are explicitly told that the halacha follows the opinion of רבה. The reason for this is that ר' אליעזר also holds that all that is required to fulfill one's obligation of מלכות is an allusion, a הזכרה, to מלכות, and in this case "הא-ל הקדוש" is considered to be a sufficient allusion to this concept, based on the pasuk he quotes. Thus both רבה and ר' אליעזר maintain that all we need is an allusion, הזכרה, and therefore we follow the halachic opinion of רבה, for רבה argues against ר' אליעזר and maintains that the allusion to kingship must be spelled out and "הא-ל הקדוש" does not suffice.

III
Is Rosh Hashanah like Rosh Chodesh?

The חיי אדם (כלל כד) states in the name of Rav Abbale Poswaller that if, on the night of Rosh Hashanah, one failed to say "המלך הקדוש", one need not repeat the Amidah prayer. The rationale behind this decision is the following. We know that on the night of Rosh Chodesh if one mistakenly omits "יעלה ויבוא", he need not repeat the Amidah prayer, since Rosh Chodesh is only proclaimed on the following morning. Thus, since Rosh Hashanah, which is also on Rosh Chodesh, really commences on the following day, failing to say "המלך הקדוש" instead of the usual "הקל הקדוש", does not necessitate that one repeat the Amidah.

However, some disagree with this attempt to equate Rosh Hashanah and Rosh Chodesh. They base their objection on a statement by Rabbenu Yona that if, on the night of Yom Tov, one failed to make the appropriate reference to Yom Tov ("מקדש ישראל והזמנים"), he must repeat the Amidah. For, even though it is true that the bais din sanctifies the Yom Tov commencing in the morning, yet because work is forbidden the previous evening, this in itself requires that the prayer mention Yom Tov. Therefore, since Rosh Hashanah is also a Yom Tov on which work is forbidden, one must say "המלך הקדוש", since this phrase also alludes to the Yom Tov.

Rav Shlomo HaKohen of Vilna upholds this decision of Rav Abbale and distinguishes between Yom Tov and Rosh Hashanah, in that Yom Tov alludes to איסור מלאכה, the prohibition against doing work. Thus the night is also included in the mention of Yom Tov, since the prohibition against doing work extends to the night as well. However, even though Rosh Hashanah is also a Yom Tov and איסור מלאכה applies at night, yet the issue here is "המלך הקדוש", which alludes to Rosh Hashanah as a unique day of Judgement, which commences only in the morning. Thus it follows that there is no legitimate reason to repeat the Amidah if one failed to say "המלך הקדוש".

Yet, as we previously discussed, some commentators make a distinction between Rosh Hashanah and Rosh Chodesh. And in this sense, "יעלה ויבוא" is not looked upon as an integral part of the Amidah, but rather it constitutes what we call "מעין המאורע", "the occasion of the day", something required to be said on that particular occasion. Thus, if one failed to recite "יעלה ויבוא" on the evening of Rosh Chodesh, this does not invalidate the prayer, although we say that the mention of the special occasion, מעין המאורע, is missing. For at night such an omission is not considered crucial. However, the phrase "המלך הקדוש" in the Rosh Hashanah Amidah, as well as alluding to the Judgement day, is also an integral part of the prayer, ממטבע התפלה, as instituted (or "coined") by our Sages. Thus we can understand why on the Ten Days of Repentance between Rosh Hashanah and Yom Kippur, failure to say "המלך הקדוש" calls for a repetition of the entire Amidah. For even though these days are not actual days of judgement, yet because the Sages decreed that "המלך הקדוש" be said during these ten days, this phrase is considered to be an integral part of the Amidah prayer on these days. This is why it must be repeated if these words were inadvertently omitted.

The issue here regarding "המלך הקדוש" on Rosh Hashanah night also depends on the question of whether or not this phrase is considered to be a "ממטבע הברכה", thereby requiring one to repeat the Amidah if it was omitted. Or is "המלך הקדוש" a הזכרה, only an allusion to the concept of kingship, and therefore not crucial on the night of Rosh Hashanah? We can say, in light of our previous discussion, that the issue depends on the difference of opinion between Tosafos, the Rambam and the Ra'avad.

The Rosh Hashanah Kiddush

I
Why mention the Exodus on Rosh Hashanah?

The "שבלי הלקט" asks the same question which was raised by his brother Rabbi Binyamin: why is the Exodus from Egypt included in the Kiddush of Rosh Hashanah and in the prayers of Rosh Hashanah and Yom Kippur? We can understand why the other holidays of Shavuos, Succos and Shabbos deal with יציאת מצרים, for the connection is explicitly discussed in the Torah itself. However, nowhere does the Torah even allude to the event of the Exodus in relation to Rosh Hashanah or Yom Kippur.

The answer of the "שבלי הלקט" is based on a statement in Mesechtas Rosh Hashanah that it was on Rosh Hashanah day that our forefathers ceased to work in Egypt. This, then, provides an allusion to the Exodus in relation to Rosh Hashanah. Regarding Yom Kippur, we know that the shofar was sounded on the Yom Kippur of the Jubilee year, יובל, to set the slaves free. And the Torah tells us that this freeing of slaves should remind us that we too were slaves in Egypt. Here, then, is an allusion to the

Exodus related to Yom Kippur. The "שבלי הלקט" writes as follows:

"תימא לאחי ר' בנימין מה שקבעו בקידוש ובתפילה של ראש השנה ויוהכ"פ זכר ליציאת מצרים. בשלמא בקידושא של שבת, שהרי בעשרת הדברות שבמשנה תורה כתיב, וזכרת כי עבד היית בארץ מצרים. שבועות נמי במשנה תורה כתיב ביה, 'וזכרת כי עבד היית' בסוף פרשת ראה, סוכות נמי כתיב ביה 'למען ידעו דורותיכם כי בסוכות הושבתי את בני ישראל בהוציאי אותם מארץ מצרים'. אבל בראש השנה ויוהכ"פ מאי זכר ליציאת מצרים איכא, והלא לא מצינו שנכתב בהם יציאת מצרים כלל.

ותירץ בר"ה נמי ראוי לומר זכר ליצ"מ לפי מה ששנינו בר"ה. תניא ר"א אומר וכו' בר"ה נפקדה שרה רחל וחנה, בר"ה יצא יוסף מבית האסורים, בר"ה בטלה עבודה מאבותינו במצרים... וביוהכ"פ נמי מצינו יצ"מ גבי שילוח עבדים במשנה תורה 'כי ימכר לך אחיך וגו' העניק תעניק לו וגו' וזכרת כי עבד היית'. ותניא ר"י בנו של ר"י בן ברוקא אומר לפי שנאמר תעבירו שופר ביוהכ"פ וכו', מיכן אמר ר"י בן ר"י בן ברוקא מראש השנה עד יוהכ"פ לא היו עבדים נפטרים לבתיהם ולא משתעבדים לאדוניהם וכו', כיון שהגיע יוה"כ תקעו ב"ד בשופר נפטרו עבדים לבתיהם וגבי שילוח עבדים כתיב כי עבדי הם אשר הוצאתי מארץ מצרים, הא למדת שבר"ה ויוהכ"פ נמי שייך לומר זכר ליצ"מ."

The obvious question here is this: The allusion to Yom Kippur only applies to the Yom Kippur of the Jubilee Year, יובל. What relevance, though, does it have to Yom Kippur every other year? And why should we mention the event of the Exodus each year when it only alludes to something that happens once in fifty years?

II
Mentioning the Exodus in Kiddush

We might suggest an answer based on the following insight of the Chasam Sofer, cited in his sefer שו"ת חתם סופר", סימן קפה. There are two classifications of Mitzvos relating to commemorating the Exodus from Egypt, זכר ליציאת מצרים. One of these is characterized by the entire Mitzva resulting directly from the Exodus. Examples of this are matzah, maror and the Korban Pesach. The second classification of commemorative Mitzvos has nothing to do with the actual Exodus, but rather the Torah requires us when performing the particular Mitzva to remember the Exodus. An example of such a Mitzva is tefillin, which has no actual relation to the story of the Exodus at all, yet we are commanded that when we put on tefillin, we must read the parasha that relates the story of the Exodus.

In light of this, we could ask the following question. When we are told to include the זכר יציאת מצרים in the Kiddush of Rosh Hashanah, to which of these two classifications does the mention of the Exodus belong? And a further question: when we mention the Exodus in this Kiddush, are we now fulfilling the Mitzva of Kiddush, which requires that we allude to this essential element of this day of Rosh Hashanah? Or are we, in addition to fulfilling the Mitzva of Kiddush, also fulfilling the separate Mitzva of remembering the Exodus from Egypt, זכר ליציאת מצרים?

The practical difference here would be that if we consider the Mitzva of remembering the Exodus as an integral part of the Kiddush and as essential to the meaning of the day, then if we fail to mention the Exodus, we have not fulfilled the central Mitzva of Kiddush. However, if we say that it is to be viewed only as an added feature of remembering the Exodus, then failure to mention it would not invalidate our fulfillment of the Mitzva of Kiddush.

In light of this, we could perhaps explain the opinions of the Rishonim regarding the statement of רב אחא ב"ר יעקב in פסחים קיז,ב that one must add the element of יציאת מצרים in the Kiddush, because we are told in regard to Kiddush "to remember", "זכר את יום השבת לקדשו", and in regard to remembering the Exodus it states: "למען תזכור את יום צאתך מארץ מצרים". Some say that this only affects Kiddush; however, others maintain that both prayer and Kiddush are meant here. In light of our above discussion, we could explain each of these positions. The one which believes that only Kiddush requires a mention of the Exodus holds that all that is required here is to add a mention of יציאת מצרים; and this requirement is fulfilled by adding this element to the Kiddush and nothing else is needed. However, the opinion that calls for a mention of יציאת מצרים in both the Kiddush and the tefillah maintains that the mention of the Exodus describes the essence of the day, and therefore it must be included in the Kiddush as well as in the tefillah; for failing to include it means that one has left out an essential ingredient of the day.

There is another practical difference between these two approaches. If we say that mentioning the Exodus in the Kiddush is crucial, for it describes the essence of the day, then we would be required to find a verse in the Torah which tells us that יציאת מצרים has relevance to this particular Kiddush. However, if we are only to *attach* a mention of the Exodus to the Kiddush, all that would be required is a logical allusion of the particular Mitzva to the Kiddush, and no specific verse from the Torah pointing to this Mitzva is needed.

We could say that the יציאת מצרים factor in the Kiddush of Rosh Hashanah belongs to this second classification, the one which alludes to attaching the יציאת מצרים factor to the Mitzva. Thus, we do not need a specific verse from the Torah to connect the Mitzva with the mention of יציאת מצרים. This, then, answers the question of the שבלי הלקט regarding the Kiddush of Rosh Hashanah.

And yet, we might say that even in relation to Shabbos and Yom Tov we mention יציאת מצרים not because it is an integral part of the Kiddush of the day, but it is rather to be viewed as a fulfillment of the Mitzva of commemorating the Exodus. This approach is based on the following rationale.

The obligation to recite Kiddush finds its source in the pasuk of "זכור את יום השבת לקדשו", that we must "remember the Shabbos day and sanctify it" in the way specified by Chazal, which was by a specific recitation. The day of Shabbos stands as a memorial to Creation — "מעשה בראשית" — and as a reminder that we were once slaves in Egypt — "כי עבד היית בארץ מצרים". Thus the question arises, which of these two factors do we relate to when we make Kiddush? Chazal tell us in Mesechtas Pesachim 117b that we must mention the Exodus when we make Kiddush because of the comparison of words in the following pasukim: "זכור את יום השבת לקדשו" and "למען תזכור את יום צאתך מארץ מצרים". Thus, if we say that the obligation to recite

Kiddush, based on the pasuk of "זכור את יום השבת לקדשו", alludes to both the Shabbos of Creation and the Exodus from Egypt (as described in the second set of Tablets), why, then, must we compare the key phrases of "זכור" and "וזכרת" to obligate us to add the Exodus factor to the Kiddush when we are already obligated because of the pasuk of "זכור את יום השבת לקדשו"? It seems that this pasuk refers exclusively to the element of Creation, מעשה בראשית, and it is only because of this comparison between "זכור" and "וזכרת" that we are obligated to include the element of "זכר ליציאת מצרים". Consequently, we might conclude that when we add this requirement of remembering the Exodus to our Kiddush, we are not to view this theme as part of the essence of Shabbos, but rather as being "attached" to the Kiddush as a "זכר", a memorial to the Exodus. From this we can see that Shabbos and Yom Tov, as well as Rosh Hashanah, require a mention of the Exodus in the Kiddush only as a means of fulfilling the obligation that when doing certain Mitzvos we should remember the Exodus, as well as fulfilling the actual Mitzva. Thus, the requirement of including a mention of the Exodus in our Kiddush on Rosh Hashanah is not based on a particular pasuk from the Torah but is rather a "זכר", a commemoration.

Various Customs of Rosh Hashanah

I
Laws versus customs

In the Shulchan Aruch, Orach Chaim 583:2 the custom of eating various foods on Rosh Hashanah night is discussed.

"יהא אדם רגיל לאכול בר"ה רוביא...וכשיאכל רוביא יאמר יהי רצון שירבו זכיותינו. כרתי, יכרתו שונאינו. סילקא, יסתלקונו אויבינו. תמרי, יתמו שונאינו. קרא, יקרע גזר דיננו ויקראו לפניך זכיותינו. הגה: ויש נוהגין לאכול תפוח מתוק בדבש ואומרים תתחדש עלינו שנה מתוקה...ויש אוכלים רמונים ואומרים נרבה זכיות כרמון..."

These foods are eaten and serve as symbols, סימנים, to evoke Heavenly mercy. In this context the Rema cites the custom of Tashlich and of not sleeping on the day of Rosh Hashanah, as follows:

"והולכין אל הנהר לומר פסוק ותשליך במצולות ים כל חטאתינו וגו'. וגם נוהגים שלא לישן ביום ראש השנה ומנהג נכון הוא."

This statement here of the Rema leads us to ask the following questions:

1) What common element is there between the Shulchan Aruch's statement that certain foods are to be

eaten on Rosh Hashanah night and the custom of not sleeping and performing the ritual of Tashlich on Rosh Hashanah day?

2) Wouldn't it have been more appropriate to mention the custom of Tashlich and not sleeping on Rosh Hashanah day later on in the Shulchan Aruch after the discussion of the Mitzva of Shofar and the prayers of Mussaf and Minchah? For Tashlich is performed after we recite Minchah. Why, then, discuss these Mitzvos prior to the Mitzva of Shofar? Indeed, the לבוש and the מטה אפרים, when they discuss these two issues, mention them after discussing the laws of Shofar and the Tefilos of Rosh Hashanah, in סימן תקצו and תקצ"ח (instead of in סימן תקפג, as the רמ"א does). We could thus ask what is the rationale for this and why does the Rema place his discussion of these customs before the laws of Shofar and the Minchah — Mussaf prayers?

II
Tashlich

We might suggest the following answer. There are many reasons given for Tashlich. They include:

1) As a memorial, זכר, to the Akeida; for the midrash tells us that when Avraham Aveinu was on his way to sacrifice his son, as Hashem commanded, the Satan tried to prevent him from going, by placing an impassable river before him. Avraham, however, would not be deterred and entered the river in an attempt to cross it. When it seemed that he would drown if he continued, he appealed to the Almighty for help and he was saved. Therefore, the Tashlich ritual is intended to recall the merit of the Akeida and the self-sacrifice of Avraham when he went forth to overcome all obstacles in order to do the will of Hashem.

2) It alludes to the theme of מלכיות, the coronation of Hashem as King on this day. For, as mentioned in the Tanach, one anointed a king by a river bank, which served as a symbol that just as a river keeps on flowing, so shall the reign of the new king be continuous.

3) It teaches man his obligation in life. For at the time of Creation the waters covered the earth and Hashem decreed that dry land should emerge, whose purpose was to afford a habitat for mankind. And from this foundation man was formed to serve Hashem as his Creator and his Master. And so, on the day of Rosh Hashanah, when we stand beside a river we are reminded of our obligation and awakened to our mission in life, which is to serve Hashem.

4) Our commentators tells us that the river beside which we recite Tashlich should have fish in it. This is to remind us that just as fish live in water and have their eyes open all the time, so, too, is Hashem forever alert, always looking after His people and attending to the needs of all mankind. And so, when we go to the river we acknowledge our belief in Divine Providence on this day of Rosh Hashanah.

5) In the prayer which accompanies the Tashlich ceremony, there is an allusion to the "Thirteen Attributes of Mercy" — the מדות הרחמים — י"ג מדות הרחמים — which is repeated three times. At this time we petition Hashem once again for His Mercy on this day of Rosh Hashanah.

6) Based on the words of the מלכיות, that points out that although the Divine Presence, the שכינה, does not rest outside the land of Eretz Yisrael (for other lands are polluted with impurity), yet because water is not subject to impurity, the שכינה does indeed rest upon rivers, as we find in the book of יחזקאל. For although the Prophet Yehezkail lived outside Eretz Yisrael, he was still able to prophesy by the rivers. We therefore visit this place of purity on this day as we seek to cleanse body and soul.

Thus we may say that the Rema here in סימן תקפ"ג is giving us a different reason for the practice of Tashlich:

"לומר ותשליך במצולות ים כל חטאתם" — to cleanse our bodies and our souls from all impurities. Thus, we symbolically cast our sins into the depths of the river. And so we might say that the common factor between the custom of Tashlich and that of eating various foods is that both serve as symbols, and that is why they were mentioned together in the same halacha. Yet the question remains, why do we also mention here the custom of not sleeping on Rosh Hashanah day?

III
Why the customs are mentioned before the laws

We might suggest a possible answer to this question why these three customs — eating various foods, Tashlich, and not sleeping on Rosh Hashanah — are mentioned together in סימן תקפג and why they precede the discussion of Shofar and the Rosh Hashanah prayers of Mussaf and Minchah.

On Rosh Hashanah we are not only required to do teshuvah and pray for forgiveness by relying solely on the Mitzvos of the day, Shofar and Prayer, but we must also show a sincere desire to cleanse ourselves, a heartfelt sense of remorse for our wrongdoings, and a resolve to improve our behavior in the coming year. This is best illustrated by our willingness to go beyond the requirements of the day. We demonstrate this by eating symbolic foods to try to persuade Hashem to intercede on our behalf. We cast our sins into the river to show that we abhor our wrongdoings of the past year. And we remain awake all day, even though sleeping on Rosh Hashanah is not prohibited on this day, to show our sensitivity to the awesome nature of this special day; for how can we sleep when our spiritual existence is at stake?

There is a similar idea to be found in the approach of the Apter Rebbe, one of the great Chassidic masters, who said that if it were possible, he would abolish all the fast days, even Tisha B'Av and Yom Kippur. Yet he would continue to fast on these two days; for who could eat when one remembers the destruction of our Holy Temple? And who would wish to eat on Yom Kippur, a day of such sanctity and solemnity?

Thus all three of these symbols — the special foods, Tashlich and not sleeping on this day — serve as additional ways of petitioning Hashem, apart from the specific Mitzvos of the day. This is why these three are mentioned together before the Shulhan Aruch discusses Shofar and tefilos, the Mitzvos of the day, for they call to our attention that we should go beyond the ordinary Mitzvos of the day if we wish to achieve forgiveness, סליחה and מחילה, on this most awesome of days.

However, if we ask why the לבוש and the מטה אפרים place these requirements after the Mitzvos of the day, perhaps they also agree that one should engage in Mitzvos above and beyond those normally required. But the major reason they placed them after the Mitzvos of the day was to show that had these customs been mentioned before the discussion of the required Mitzvos of the day, this might lead to the mistaken impression that it would be sufficient on this day to follow these customs instead of fulfilling the required Mitzvos. And so, we are first told that these customs have relevance only if they are performed in their proper time and perspective — after we have already fulfilled the crucial Mitzvos of the day. For we must hear the shofar as prescribed by our Sages — "מאה קולות" and we must have intense concentration in prayer, especially during the מלכיות זכרונות ושופרות. And the customs of Rosh Hashanah represent additional observances, and they only have relevance after the central Mitzvos have been fulfilled, since they are not ends in themselves.

Why No Hallel on Rosh Hashanah?

I
The Days of Awe require solemnity,
not unbounded joy

At the beginning of the Gemara in ערכין י, ב we find two prerequisites before Hallel can be said.

1) the day must be called a מועד, a festival

2) work is prohibited on this day

Despite the fact that both these prerequisites are met on Rosh Hashanah, the Gemara asks why Hallel is nevertheless not recited:

"ראש השנה ויום הכפורים דאיקרו מועד ואיקדוש בעשית מלאכה לימא? משום דר' אבהו דאמר רב אבהו: אמרו מלאכי השרת לפני הקב"ה מפני מה אין ישראל אומרים שירה לפניך בראש השנה וביום הכפורים? אמר להם: אפשר מלך יושב על כסא הדין וספרי חיים וספרי מתים פתוחין לפניו וישראל אומרים שירה לפני..."

"Then let the Hallel be said on the New Year and the Day of Atonement, both of which are called 'festivals' and are sanctified by the prohibition against working. That is not possible, because of what R' Abbahu said: The ministering angels said before the Holy One, Blessed be He: Why do not the Israelites sing a song before You on the New Year and the Day of Atonement? He answered them: Would that be possible, the King sits on the Throne of Judgement with the books of those destined to live and those destined to die before Me and Yisrael singing a song before Me?"

The Rambam in Hilchos Channukah, Chapter 3, Halacha 6 addresses this question why there is no Hallel on Rosh Hashanah and Yom Kippur:

"אבל ראש השנה ויום הכפורים אין בהם הלל לפי שהן ימי תשובה ויראה ופחד לא ימי שמחה יתרה."

"But Rosh Hashanah and Yom Kippur do not have Hallel because they are days of repentance and fear and not days of added joy."

But what is the significance of this statement of "לא ימי שמחה יתרה" here? We might suggest an explanation of the Rambam's words here based on the following insight presented in the sefer of the "עמק ברכה" (עמ' קח-שמחת יום טוב) where we are told the following.

The Rambam in Hilchos Yom Tov, Chapter 6, Halacha 17 states:

"שבעת ימי הפסח ושמונת ימי החג עם שאר יום טוב חייב אדם להיות בהן שמח וטוב לב."

Here, says the עמק ברכה, the Rambam was alluding to that which the Gemara in ערכין יא,ב addresses when it says: "מנין לעיקר שירה מן התורה". "From where do we know that the Torah called for *songs* to be rendered?" And רב מתנה answers this by stating:

"מהכא: 'תחת אשר לא עבדת את ה' אלקיך בשמחה ובטוב לבב'. איזהו עבודה שבשמחה ובטוב לבב, הוי אומר זה שירה."

"Rav Masneh said it is derived from here: 'Because you did not serve Hashem in joyfulness and gladness of heart' (Devarim 28:47). Now which service is it that is deemed 'in joyfulness and gladness of heart', you may say it is song — *shirah*."

The Gemara then asks: But perhaps it means the words of the Torah, as it is written: 'The precepts of the Lord are right, rejoicing the heart.' To which the Gemara answers: "Torah is described as 'rejoicing the heart', but not 'gladdening the heart'."

"משמחי לב איקרי 'טוב לב' לא איקרי."

The Gemara again asks, perhaps we mean Bikkurim, "ושמחת בכל הטוב", "and you shall rejoice in all the good." To this the Gemara answers: "They [Bikkurim] are called 'good', but not 'gladdening the heart'."

Thus we have here three levels of joy, שמחה:

1) *Simchas Bikkurim*, which is referred to as "joy and good" but not "gladdening the heart".

2) *Simchas HaTorah*, which is *only* referred to as "gladdening the heart".

3) And *Simchas Shirah*, "song", which has all the requirements of "joy, good and gladdening the heart".

What the Rambam was referring to in Hilchos Yom Tov when he said that Yom Tov calls for "שמח וטוב לב", "joy and gladness of heart", was שירה, "song", for that represents the highest level of joy one can realize in this world, and as Rashi points out, "ultimate joy results in song." (op. cit.)

With this in mind, we can understand what the Rambam meant here in Hilchos Channukah when he stated that Rosh Hashanah is not a day of "שמחת יתרה", on Rosh Hashanah we are not required to reach the highest level of joy. Therefore Hallel, which is an expression of that ultimate level of joy, is not called for either on Rosh Hashanah or on Yom Kippur. The reason for this is that these days require a serious frame of mind rather than extreme expressions of joy.

II
Hallel not appropriate when our lives hang in the balance

According to the Gemara, Hallel is not appropriate on Rosh Hashanah because "the books of life and death are opened before Him". Perhaps we could explain this rationale in the following way.

In Psalm 13:6, King David declares:

"ואני בחסדך בטחתי יגל לבי בישועתך, אשירה לה' כי גמל עלי."

"As for me I trust in Your kindness, my heart shall rejoice in Your salvation. I will *sing* to Hashem, for He dealt kindly with me."

Rav Chaim Brisker deduces a halacha from this verse. If one is saved from a situation of danger, he is obligated to express gratitude to Hashem in the form of shirah, Hallel, only *after* he has been rescued from that situation of danger. Consequently, even if a prophet tells a person that he is going to be rescued and that person experiences a feeling of relief and optimism that everything will soon be well, he is still not obligated to express his gratitude until the foretold relief and salvation has actually come about. We understand the halacha from this verse in the following way. Although I trust in Your kindness and *already* rejoice when I believe that You will save me; yet *"I will sing to Hashem"* only *after* He has *"dealt kindly with me."*

Thus we see that shirah, Hallel, is not to be said in the instance of pure faith, בטחון, but rather only after the miracle has actually transpired.

And so we might interpret the Gemara here as saying: since the books of life and death are opened before Him, although we have pure faith in Him, we adorn ourselves as the halacha requires, by washing and putting on fresh clothes, etc., in anticipation of being granted life; yet this is only an expression of faith and until we are actually granted salvation we do not sing shira. And that is precisely the reason why Hallel is not recited on Rosh Hashanah.

III

Do the angels say Hallel on Rosh Hashanah?

Tosafos, in ערכין י,ב, (ד"ה אמרו) comments on the question of the angels as to why Yisrael does not recite Hallel on Rosh Hashanah. He asks why they do not question why they, too, are not permitted to say Hallel. He concludes that perhaps the angels do in fact recite Hallel on Rosh Hashanah even though Yisrael does not.

In the sefer "מאורי המועדים", which contains insights by Rav Dovid Soloveitchik, שליט"א, he questions this assumption by the Baalei Tosafos and contends that the angels do not recite Hallel on Rosh Hashanah. He bases this on the statement of Rav Chaim of Volozhin in "נפש החיים" (שער-א, פרק יא-יב). There we read that the Gemara in Hullin (91b) tells us that the angels above do not sing shirah unless they are first preceded by Bnai Yisrael singing shirah below in this world. Rav Chaim explains the rationale behind the words of the Gemara in the following way:

"לא שהם חולקים כבוד לישראל, אלא שאין בכחם ויכלתם כלל מצד עצמם לפתוח פיהם להקדיש ליוצרם עד עלות קול קדושת ישראל אליהם מלמטה."

"The angels follow Bnai Yisrael not as a mark of respect, but rather they are unable to open their mouths to offer praise until Yisrael first offers praise to Hashem."

Thus we see, concludes Rav Dovid Soloveitchik, that unless Bnai Yisrael first offers shirah, the angels cannot do so. This means that since Bnai Yisrael do not sing Hallel on Rosh Hashanah, then we can assume that the angels are not able to sing Hallel, and this contradicts the contention of the Baalei Tosafos here.

This approach of Rav Soloveitchik was already anticipated by the ערוך לנר in his commentary to Rosh Hashanah 32b (ד"ה מפני מה וכו').

However, in "ובחרת בחיים", a commentary on the "נפש החיים" by Rav David Goldberg, the author points to the *Yalkut Shimoni* (פ' בשלח אות רמב), which reads as follows:

"כיון שעלו ישראל מן הים באו ישראל ומלאכי השרת לומר שירה. אמר הקב"ה למלאכי השרת הניחו לישראל תחילה שנאמר 'אז ישיר משה'. נמצאו הנשים ומלאכי השרת עומדים מי יקלס תחילה. אמר רב חייא בר אבא עשה שלום ביניהם."

"After Bnai Yisrael emerged from the Sea, both Bnai Yisrael and the angels sought to offer shirah. Said Hashem to the angels, 'Let Yisrael sing first.' Then the women and the angels were at odds as to who should sing first; and in order to appease the angels, they were allowed to offer shirah before the women."

This leads to the opposite view. For we see here that the angels wished to recite shirah *before* Bnai Yisrael. This seems to imply that they were not dependent on Bnai Yisrael offering shirah first, which seems to contradict the contention of the נפש החיים. We may conclude from this that we must distinguish between *Kedushah* and *shirah*. For the נפש החיים said that קדושה, a דבר שבקדושה, cannot be offered by the angels unless Bnai Yisrael recite it first. For Kedushah "rises from one world to another", and only Bnai Yisrael has the ability to have the Kedushah ascend from one world to the next.

"כי ענין אמירת הקדושה היא העלאת העולמות והתקשרותם כל העולם בעולם שמעליו...[ואולי מזה יצא מנהג של ישראל שנוהגים להעלות עצמן בעת אמירת הקדושה] וזה אין בכח שום מלאך ושרף לעשותו בעצמו תחלה כנ"ל לזאת לא יפתח פיו עד עלויית הבל פיהם של קדושת ישראל קבוצי מטה."

This thinking only applies to the Kedushah. An angel on his own does not have the power to elevate the Kedushah, and therefore he must first wait for Bnai Yisrael to offer shirah by reciting the Kedushah. However, in relation to simply singing the praises of Hashem, שבחות, they can do this on their own. This is the reason they sought to sing the "Song of the Sea", "אז ישיר", before Bnai Yisrael. From this we must conclude that Hallel on Rosh Hashanah may be sung by the angels independently of Bnai Yisrael.

We might suggest the following answer to the question raised by the *Yalkut Shimoni*.

Chazal tell us in Hullin 91 that angels cannot form a *minyan*. Thus we might say that whenever shirah requires a minyan, as for example, when Kedushah is to be recited, then the angels must wait until Bnai Yisrael first offer shirah and recite the Kedushah, and only then can they join them in offering shirah. However, when shirah does not require a minyan, the angels can initiate it on their own. Therefore, since Hallel does not call for a minyan, the angels sought to offer shirah first when Bnai Yisrael emerged from the Sea. And on Rosh Hashanah, when Hallel does not require a minyan, even though Bnai Yisrael cannnot say Hallel, the angels may recite it. This way of thinking justifies the conclusion of Tosafos.

IV

These angels are no friends of ours

Who are these pious angels, "מלאכי השרת", who ask why Bnai Yisrael are not singing shirah today on Rosh Hashanah? At first glance, they appear to be upstanding Heavenly creatures who feel it proper that Hallel should be said on this day the world was created. Yet, on closer scrutiny, we may perhaps find that these so-called angels are "no friends of ours!" For they criticize and try to "cause trouble" for Klal Yisrael.

We are told in Midrash Rabbah, Ve'Eschannan 2:14, that before the High Holy days the angels ask Hashem "When is Rosh Hashanah? When is Yom Kippur?" To which Hashem replies, "Let us descend to the Bais Din on the earth below and hear when they proclaim these holy days."

This dialogue between the Almighty and the angels can be explained in the following way. These angels wished to give testimony against the Jewish people on the Day of Judgement. They cannot wait to speak evil against them. Thus they ask, when is Rosh Hashanah? When is Yom Kippur? that they might speedily present their case against Bnai Yisrael.

Hashem answers them by saying, let us descend to the world of man and there you will see how difficult it is to try to live as a righteous human being and as an observant Jew while trying to contend with the harsh realities of the materialistic world. It is all very well for you to want to judge, but you do not know what it is like to have to cope with the trials and tribulations of life in this world below.

We might suggest that these are the same angels who are taunting Hashem by asking: Why aren't Bnai Yisrael saying Hallel today? Surely, today is a holiday which calls for shirah; why, then, are they not reciting it? This is said as criticism, to emphasize the inadequacies of Bnai Yisrael and their ingratitude to the Creator. To these angel critics, the Almighty answers: It is appropriate for *you* to want to sing shirah on this day, for your very existence is not threatened, and you do not have to stand up and be judged on this day. But for Bnai Yisrael this is a day of great fear and trembling, when they must stand before the Heavenly Tribunal and their future is at stake. How, then, are they to sing shirah on such a day?

V

The psalm of the day versus Hallel

As we have discussed, Hallel is not said on Rosh Hashanah or Yom Kippur because the seriousness of the day overshadows its joy, "ספרי חיים וספרי מתים פתוחין". This leads the Griz HaLevi, quoting his father, Rav Chaim Brisker, זצ"ל, to ask: if Hallel cannot be said because the day is not one of complete joy, then it should follow that the שיר של יום, the daily psalm, which accompanies the daily Tamid sacrifice, should also not be said, since "שיר" requires "שמחה"; and yet we find that we do indeed recite the שיר של יום on the day of Rosh Hashanah. And Rav Chaim answered that we must distinguish between these two prayers, *Hallel* and the *Psalm of the Day*. Hallel calls for total joy, שמחה שלימה; but because the books of life and death lie open before us, this prevents that state of ultimate joy being reached. This is why it is inappropriate for us to recite Hallel on Rosh Hashanah. However, regarding the daily psalm, even a subdued level of joy is sufficient, and therefore we recite it on both Rosh Hashanah and Yom Kippur.

In truth, there is a vast difference between Hallel and the Psalm of the Day. We recite Hallel on a festival, מועד, as we know from the Gemara in ערכין, י,ב which asks why Hallel is not recited on either Rosh Hashanah or Yom Kippur, even though they are both called "מועדים". The answer, as we have indicated, is that since the essential mood on these days is that of judgement, משפט, we do not have that supreme level of spiritual joy which would obligate us to say Hallel. On the other hand, the fact that today is a day of judgement, and joy must be subdued (since the books of life and death lie open before us) does not affect the requirement of reciting the שיר של יום which must accompany the קרבן תמיד.

Tosafos in ערכין י,ב tells us that the angels do indeed recite Hallel on Rosh Hashanah, even though we do not. This leads us to ask the following question. On the seventh day of Pesach at the time Bnai Yisrael miraculously crossed the Red Sea and all the Egyptians were drowned, Chazal tell us that the angels wanted to sing *Shiras HaYam*. However they were prevented from doing so by Hashem Himself, who told them, "How can you wish to sing when my creatures are being drowned in the sea? "מעשה ידי טובעין בים ואתם אומרים שירה?"

We can ask a similar question of them on the day of Rosh Hashanah. How can you wish to sing when the whole world stands in judgement before the Divine Court, with their lives hanging in the balance between life and death? How, then, were the angels allowed to say Hallel in such a situation?

We might suggest, in answer to this question, that the obligation which allows Hallel to be said on the seventh day of Pesach is "באיבוד רשעים רנה", which explains that when the wicked are destroyed, shirah (Hallel) is in order. But this applies only to human beings, whose lives were in danger because of the wicked Egyptians. For the angels another perspective is required. They are told: Bnai Yisrael, who are now saved from the wicked destroyers, can and must sing Hallel, since they have experienced salvation. But *you* were never in danger. Therefore how can you rejoice when My creatures are being destroyed?

On Rosh Hashanah, though, the reason for Hallel is that it is a festival, מועד. Therefore the angels, who are not themselves affected by judgement (even though there is a school of thought which suggests that they, too, are judged on this day) are obligated (מחויב) to say Hallel, despite the fact that human beings, who are subject to judgement, are not.

The Order of the Mussaf Amidah Prayers

I
Why does the Mishna tell us what we already know?

The Mishna in the fourth chapter of Mesechtas Rosh Hashanah (4:5) tells us what is to be included in the Mussaf Amidah prayer:

"סדר ברכות: אומר אבות וגבורות..."

"This is the order of the blessings: he recites the blessings called 'Avos', then the blessings of 'Strength'..."

But why, asks the Ritba, did the Mishna need to tell us that these blessings must be included in the Rosh Hashanah Shemoneh Esreh? Isn't this already self-evident; for they are said all year round in every Amidah prayer? The Ritba then suggests an answer. The Tanna of the Mishna emphasized this to inform us that although here in the Mussaf prayer we add on other sections which are never included in the regular prayers the rest of the year, such as מלכיות זכרונות ושופרות, yet in the opening sections of the Amidah, which include the אבות and the גבורות, nothing should be added. Indeed, "זכרנו לחיים" and "מי כמוך" do not belong here, and they should not be included, for we are told that in the first three berachos of the Shemoneh Esreh we are not to offer any petitions (ברכות לד,א). However, concludes the Ritba, in Mesechtas Sofrim 19:8 it does state that we are permitted to add these additional petitions in the first section. Nevertheless, this only applies to the first two days of Rosh Hashanah, maintains the Ritba. However, during the Ten Days of Repentance, עשרת ימי תשובה, they should not be said.

A similar question is asked by the פני יהושע. Commenting on the question raised at the very beginning of the Gemara: "ת"ר מנין שאומרים אבות..." "How do we know we are to say *Avos*, etc....", this commentator asks: Since the Mishna is exclusively concerned with the structure of the Mussaf Shemoneh Esreh, why focus on the sources of the Avos, etc. which remain the same for the Shemoneh Esreh all year round?

To answer the Ritba's question why the Mishna needed to inform us to include the Avos and the other blessings in the Rosh Hashanah Shemoneh Esreh, we may remember that the sefer "בית אלקים" points out that the section of praise which precedes that of petition in our prayers was never meant as a means of "flattering" Hashem before we ask Him to fulfill our requests, but only to remind us that He has the *ability* to meet our needs because of His greatness, and that is why we are praying to Him.

With this in mind, we might add that perhaps on Rosh Hashanah we add the section of מלכיות to emphasize the same point — God's greatness and His ability to fulfill our petitions. Thus we might think it unnecessary to recite the sections of אבות and גבורות, and that is the reason the Tanna of the Mishna needed to specify that these sections which we recite every day of the year are also required on Rosh Hashanah, even though we have an added section which seemingly articulates the same principle. The פני יהושע gives a similar answer here as well.

II
Prayer at a time of dire need

We can defend the practice of adding זכרנו and מי כמוך in the first section of the Amidah prayer, even though this section seems dedicated exclusively to praise and not petition, by citing the following two classic answers.

1) "צבור שאני"— The Gemara indicates, by the words: "אל ישאל אדם", that an *individual* should not petition for his own needs in the first section of the Amidah; however, a

congregation, צבור, may do so. In fact, the wording of the זכרנו section reflects this, when it says: "Remember *us*".

2) "תפלה בעת צרה מותר" — we are permitted to petition Hashem, even in the first section of the Amidah (which includes Avos, etc.) if we should find ourselves in an emergency or a desperate situation, such as on the day of Rosh Hashanah, when our very life hangs in the balance.

Based on this approach of "תפלה בעת צרה שאני" — that prayer during a time of dire need allows us to waive all restrictions — we could perhaps answer the following question. There is a well-known difference of opinion between the Rambam and the Ramban as to whether prayer is decreed by the Torah or only ordained by the Rabbis, "תפלה מדאורייתא או מדרבנן". The Rambam believes that it is commanded by the Torah, and he bases this on the pasuk of "ולעבדו בכל לבבכם", "And you shall serve Him with all your heart". Chazal comment on this by saying: "איזהו עבודה שבלב — זו תפלה". "How does one serve Hashem with his heart — by praying." (Taanis 2a)

The Ramban, on the other hand, dismisses all proofs which purport to show that prayer is commanded by the Torah, and he contends that it is rather ordained by the Rabbis. He admits, though, that biblically ordained prayer does exist, and that is תפלה בעת צרה, prayer in a moment of extreme distress. But the question arises, in this case of prayer at a time of distress, does the Ramban believe that it must follow the prescribed form (as set down by the Rambam in Hilchos Tefillah 1:3 to include: שבח, צרכיו והודאה, praise followed by petition, and finally thanksgiving) even though prayer in general, which he believes to be predominantly rabbinically ordained, need not follow such a format? Or because it is a prayer uttered at a moment of distress, is petition enough, without the prior requirement of praise?

If we view the Amidah Mussaf prayer as תפלה בעת צרה, we can conclude from the words of the Tanna of the Mishna that this was the purpose of stating here the requirements of אבות, גבורות, etc., to teach us that prayer on Rosh Hashanah is "prayer in a moment of distress" and requires the introduction, as in all other prayers, of praise before we ask for our petitions to be granted.

If this is so, then we can answer all the questions raised by the Ritba and the פני יהושע, as to why the Tanna had to mention the need for אבות, גבורות, etc. Since our prayers on Rosh Hashanah are considered to be תפלה בעת צרה, we might think that Avos, etc. were not required as in prayer which follows the normal sequence during the rest of the year. Thus, the Tanna finds it necessary to inform us that even for prayer at a time of distress, in order for it to be valid, it must follow the prescribed order of all prayer, which is to begin with praise (Avos, etc.) and only then can we proceed with our petitions. This, then, answers the question raised by the פני יהושע.

The Akeida And Its Implications For Us

I
The Shofar Reminds Hashem of the Akeida

The story of the sacrifice of Isaac, the Akeida, is one of the most important themes in the Rosh Hashanah Machzor. It provides the justification for us to approach Hashem with our petition for mercy on this day of judgment. We fulfill the Mitzva of sounding the shofar with a ram's horn, for it too alludes to Avraham and Yitzchak's self sacrifice, מסירת נפש. This is explictly stated in Mesechtas Rosh Hashanah 16a:

> "תקעו לפני בשופר של איל כדי שאזכור לכם עקידת יצחק בן אברהם ומעלה אני עליכם כאילו עקדתם עצמכם לפני."

"Why do we blow on a ram's horn? The Holy One, Blessed be He said: Sound before Me a ram's horn, so I will remember on your behalf the binding of Yitzchak, the son of Avraham, and account it to you as if you had bound yourselves before Me."

The Magen Avraham states, in סימן א ס"ק ז:

"כתב רבינו בחיי פ' צו שאין די באמירת פרשת העקידה אלא בביאור הפרשה, כי מתוך שמתבונן במה שיורו הפסוקים ואל מה שירמז אז יכיר ויבחין נפלאות תמים דעים ויתחזק לבו באמונת השי"ת ועבודתו וכו'."

"Rabbenu Bachya writes that it does not suffice merely to recite the chapters of the Akeida, but it is incumbent to delve into this chapter and study the messages and allusions of this story. This will thereby lead one to have stronger faith and to serve Hashem with greater dedication."

Our gedolim have much to tell us of the significance of the Akeida and what we can learn from it.

The Chasam Soifer:

The Akeida Teaches אמונת חכמים

In the concluding beracha of the זכרונות section of the prayers for Rosh Hashanah, we read the following words:

"ותראה לפניך עקדה שעקד אברהם אבינו את יצחק בנו על גבי המזבח וכבש רחמיו לעשות רצונך בלבב שלם, כן יכבשו רחמיך את כעסך מעלינו..."

"Let there appear before You the Akeida, when Avraham, our father, bound Yitzchak, his son, upon the altar, and he suppressed his mercy to do Your will wholeheartedly. So may Your mercy suppress Your anger against us."

When we speak of the Akeida, we mention the part played by Avraham. Yet at the conclusion of this beracha we find that it is referred to as "the Akeida of Yitzchak".

"ועקידת יצחק לזרעו היום ברחמים תזכור."

"And may You mercifully remember, today, the Akeida of *Yitzchak* for the sake of his offspring".

Why the change here from invoking Hashem's mercy because of the merit of Avraham (as we do at the beginning of this beracha) to asking Him to spare us for the sake of Yitzchak and his offspring?

This question was asked by the Chasam Soifer in his responsa (שו"ת חתם סופר, או"ח סימן רח), and here is his answer:

"ואין מן התימא על אברהם ששמע מן הקב"ה עצמו, אבל מהתימא על יצחק שקיבל מאברהם מה שהוא נגד השכלתו וא"א לשמוע כלל. מ"מ לא הרהר גם אחרי דברי חכמים ושמע ופשט צווארו... בהא סלקינן יצחק מסר נפשו על דברי חכמים במה שהוא חוץ לשכל ולא הרהר אחר חכמים, משום הכי 'ועקידת יצחק תזכור' להשומעים לתורה שבעל פה ואינם מהרהרים אחרי דברי חכמים ותקנותיהם וגזירותיהם. אבל מי שאינו בכלל זה אין לו חלק בתפלה זו."

"There is no problem as far as Avraham is concerned, although we were never meant to sacrifice a human being, yet since he heard it from Hashem Himself, he complied with the directive. However, as for Yitzchak, who did not hear directly such a command, why did he agree to be offered as a human sacrifice? The answer is simply that he had perfect faith and was willing to follow the words of the Sages. Therefore he offered himself as a sacrifice. This is the reason we stress the merit of Yitzchak in the concluding beracha, to point out that this merit of the Akeida is to be extended only to those who adhere to the words of the Sages and their decrees. However, those who do not adhere to their words have no share in this merit."

The Bais HaLevi: The Merit of the Akeida

The Bais Halevi, in Parashas Vayera, asks a question similar to that of the Chasam Soifer.

"The Torah depicts the Akeida primarily as a trial for Avraham rather than for Yitzchak, as it says, in Bereishis 22:1, "and Hashem tested *Avraham*", whereas we pray: 'Remember the Akeida of *Yitzchak* mercifully on behalf of his offspring."

The apparent contradiction here can be reconciled in the following way. Avraham's trial was to slaughter his only son, born to him when he was a hundred years old. However, Yitzchak's trial was seemingly more difficult — to submit to being slaughtered. We know that one can easily stumble as a result of the pressure of having to earn a livelihood and because of one's love for his children. Yet even those who violate the Torah out of love for their children would be willing to die for the sanctification of Hashem's name. In other words, it is easier to give up our lives than to live without our loved ones, which was what Avraham was being asked to do.

Therefore, the Torah views his test as greater than that of Yitzchak, who was "only" being asked to sanctify His name. If this is so, why do we invoke the merit of

Yitzchak in our prayer, rather than that greater merit of Avraham? Indeed, why invoke the merit of our ancestors at all? We know that even the great merit of Avraham could not redeem Ishmael.

We draw strength from the merits of our ancestors because a measure of their exemplary attributes has been passed down to us. As we say in our prayer, "מה יפה ירושתינו", "how beautiful is our inheritance". Yitzchak's achievement of *mesiras nefesh* has been followed often. Jewish history is replete with examples of Jews — even simple Jews — who were able throughout the ages to emulate the self sacrifice of Yitzchak and give up their lives to sanctify God's name.

We pray in the merit of Yitzchak, that we may emulate his level of self sacrifice. Avraham's greater level is one we can never hope to aspire to, and although we stand in awe of it and marvel at the exalted level a human being is capable of reaching, we nevertheless associate ourselves in the final reckoning with Yitzchak, and not with Avraham.

II
The Akeida: reaching great spiritual heights

The following insight of HaRav Shimon Schwab, ז"ל, helps us answer the question raised by the Chasam Soifer as to why we conclude the beracha by mentioning Yitzchak rather than Avraham.

Rashi comments on the pasuk in Bereishis 22:2:

"ויאמר קח-נא את בנך", "And He said: please take your son".

"קח-נא: אין נא אלא לשון בקשה. אמר לו: בבקשה ממך עמוד לי בזו הנסיון, שלא יאמרו הראשונות לא היה בהן ממש."

"The term 'נא' denotes a request. Hashem said to him: 'I request of you' to withstand for My sake, so people will not say 'the first trials did not have any reality in them.'"

Rav Schwab points out that this comment of Rashi, which finds its source in Mesechtas Sanhedrin 98b, is at first sight difficult to understand. Why, if Avraham failed to pass this last test, would all his previous tests be discounted? Surely they should have been accounted to his credit on their own merits. The answer must be that the main purpose of this final test was to see if Avraham had the ability to be able to bequeath to his descendants the spiritual levels that he reached. All the other tests which came before were intended to prepare him for attaining those levels. Thus the Akeida was the ultimate purpose of all Avraham's tests. And if he succeeded in attaining that level he would then be able to transfer to his descendants the ability to emulate this measure of supreme self sacrifice and total dedication to Hashem's will, even to the point of giving up one's life. And thus we can understand that if Avraham had failed this test, even though he personally would have reached a very high spiritual level, yet from a wider perspective, his efforts would have been considered a failure, since his descendants would not have his example of the supreme act of self sacrifice in order to follow in his footsteps. This ultimate test met with success when Yitzchak joined Avraham. For he understood what was required of him and acquiesced wholeheartedly, without questioning his father on earth or his Father in Heaven. Thus Yitzchak, and in his merit, all the generations who came after him, became a full partner in meeting the challenge of the Akeida. This is indicated when the Torah tells us: "וילכו שניהם יחדיו". They went together hand in hand, father and son, both fully aware of what this difficult test required, even though it seemed to contradict everything they had always believed.

This explains why we stress the role of Yitzchak in our concluding prayer, for it was because of him that the test was successful. And just as he followed in his father's footsteps, so, too, do we, Yitzchak's descendants, follow in his footsteps. The Bais HaLevi points out that this accomplishment of Yitzchak became ingrained in the

Jewish character. And so we emphasize the role and merit of Yitzchak in this crucial prayer which exemplifies what is required of us on the day of Rosh Hashanah.

III

We Sacrifice Ourselves in Total Commitment

to Hashem

At the end of the story of the Akeida, Hashem tells Avraham: "כי עתה ידעתי", "For now I know". Rashi comments as follows:

"אמר רבי אבא: אמר לו אברהם, אפרש לפניך את שיחתי. אתמול אמרת לי 'כי ביצחק יקרא לך זרע.' וחזרת ואמרת: 'קח-נא את בנך'. עכשיו אתה אומר: 'אל תשלח ידך אל הנער'? אמר לו הקב"ה: לא אחל בריתי ומוצא שפתי לא אשנה, לא אמרתי לך שחטהו אלא העלהו אסקתיה אחתיה."

"Rebbe Abba said: Avraham said to Hashem, I shall declare before You my complaint. Yesterday you said to me, 'For Yitzchak will be called thy seed'. Then You retracted and said, 'Take now thy son'. Now You say, 'Lay not thy hand upon the lad.'

The Holy One, Blessed be He, said to him: I shall not profane My covenant and the utterance of My lips, I shall not change. When I said to you, 'Take thy son', I did not say to you 'slay him', but 'bring him up'. You have brought him [upon the altar]; now bring him down."

There is an obvious difficulty here, for in the initial command to bind Yitzchak on the altar, Hashem's words were: "והעלהו שם לעולה" (שם, כב,ב). The literal translation of this is: "and offer him there as a burnt offering" (עולה). How, then, could Hashem justify Himself by saying, "I didn't mean for you to slay him, but to bring him up upon the altar"?

The Chasam Soifer, in the previously cited responsa (רח), explains the dialogue that took place here between Avraham and Hashem.

"הנה אברהם אבינו וגם יצחק בנו חכמים גדולים היו...והנה האנשים האלה השכילו ענין וסוד הקרבנות שהיו בונין מזבחות והקריבו קרבנות וידעו עד היכן הדבר מגיע ומה שאפשר להשכיל בו כי אע"פ י שנתן הרמב"ם במורה טעמים להשקיט לב ההדיוטים מ"מ בסוף הלכות מעילה כתב שהוא חק וסוד שלא נגלה לנו. ומכל מקום האבות שבנו מזבחות ידעו וכמ"ש רמב"ן פ' ויקרא. והם ידעו והשכילו שא"א בשום אופן בעולם כלל וכלל שירצה השי"ת בקרבן האדם, שאלו לא הי' השכילו כן, כבר היה אברהם מקריב את ישמעאל בנו או אפילו יצחק אלא שזה אי אפשר בשום אופן בעולם.

והנה כשאמר לו הקב"ה 'קח נא את בנך את יחידך והעלהו לי לעולה' ע"כ יאמר שטעה בהשכלתו ומכיון שטעה אפשר ח"ו הכל טעות שהתקוטט

עם אנשי דורו על האמונה. ולא יעלה על הדעת שמא אמר הקב"ה רק 'העלהו' ולא להקריבו אין דרכו של הקב"ה חלילה לדבר בלשון שיטעה בו הנביא, ואברהם הבין שלשון 'העלהו לעולה', הוא לשון עולה ממש שהוא כליל לה'. ומ"מ בתום לבבו לא הרהר כלל אעפ"י שהי' חוץ להקיש הסוד שהבין מן הקרבנות.

ואין זה מן התימא על אברהם ששמע מן הקב"ה עצמו אבל מהתימא על יצחק שקיבל מאברהם מה שהוא נגד השכלתו...והאמת בזה שבוודאי הי' יצחק עולה כולו כליל כי בן אדם הנותן נפשו לשחיטה והקטרה בלי שום ציפוי שימלט נפשו ע"ד [על דרך] אליך ה' נפשי אשא, הרי נפשו כולו כליל לה' ית'. ולא דמי לקרבן בהמה שצריך הפשט וניתוח וכליל לאישים ואז תועלה נפש הבהמה לריח ניחוח אבל לא כן נפש האדם בחיים חיותו נדבק בהי"ת על ידי מחשבתו ובתנאי שיהי' מסירת נפש ממש. וא"כ היינו <u>'העלהו לי לעולה'</u>, והרי העלהו, והי' לעולה. ואע"פ שזה פשוט לכל מבין ומשכיל מ"מ העלים הקב"ה מחשבה זו מאברהם ויצחק אע"פ שהיו חכמים גדולים מ"מ כתיב יצפון לישרים תושי', כי לולא שהעלים מהם סברא זו לא הי' מסירת נפש שלימה, כי ידע שלא ימות, ע"כ לא הבינו תוכן הדבר עד אחר המעשה."

"Our Patriarchs understood the secret purpose and meaning of offering sacrifices on the altar. They clearly understood that it was impossible for Hashem to desire human beings to be offered as sacrifices upon the altar. For if this would have been His Will, then Avraham himself would have sacrificed his own son Yishmael or even Yitzchak. Therefore, when Avraham was told to sacrifice his son Yitzchak, though it contradicted all he had come to believe, he willingly agreed, in his simple faith, to offer Yitzchak up as a sacrifice. Avraham was aware that Hashem does not issue directives in which a prophet can be misled, and thereby this command must be taken literally — offer your son as a sacrifice.

However, what Hashem desired was not that a human being should be sacrificed, but rather that Avraham should be willing to do so wholeheartedly, without any hope of Hashem retracting this command. Hashem hid this true desire from Avraham, for had he known that Yitzchak would not be slaughtered, then there would not be a test here at all.

Thus we see that the real test of the Akeida was Hashem's desire for Avraham's total commitment, his willingness to give up everything for Hashem. For unlike an animal offering, which calls for actual sacrifice, this offering of Yitzchak alludes to surrendering one's will for the sake of Heaven."

This insight of the Chasam Soifer helps us understand the halacha that Selichos prayers must be said at least four days before Rosh Hashanah. The reason for this is explained in the sefer "אליהו רבה" (cited in the Mishnah Berurah, סימן תקפא, ס"ק ו'):

טעם שקבעו ד' ימים שכן מצינו בקרבנות שטעונים ביקור ממום ד' ימים קודם הקרבה. ובכל הקרבנות בפרשת פנחס כתיב 'והקרבתם עולה' ובראש השנה כתיב 'ועשיתם עולה' ללמד שבראש השנה יעשה אדם עצמו כאלו מקריב את עצמו, ולכן קבעו ד' ימים לבקר כל מומי חטאתו ולשוב עליהם.".

"Four days are required before Rosh Hashanah [to say the Selichos prayers], for we find that the law requires an animal to be tested four days prior to its being offered as a sacrifice [to be sure that no blemish is present], and therefore in relation to all the other occasions when a sacrifice is offered, the expression written in the Torah reads "והקרבתם", "and you shall bring forth [an animal] for a sacrifice". However, in relation to Rosh Hashanah, the word used in calling for a sacrifice is "ועשיתם", "and *you* should make", which is taken to mean that man himself should serve as the sacrifice, and therefore, just as an animal sacrifice calls for four days inspection, so the "human sacrifice" calls for introspection to rectify all a person's blemishes."

And so on Rosh Hashanah we are called upon to offer ourselves as a sacrifice. In light of the lesson we learn from the Akeida, this can be understood to mean that we surrender our will and resolve to serve Hashem wholeheartedly. This is the "human sacrifice" which Hashem requires of us on this special day.

IV
Reconciling Contradictions

There seem to be two contradictions which arise from the dialogue between Avraham Aveinu and Hashem regarding the sacrifice of Yitzchak. Avraham tells Hashem that he was first commanded to "Take now your son"; and this was later contradicted when Hashem cautioned Avraham by saying, "Lay not your hand upon the lad". At this point Hashem claims that He never intended for Avraham to slay Yitzchak. This leads to several questions.

1) Why did Avraham wait until after the actual Akeida to confront Hashem with these two contradictory statements? Why did he not raise the matter earlier?

2) Avraham appears to be complaining against Hashem. But is he really challenging Hashem's authority with these seemingly impertinent questions?

The truth is we are not meant to see Avraham as questioning Hashem or complaining, and this becomes clear when we view this episode in light of an insight of Rav Chaim Brisker. He recounts that he was once asked by a chassid why *misnagdim* ask so many questions and try to answer them with *pilpul*. Why question Hashem, he asked? Didn't He clearly set out His commandments in the Torah for us to follow? What more is there to ask?

Rav Chaim remarked that in a sense this man was right, for certainly we are expected to adhere to the written word of Hashem. And yet the Torah itself sets down guidelines as to when it is appropriate to ask questions and when not. These guidelines are delineated for us in the ברייתא דר' ישמעאל, where we are told the following:

"שני כתובים המכחישים זה את זה עד שיבוא הכתוב השלישי ויכריע ביניהם."

"Two passages contradict one another...until a third passage comes to reconcile them."

As long as we do not have this "third passage" available to us to reconcile the apparent contradiction, we do not have the right to question the contradiction that stands before us. For we must be reconciled that this is what the Torah says and we may not contradict Hashem. This is to be viewed as a dictate from Hashem, "גזירת הכתוב", which we must unquestioningly follow. However, if we become aware of an answer to this apparent contradiction by means of a third passage, "הכתוב השלישי", where the Torah itself offers a resolution to the conflicting statements, then we may proceed to question the contradiction. For now this question becomes a "חלק התורה", an integral part of the Torah.

We can now try to appreciate the answer offered by exploring its deeper meaning. We learn this approach from the actions of our patriarch Avraham. When he heard the apparent contradictions of Hashem telling him to "Take now your son" and slaughter him, and His previous assurance that "Yitzchak shall be called your seed", Avraham did not ask any questions. Only after he heard the "הכתוב השלישי" — that he was not to offer Yitzchak as a sacrifice after all — did he venture to question the apparent contradiction. For only now was he given permission to ask and to delve into the deeper meaning of the situation. And he discovered that the true answer was "אסקתיה, אחתיה", what Hashem really desired was for Avraham to bind Yitzchak on the altar but not to actually sacrifice him.

In light of this explanation of the events of the last phase of the Akeida, we become aware that Avraham was not complaining to Hashem about what must have been a painful contradiction, but rather he truly desired to understand the deeper meaning behind the seemingly confusing turn of events, so that he could better appreciate Hashem's Will.

Thus the story of the Akeida teaches us when and how to question. And when we ask a question of faith we should do so not to confront Hashem or to challenge Him. But rather our attitude should be that we are searching to gain a deeper understanding of Hashem's ways and what He requires of us.

The true spirit of how to question is exemplified in the prayer of Ain K'Elokeinu, where we first declare our belief in the uniqueness of Hashem, when we say, "there is none like our God", "אין כאל-הינו" and only then do we proceed to question His ways, with the statement of "מי כאל הינו". And finally, after all our questions are asked and answered, His uniqueness remains unchallenged and unmatched.

Gaining a Torah perspective

This insight of Rav Chaim Brisker's was challenged by the following question of HaRav David Moshe Soloveitchik, in his sefer "מאורי המועדים" (עמ' קכו):

"Rav Baruch Zeldovitz asked of Rav Chaim that Avraham Aveinu was not aware as yet that this 'third passage', "הכתוב השלישי" (of "אל תשלח ידך") contained the answer to the contradiction of Hashem's previous two statements. If so, how did Avraham attempt to ask a question, for his question would not be viewed as an integral part of Torah? Rav Chaim answered that Avraham was so sensitive to Torah thought that it did not even enter his mind to question Hashem's ways until the "third pasuk" appeared. Only after that, even though he was not yet aware of it, did he question the contradiction. Now he sensed that there was indeed a question to be asked, and he saw it as an integral part of Torah, and therefore he was prepared to raise the question.

From this we learn an important lesson in how to ask questions. We must first adopt a Torah perspective and develop the sensitivity to attune our questions to Torah values. For sometimes our questions arise from a lack of sensitivity or sufficient Torah knowledge. For we may not understand that a הכתוב השלישי has already been offered to our question. Therefore, we should seek to understand those answers which have already been given rather than dwell on the questions for their own sake.

V

The test of the Akeida: Rav Shach's view

Rav Eliezer Shach, שליט״א, suggests yet another lesson which can be learned from the Akeida. He bases this on an insight offered by Rav Yehoshua Leib Diskin, which is derived from the Rambam's contention that only Moshe Rabbenu was able to see the prophecies vouchsafed him by Hashem with clear vision, באספקלריה המאירה. All the other prophets, including the Avos, received their prophecies on a lower level of clarity, באספקלריה שאינה מאירה, as though they were seeing their visions through a refracted lens. (See *The Commentators' Gift of Torah*, pp. 117-121.) When Avraham Aveinu was told to sacrifice his son, it would seem that all the details were spelled out for him and there was no margin of choice or possibility of error left. For he was told explicitly, "Take your son, your only son, the one whom you love, Yitzchak." Why then, asks Rav Shach, was Avraham accorded such great merit by Hashem for what he did if he was only following His explicit commands and there was no room left for any variant interpretation on Avraham's part? In what sense was this considered such a great test?

The answer to this, contends Rav Shach, in light of Rav Yehoshua Leib Diskin's explanation, is that

Avraham's prophetic vision was of a slightly unclear nature (as if through the medium of a translucent mirror) like that of any other prophet. The Rambam attests to this in Hilchos Yesodei HaTorah (7:5) when he writes; "all of what we have said described the prophetic method of the earlier and later prophets."

From this we understand that the prophecy concerning the sacrifice of Yitzchak required *interpretation* by Avraham. What he was shown was in the nature of a dream or a parable, and it was a measure of Avraham's greatness that he was able to confront this vision with unflinching honesty and to accept that Hashem wanted him to take his only son, whom he dearly loved, and sacrifice him as a burnt offering. Because of the pure and luminous nature of his soul he interpreted his vision accurately, unmoved by motives of self-interest, nor did he seek a more favorable interpretation, for which the possibility existed had he been less committed to truth. This, concludes Rav Shach, constitutes Avraham's greatness in facing the test of the Akeida.

We read the story of the Akeida each day in our morning prayers to challenge us to be honest with ourselves, as Avraham was, and to see events in our lives as they really are and not to delude ourselves. Thus we are here being challenged to face situations which may not be ideal with faith that Hashem has our ultimate welfare in mind and that things will work out for the best in the end, as they did for Avraham Aveinu. And so we can appreciate the proximity of the Akeida to the prayer of "לעולם יהא אדם...ודובר אמת בלבבו", "Always should a man be God-fearing ... he should acknowledge the truth and speak the truth in his heart." This is an expression of the importance of being honest with oneself and with God.

"למנצח": Before Sounding the Shofar I
"To sing" or "to prune"?

Before we sound the shofar, we recite Psalm 47 seven times. This psalm, which begins with the words "למנצח לבני קרח מזמור", speaks about the sounding of the shofar both on Rosh Hashanah and in the future Messianic age. In the seventh verse we read:

"זמרו אלקים זמרו, זמרו למלכנו זמרו".

The word "זמרו" can be understood in one of two possible ways:

1) to sing or make music

2) to prune, "זומר", is from the same root as "זמרה", to sing.

If we take the word "זמרו" to refer to singing, then we can understand the verse to mean: "Sing for Hashem, make music for our King, make music."

The purpose of "making music" is to rejoice in our King on this day of Rosh Hashanah. This concept is explained by the Sforno in Vayikra 23:24. Commenting on the pasuk, "זכרון תרועה", the Sforno says:

"A memorial of the trumpet, a signal for the king, by which the people rejoice in their king, as it says: "הרנינו

"לאלקים עוזנו הריעו", 'Sing aloud to Hashem, our strength; make a joyful noise' (Ps. 81:2). This is done because He sits on the Throne of Justice, as we know from tradition (Rosh Hashanah 8b). And it says:

"תקעו בחדש שופר בכסה ליום חגנו כי חק לישראל הוא משפט לאלקי יעקב".

" 'Blow a shofar at the new moon, at the full moon of our festival day. For this is a statute for Yisrael, an ordinance of the God of Yaakov (Ps.81 4-5)'. It is therefore fitting that we rejoice more so at this time when He is our King, Who will lean towards kindness and will judge us favorably, as it says: "כי ה' שופטנו, ה' מחוקקנו, ה' מלכנו הוא יושיענו".

'For Hashem is our Judge, Hashem is our Ruler; Hashem is our King; He will save us.' " (Isaiah 33:22)

It was the custom of the Gaon of Vilna to be very joyful at this time when the shofar was being sounded, for he maintained that just as we are joyful when a new king is coronated, so too on the day of Rosh Hashanah, when we coronate Hashem as our King, we must rejoice in full measure.

And so we must "sing" and "make music" when we come to sound the shofar, for this is a time of great joy as we ceremonially install Hashem as king over all Creation; and singing to Him gives Him honor, "זמרו למלכנו זמרו".

If, on the other hand, we understand "זמרו" to mean "to prune", then we can understand this in light of the קדושת לוי, who views the name of God, "Elokim", as alluding to the Divine attribute of strict justice. He explains this as follows:

"והנה ידוע שאלקים מרמז על דין, וזהו זמרו, כלומר תראו לחתוך זה המידה, שלא יישב במידת דין וכו' רק כאב את בן, והוא יציל אותנו מכל דופי."

Since Hashem judges us according to this attribute of strict justice, we must do something to alter this so that He will judge us more favorably, employing instead His attribute of mercy.

This insight of the Kedushas Levi is derived from a Midrash in Vayikra (29:3) which tells us:

"יהודה ב"ר נחמן פתח (תהילים מז) עלה אל-הים בתרועה ה' בקול שופר. בשעה שהקב"ה יושב ועולה על כסא דין בדין הוא עולה, מה טעם עלה אל-הים בתרועה. ובשעה שישראל נוטלים את שופריהן ותוקעין לפני הקב"ה הוא עומד מכסא הדין ויושב בכסא רחמים דכתיב, ה' בקול שופר, ומתמלא עליהם רחמים ומרחם עליהם והופך עליהם מידת הדין לרחמים אימתי בחודש השביעי."

"Yehudah ben R' Nachman opened his discourse with the text: 'Hashem has gone up amidst shouting, the Lord amidst the sound of the horn.' (Ps. 47)

When the Holy One, Blessed be He, ascends and sits upon the Throne of Judgement, He ascends with the intent to rule using strict justice.

What is the reason for this statement? "Elokim" [which describes Hashem according to His attribute of justice] goes up amidst shouting. But when Yisrael take their horns and blow them in the presence of the Holy One, Blessed be He, He rises from the Throne of Judgement and sits upon the Throne of Mercy, for it is written: 'Hashem amidst the sound of the horn', and He is filled with compassion for them, taking pity upon them and changing for them the attribute of justice to that of mercy. When? In the seventh month."

II
Both interpretations are intended

Rav Dov Karrelenstein, שליט״א, in his sefer (קונטרס חידושי תורה בעניני הימים נוראים) attempts to show that both interpretations of the word "זמרו" are alluded to here in the psalm. This view is based on the following insight of the who (לרבינו יונה, שער ד' אות י"ב) שערי תשובה commentator writes as follows:

"ואם תמצא את החוטא תלאה ותקרה אותו צרה ויצדיק עליו את הדין, ויקבל המוסר באהבה, יהי' זה לו למגן מן היסורים הרבים הראוים לבוא עליו, כמו שנאמר (תהילים ע): כי חמת אדם תודך, שארית חמות תחגר, פירוש, כאשר צער האדם יודה אותך, כלומר, שיודה אותך האדם בעת צרה וכו'. שארית חמת שהיו מפתחות לבוא על האדם וכו' תחגור אותם ולא תביאם עליו וכו' ונאמר, אודך ה' כי אנפת בי, ישב אפך ותנחמני."

"And if the sinner is beset with hardships and visited with trouble, and he justifies the punishment accorded to him and accepts the chastisement with good will, this will serve as protection against the many afflictions which by right should come upon him, as it is said: 'When the suffering of man shall praise Thee.' (Ps. 76:11). 'When the suffering of man shall praise Thee', i.e., when a man shall praise You in the time of his suffering, the residue of wrath that had been unleashed to come upon him, 'You will gird', and withhold and not bring it upon them..."

Consequently, if one justifies appropriate punishment brought upon him, this can serve as an assurance that further punishment will cease. Accepting fitting punishment is alluded by the Rambam in Hilchos Berachos 10:3, where he writes:

"ובכלל האהבה היתירה שנצטווינו בה, שאפילו בעת שייצר לו, יודה וישבח בשמחה."

"Included in this extra dimension of love [of Hashem] that we were commanded to express is to acknowledge and praise Hashem with happiness even at one's time of difficulty."

In light of this, we can understand the words, "זמרו אלקים זמרו", to mean that even at the moment of strict judgement (the attribute of דין, as alluded to by calling Hashem "אלקים") one must sing to Hashem and praise Him for whatever punishment we receive, as we do for any reward. When we do this it signifies that we accept His judgement, whatever it may be, and we thereby succeed in "pruning" the attribute of strict justice and transforming it into the attribute of mercy. In this way, both meanings of the word "זמרו" are applicable here.

III
The shofar: from justice to mercy

We might suggest that the first part of the statement "זמרו אלקים זמרו" alludes to the insight of the Kedushas Levi that at a moment of strict justice (אלקים) we must do something, such as sound the shofar, to remove the Divine attribute of justice and replace it with that of mercy. After this, we are then told to make music and sing, "זמרו למלכנו",

"זמרו" for we rejoice in the knowledge that we are ruled by a King Who judges us with the attribute of mercy. This explains the rationale of those who say, before blowing the shofar: "עלה אל-הים בתרועה ה' בקול שופר", "God has ascended with a blast, Hashem, with the sound of the shofar".

This verse is recited to allude to the sounding of the shofar, and it is characterized by a change in God's name from אלקים, which signifies strict justice, to ה', which is a representation of Hashem in His attribute of mercy.

There are other indications that both meanings of "זמרו" — "to sing" and "to prune"— are intended. For example, in the Morning Prayers, the section referred to as פסוקי דזמרה is sometimes defined as alluding to the fact that these verses help us "to prune" extraneous thoughts from our minds and focus our attention on our morning prayers. Other commentators, though, interpret this term, פסוקי דזמרה, literally, as a collection of verses (פסוקים) from the Book of Psalms and from Nach, which sing the praises of Hashem. We could combine the two interpretations, and say that through song, "זמרה", we are able to prune the obstacles which stand in the way of proper concentration in prayer. In this way, we see how "זמרו" alludes to both concepts of שירה and זומר.

IV
The shofar itself is a form of song

We might suggest yet another reason why we are commanded here "to sing" and make music. Rav Yosef Dov Soloveitchik (see "נוראת הרב", חלק א, עמ' 66-78) believes that the shofar contains two mutually exclusive motifs: שירה, song, and צעקה, crying out. We have two separate obligations to sound the shofar on Rosh Hashanah, חובת תקיעת שופר, and these are based on two pasukim from the Torah.

1) "יום תרועה יהי' לכם" "It is a day of sounding the shofar for you." (Bamidbar 29:1)

2) "וביום שמחתכם ובמועדיכם ובראשי חדשיכם ותקעתם בחצצרות..."

"And on the day of your gladness, on your festivals, and on your new moons, you are to sound the trumpets." (Bamidbar:10:10)

Although neither the shofar nor the day of Rosh Hashanah is specified in these verses, yet both are alluded to here.

1) The positive commandment, עשה, of sounding the shofar on Rosh Hashanah, יום תרועה, is rooted in the special

sanctity of Rosh Hashanah day, קדושת היום. The obligation to offer praise on this day, קיום שירה, results from the fact that it is a new month, and so the קדושת היום of Rosh Chodesh merges with that of Rosh Hashanah. It is specifically the קדושת ראש חודש which precipitates חובת שירה, the obligation to offer songs of praise on this day.

2) שירה is expressed differently in the גבולין, outside the boundaries of the Bais HaMikdash, than it is inside. Within the Mikdash, שירה is expressed both by the shofar and the trumpet, שופר וחצוצרות. However, outside its confines, it is expressed exclusively by the shofar. The Gemara in Rosh Hashanah 30b, tells us that the psalm of the day, שיר של יום, which constituted the daily song of praise, was "תקעו בחודש שופר". On all other holidays the unique psalm of the day was recited only at Mussaf, whereas in Shacharis, they recited the regular psalm of that particular day of the week, שיר של יום. For example, on Pesach morning they recited the day's שירה on the daily sacrifice, תמידים, but at Mussaf they sang "בצאת ישראל". On Rosh Hashanah they sang a different שירה for the תמידים as well. This is the only holiday when this occurred. Even on Yom Kippur, they sang the regular שירה. What was the reason for this? It was because on Rosh Hashanah there is

a special obligation of שירה, and therefore the song of praise which accompanies the daily תמידים sacrifice, שירה על הקרבן, becomes the song of praise for Rosh Hashanah, שיר של ראש השנה, which is from Psalm 8, and reads: "תקעו בחודש שופר". This reinforces the idea that the sounding of the shofar is not simply a Mitzva of shofar, but also fulfills the Mitzva of שירה, and it is connected to the sanctity of the day of the new month, קדושת ראש חודש.

This way of looking at the obligation of shofar, to include the obligation of שירה as well, helps us understand why "זמרו", "to make music", is linked with the sounding of the shofar. For it reminds the listeners that sounding the shofar, תקיעת שופר, fulfills not only the Mitzva of shofar, but also the requirement to offer songs of praise on this day.

Sources for the Ten Verses:
מלכיות זכרונות ושופרות

I
Why ten verses?

The Mishna in Rosh Hashanah 32a states:

"אין פוחתין מעשרה מלכיות, מעשרה זכרונות, מעשרה שופרות."

"They recite no fewer than ten verses relating to *Kingship*. Ten verses for the section of *Remembrances*; and ten for the section of *Shofaros*."

The Gemara asks: "?הני עשרה מלכיות כנגד מי"

"The requirement of reciting ten verses for *Kingship*; from where do we know this?"

But why does the Gemara question the source of מלכיות alone? Why not also זכרונות and שופרות? Do they not also require clarification?

This question was anticipated by earlier commentators, who all seem to agree that "כנגד מי" includes not only מלכיות, but the other two sections of זכרונות and שופרות as well. For example:

1) The Ramban, Rashba and Hiddushei HaRan all read the Gemara here as: "הני עשרה כנגד מי", without the

word "מלכיות". (See Footnote 94 in the Mossad HaRav Kook edition of "חידושי הרשב״א" here). This means that the question covers all three sections (זכרונות and שופרות, as well as מלכיות). And similarly, the text of רבנו חננאל, which is printed in our pages of the Gemara, reads as does the text of these Rishonim.

2) The "ענף יוסף", in his commentary of the Gemara, quoted in the "עין יעקב", also asks the same question.

"יש להרגיש על לשון הש״ס הני עשרה מלכיות כנגד מי, ולא שאלו על עשרה זכרונות ולא על עשרה שופרות כנגד מי"."

And he answers that when the Gemara responds to its question of "כנגד מי", it offers the source of all three sections of מלכיות זכרונות ושופרות.

"אמר רב: כנגד עשרה הלולים דכתיב בהו הללו בתקע בשופר.
רב יוסף אמר: כנגד עשרה הדברות שנאמרו לו למשה בסיני.
ר' יוחנן אמר: כנגד עשרה מאמרות שבהן נברא העולם."

The Gemara here cites three opinions regarding the sources for the ten pasukim:

1) According to Rav: they correspond to the ten times the word "הללו" (praising Hashem) is repeated in Psalm 150, which includes the pasuk of "Praise Him with the sound of the Shofar".

2) According to Rav Yosef: they correspond to the Ten Commandments.

3) According to Rav Yochanan: they correspond to the Ten Divine Utterances with which Hashem created the world.

Thus we can see that:

Rav Yochanan alludes to the מלכיות; for since He created the world it is appropriate that we praise Him.

Rav Yosef alludes to the זכרונות, our obligation to constantly remember the Giving of the Torah on Mount Sinai.

Rav refers to the שופרות, for in the ten praises cited here the sounding of the shofar is included.

Thus we have not three different opinions of where the source is for the ten verses of מלכיות, but rather each is citing a source for one of the sections of מלכיות זכרונות ושופרות. And again we see that the Gemara is not addressing מלכיות exclusively, but refers rather to all three sections of verses. And so the Yerushalmi quoted here in the commentary of רבינו חננאל, printed in our Gemara, cites three different pasukim, each fitting either the מלכיות שופרות or זכרונות.

"הני עשר מלכיות כנגד עשר קלוסין שאמר דוד בהללויה הללו א-ל בקדשו וגו' עד כל הנשמה תהלל י-ה.

עשרה זכרונות כנגד עשרה וידוין שאמר ישעיה רחצו הזכו מה כתיב בתריה למדו היטב דרשו משפט אשרו חמוץ לכו נא ונוכחה.

י' שופרות כנגד י' שופרות ופר ואיל ושעיר..."

II
Petition or praise?

Consequently, we see that in reality the question of the Gemara regarding the source of these ten pasukim alludes to the pasukim of the זכרונות and the שופרות as well as the מלכיות.

Yet we might also defend the text which stresses only מלכיות, and attempts to locate its source, without trying to find the source for the זכרונות or the שופרות. This view assumes the following. First, that מלכיות corresponds to that section of the Shemoneh Esreh which is referred to as praise, שבחות. In the previous Mishna, found on the same page as our Gemara of Rosh Hashanah 32a, we find an argument between ר' יוחנן בן נורי and ר' עקיבא as to where to place the section of מלכיות. Rav Yochanan is of the opinion that we should link the מלכיות with the קדושת השם, the third section of the Amidah. As we know, the first three sections of the Amidah are referred to as praises, שבחות. This means that, according to Rav Yochanan, מלכיות are to be considered part of that section of praise.

Rabbi Akiva, on the other hand, maintains that the מלכיות section is to be linked with the קדושת היום, the section which proclaims the uniqueness of the day. The rationale behind linking these two sections is to justify sounding the shofar here. If we were to join the מלכיות with the קדושת השם, then it would not be possible to sound the shofar when reciting מלכיות. The reason for this is that we are not allowed to sound the shofar during the first section of the Amidah prayer, for this section is reserved for שבחות, praise of Hashem. The sounding of the shofar constitutes petition, for it is essentially a silent cry asking the Almighty to respond to our prayers, and we are not allowed to petition during this first part of the Amidah, which is exclusively dedicated to praise. And yet, even Rabbi Akiva agrees that the pasukim of the מלכיות are to be viewed in some sense as praise, otherwise we could never think of linking them with the first section of the Amidah at all.

Chazal tell us that had Moshe Rabbenu not referred to Hashem in his prayer (in Parashas Ve'Eschanan) as "הא-ל הגדול הגבור והנורא", we would never have been allowed to utter these praises and include them in our prayers. For it is forbidden to elaborate on the praise of Hashem unless we find a precedent in the Torah. Thus if the מלכיות are to be viewed as an exercise in praise, then the question would arise, how are we allowed to recite ten verses of praise — the מלכיות — for wouldn't this constitute elaborating on the praise of Hashem, which is strictly forbidden? To this question the Gemara responds that we do indeed have a source which establishes a precedent of allowing ten verses of praise to be recited. This accounts for the מלכיות. However, regarding the זכרונות and the שופרות, which fall into the category of "petition" and not "praise", there is no need to find a source, for there is no restriction placed on elaborating *petitions*, but only praise.

The Ten Verses of the מזו"ש: An Overview

I
Why quote the Writings before the Prophets?

Kisvei HaKodesh, the Holy Scriptures, are divided into three parts: Torah, Prophets and Writings, = תנ"ך תורה, נביאים וכתובים. There are two possible explanations as to why the Prophets are placed before the Writings.

1) The sanctity of the Prophets is greater than that of the Writings, either because it was composed from a higher degree of prophecy (See *The Commentators' Gift of Torah*, pp.75-108, "The Division of Tanach".)

2) The acronym תנ"ך, which places נביאים before כתובים, is to be viewed as a chronological ordering. The Torah of Moshe Rabbenu came first, then the Prophets, beginning with Yehoshua, and finally the Writings of the later prophets.

In the Mussaf of Rosh Hashanah when we add the blessings of מלכיות זכרונות ושופרות we also recite ten verses from the Tanach referring to these three themes. We first quote verses from the *Torah*, then from the *Writings*, and finally, from the *Prophets*. But why do the verses from the Writings precede those from the Prophets? Tosafos, in

Mesechtas Rosh Hashanah 32a asks a further question. The order here seems to contradict that which is stated in Mesechtas Megillah 31a. There the Gemara states:

"אמר ר' יוחנן: בכל מקום שאתה מוצא גדלתו של הקדוש ברוך הוא, שם אתה מוצא ענותנותו. דבר זה כתוב בתורה, ושנוי בנביאים ומשלש בכתובים..."

"Rav Yochanan said: Wherever you find the greatness of the Holy One, Blessed be He, there you will find His humility. This is so written in the *Torah*, repeated in the *Prophets*, and stated a third time in the *Writings*..."

Thus we see that the Prophets take precedence over the Writings. Why, then, on Rosh Hashanah, do we first quote from the Writings and only afterwards from the Prophets? Tosafos answers:

"ויש לומר משום דקראי דתהילים...קדמו לנביאים..."

The verses from the Writings take precedence over those from the Prophets because all the verses here are from the Book of Psalms, which was written before all the verses from the Prophets quoted here. For King David, who composed the Book of Psalms, lived before Isaiah, Yirmeyahu, Yechezkail, Zecharyah and Ovadiah, the prophets from whose books the verses from the Prophets were culled.

There are other insights to explain why the verses from the Writings here precede those from the Prophets; whereas on all other occasions the order is reversed.

1) רבינו מנוח, in his commentary, Hilchos Shofar 3:8, offers a unique answer. He writes:

"ויש לומר כיון דקי"ל דאם השלים בנביא יצא כמ"ש הרב, זמנין דמשתלי ולא ישלים בתורה, ואם יאמרו נביאים ואחר כך כתובים, נמצא משלים בכתובים ולא יצא. אבל עכשיו שאומר נביאים אחר כתובים אע"ג דמשתלי ולא ישלים לומר ובתורתך כתוב לאמר יצא דהא השלים בנביאים..."

"Since the law reads that if one concluded with a verse from the Prophets one has fulfilled his obligation, thus, in an instance in which one forgot to complete the last of the ten verses with a verse from the Torah yet did conclude with a verse from the Prophets, he has discharged his obligation. To assure this, we quoted the Writings before the Prophets, for had we followed the usual manner of ending with Writings, one would thereby not have discharged his obligation, for he would have concluded with a verse from the Writings."

2) The קרבן נתנאל suggests the following answer.

"ולי נראה דהיינו טעמא דפסוקים של כתובים בעצם ראשונה, שאינם אלא שבחים והמה מוקדמים בזמן שהוה ויהי'. משא"כ פסוקי דנביאים שעדיין לא נתקיימו עד אחרית הימים ע"כ לאחרונה יסעו".

"Since the name of 'ה alludes to the Almighty as being 'Hashem' of the past, present and future, thereby Torah, which alludes to the past (history) comes first; Writings, which allude to the praise of Hashem and therefore are considered as relating to the present, comes next. And the Prophets, whose prophecies as yet have not been fulfilled but will take place in the future, come last."

II

The book or the concept?

The נודע ביהודה (מה"ת או"ח סימן כ) asks the following question, based on the formula set down here by the Ba'alei Tosafos that we follow chronological order. Psalms come first, and therefore we begin with the Writings. Why, then, in the *Av HaRachamim,* which we say on Shabbos morning, do the verses from the Prophets come before those of the Writings, when all the verses are from the Book of Psalms?

"ועל ידי עבדיך הנביאים כתוב לאמר: ונקיתי לא נקיתי וגו' ". (יואל ד,כא')

ובכתבי הקודש: [כתובים] "נאמר: למה יאמר הגוים וגו'". [תהילים עט,י] ואומר: "כי דורש דמים אותם זכר וגו'". [תהילים ט, יג] ואומר: "ידין בגוים וגו'" [תהילים ק,ו-ז]

"And by Your servants the *Prophets* it is written saying: I will avenge their blood, which I have not avenged, etc." Joel 4:21.

"And in the Holy Writings it is said: Why should the nations say, etc." *Psalms* 79:10.

"And it is further said: the avenger of bloodshed is mindful of them..." *Psalms* 9:13.

"And it is further said: He will render judgement upon the nations, etc." *Psalms* 110:6-7.

Thus we see *all* the verses of the Writings here are from the Book of Psalms. Why, then, do they not precede the verses from the Prophets, which contain a verse from the Book of Yoel, a much later prophet?

Before attempting to answer this question of the נודע ביהודה we must first ask another question. It seems from the formula cited by the Ba'alei Tosafos that we have a contradiction here. For the very quotation he uses to pose his question — that we see from the statement of Rav Yochanan that Prophets precede Writings — seems to contradict his own position, that we follow a chronological order. For Tosafos bases his question here on the sequence mentioned in Mesechtas Megillah 31a, where we read the following:

שנוי בנביאים: דכתיב: "כי אמר רם ונשא וגו'" ישעיה ז:טז

משלש בכתובים: "שירו לאלקים, זמרו לו וגו'" תהילים סח:ה.

וכתיב בתריה - "אבי יתומים", תהילים סח:ו.

"It is repeated in the *Prophets*, as it is written: "For so says the exalted and uplifted One, etc." *Isaiah* 57:15.

Written a third time in the *Writings:* "Sing to Hashem, etc." *Psalms* 68:5. Afterwards it is written: "Father of orphans, etc." *Psalms* 68:6.

Thus, according to Tosafos, why do we find the Prophets first, when all the verses of the Writings are from the Book of Psalms, which chronologically comes before the Prophet Isaiah?

To answer this apparent contradiction, we might say that there are two separate issues here.

1) If the issue touches upon the *book* itself, and the question is which book takes precedence; that of the Prophets or of the Writings, then we can say that Prophets takes precedence over the Writings, since the initial book of the Prophets was written by Yehoshua, who preceded all the later prophets; or is it simply because the Books of the

Prophets are considered to have greater sanctity than those of the Writings?

2) However, if the issue is not that of the book, but rather a quotation to be recited orally, then we apply the position of Tosafos, that although one quotation may find its source in the Prophets, yet since another quotation from the Writings was written by a prophet who may have preceded the one who wrote the quotation from the Prophets, we follow the chronological order.

Thus, the issue in Mesechtas Megillah 31a is the *book*, that is, the category of Kisvei HaKodesh, as it says: "ושנוי בנביאים", "Repeated *in the Prophets*:" "משלש בכתובים" "And it is stated a third time *in the Writings*." Thus we emphasize the idea that Hashem's humility is spelled out in all the *books* of Tanach.

Whereas the issue regarding the *concepts* of מלכיות זכרונות ושופרות, Kingship, Remembrance and Shofar are cited in pasukim which refer to these concepts. Since here the focus is on the pasukim rather than on the books, we consider the chronological order of the pasukim. And so, regarding the pasukim of מלכיות זכרונות ושופרות, all of them come from the Book of Psalms, and therefore they precede the quotations from the Prophets.

III

Oral recitation and chronological order

Based on this, we can now attempt to offer a new insight into the question raised by the Avudraham. He asks: Why, in the Mussaf prayer of Rosh Hashanah, in the מלכיות, etc., when we recite the verses from the Prophets, do we say: "ועל ידי עבדיך הנביאים כתוב לאמר".

"Through Your servants, Your Prophets, it is written."

Whereas, when quoting verses from the Writings, we say: "ובדברי קדשך כתוב לאמר".

"In Your Holy Writings the following is written."

Why do we not also say, when reciting the verses of the Prophets, "ובדברי קדשך כתוב לאמר", "In Your Holy Writings it is written". Why is there a difference in the manner in which we introduce the Prophets and the Writings? (See *The Commentators' Gift of Torah*, pp. 85-86).

In light of our above discussion, we might answer that had we stressed here the *Books* of the Prophets by using the same phrase as we did when we referred to the Writings: "ובדברי קדשך כתוב לאמר", then, despite the fact that the quotations from the books of the Writings chronologically precede those of the Prophets, we still would not have placed the Writings before the Prophets (as we do in the Mussaf prayers). For, as we have discussed, if the *book* is stressed, then the Prophets would take precedence, even when the quotations from the Writings chronologically precede those of the Prophets.

Therefore, when we say here in the Mussaf prayers: "ועל ידי עבדיך הנביאים", we are stressing the *oral recitation* of the prophets. This is similar to the approach of the Avudraham and Rav Chaim Brisker, since both of them answer the question posed by the Avudraham by saying that Prophets are alluded to here, in the sense that the prophet initially relayed his message *orally* and only afterwards committed it to writing. This is why we say, "ועל ידי עבדיך הנביאים וגו'", in order to emphasize the oral recitation of the prophet. Regarding the Writings, on the other hand, the prophet first committed his prophecy to writing. And this explains why we say here in relation to the Writings, "ובדברי קדשיך כתוב"; in other words, we stress the book. Thus, when the issue is oral recitation from the Prophets, the chronological order takes precedence.

Why, then, in *Av Harachamim*, do we say, in relation to the Prophets: "ועל ידי עבדיך הנביאים וגו'"? We suggested that here we stress the *book* and not the oral recitation. To this we might answer based on the insight of the "עיון תפלה" in his comments to this statement here of "ועל ידי עבדיך הנביאים וגו'". Why do we here refer to the Prophets in the plural — נביאים — when the quotation is from only the Book of Yoel? Wouldn't it have been more appropriate to have said, "ועל ידי נביאך", "And by Your *prophet*", as we find in the Kedushah of the Shemoneh Esreh, when we say: "ועל ידי עבדך", "Spoken by Your prophet," which is a reference to the Prophet Ezekiel (3:12)?

According to the "עיון יעקב", the answer must be based on what Rashi says in Baba Basra 15a: Since each of the Books of the Twelve Minor Prophets, תרי עשר, are brief, it was feared that if each one was written separately it could get lost; therefore their composition was delayed to the period of the Anshei Knesses HaGadolah, which incorporated each of these smaller prophecies into one book called "תרי עשר". And so, when we say here "ועל ידי עבדיך הנביאים", this refers to the *Anshei Knesses HaGadolah*, who wrote the book of Yoel and joined it with eleven other prophecies to make up the book of the twelve minor prophets, "תרי עשר".

This means that when we say here in the *Av Harachamim*, "ועל ידי עבדיך הנביאים כתוב וגו'" this does not refer to the oral recitation of the prophet, but rather to the *books* written by the Anshei Knesses HaGadolah. However, when we say this in our Rosh Hashanah prayers: "ועל ידי עבדיך הנביאים" we are alluding to the oral recitation of the prophets. And when the issue is oral recitation, then the chronological order takes precedence.

IV
Written text versus oral recitation

Elsewhere (See *The Commentators' Gift of Torah*, pp. 89-90 and in my sefer "אהל רבקה", עמ' קלח-ט) we have cited the insight of Rav Chaim Brisker regarding the difference between the Prophets and the Writings. Rav Chaim maintains that the books of the Prophets are characterized by revelations spoken by the prophet and only later committed to writing. The Writings, on the other hand, were prophecies originally written down by Divine command and only later read from their manuscripts. He writes as follows:

"שנביאים היינו שהנביא היה צריך לומר את הנבואה בעל פה אבל כתובים היה הדין שמתחילה היה צריך לכתוב את הנבואה על הספר ואחר כך היתה נקראת מתוכה. וכן איתא בירמיה דנאמרו לו ב' נבואות למסור למלך יהויקים. אחת אמר לו מיד בעל פה והשניה צוה ברוך לכותבה על הספר ואחר כך מסר אותה בכתב אל יהויקים והיא היתה מגילת קינות דהיא מכלל הכתובים"

Based on the above, we can now answer the question of the Avudraham as to why we say regarding the Prophets, "ועל ידי עבדיך הנביאים", for here we stress the role of the prophet in relation to his oral recitation. When we introduce the Writings, however, the stress is on the written text, which was the essential factor in the revelation, and therefore it is appropriate to say, "ובדברי קדשך כתוב לאמר", "In Your Holy Writings the following is written."

If the issue is the *book*, then we say the Prophets take precedence over the Writings; however, if the issue is not the book itself but rather a quotation which is to be recited orally, then we follow the chronological order. And if the author of the Writings preceded the author of the Prophets chronologically, as we find in the Rosh Hashanah liturgy, then the Writings takes precedence.

Consequently, we can say that when we read in the prayers here that quote the verses from the Writings, "ובדברי קדשך כתוב לאמר", it would seem that the essential issue is the book itself. And so we are confronted with the question why the Writings precede the Prophets. Therefore we say "ועל ידי עבדיך הנביאים" to show that we wish to stress here the oral recitation, which means that the chronological order takes on primary importance. In this instance, the Psalms by King David, which come from the Writings, precede the quotation of verses from the later prophets. This explains why it is necessary to spell out the role of the prophet in the Books of the Prophets, even though this may not seem to be the appropriate place for this. But in light of our above discussion we can understand why it was necessary to do this here, in order to justify placing the Writings before the Prophets.

Outline of the Verses of the מזו״ש

In each of the blessings of the מלכיות זכרונות ושופרות, ten verses are to be recited, three from the Torah, three from the Writings, three from the Prophets, and a concluding verse from the Torah. The following table shows how these pasukim are put together.

פסוקי מלכיות

תורה	מקור
1) ה' ימלוך לעולם ועד.	שמות טו, יח
2) לא הביט און ביעקב ולא ראה עמל בישראל, ה' אלקיו עמו ותרועת מלך בו.	במדבר כג, כא
3) ויהי בישרון מלך בהתאסף ראשי עם יחד שבטי ישראל.	דברים לג, ה

כתובים	מקור
1) כי לה' המלוכה ומושל בגויים.	תהילים כב, כט
2) ה' מלך גאות לבש, לבש ה' עוז התאזר אף תיכון תבל בל תמוט.	תהילים צג, א
3) שאו שערים ראשיכם והנשאו פתחי עולם ויבא מלך הכבוד.	תהילים כד, ז
מי זה מלך הכבוד ה' עזוז וגבור ה' גבור מלחמה.	תהילים כד, ח
שאו שערים ראשיכם ושאו פתחי עולם ויבוא מלך הכבוד.	תהילים כד, ט
מי הוא זה מלך הכבוד ה' צבאות הוא מלך הכבוד סלה.	תהילים כד, י

The Commentators' Machzor Companion

מקור	נביאים
ישעיהו מד	1) אני ראשון ואני אחרון ומבלעדי אין אל-הים.
	2) ועלו מושיעים בהר ציון לשפוט
עובדיה א, כא	את הר עשיו והיתה לה' המלוכה.
	3) והיה ה' למלך על כל הארץ ביום ההוא
זכריה יד,ט	יהי' ה' אחד ושמו אחד.

מקור	תורה
דברים ו', ד	4) שמע ישראל ה' אלקינו ה' אחד.

פסוקי זכרונות

מקור	תורה
	1) ויזכר אלקים את נח ואת כל החיה ואת כל הבהמה אשר
בראשית ח, א	אתו בתיבה ויעבר אלקים רוח על הארץ וישכו המים.
	2) וישמע אלקים את נאקתם ויזכר אלקים
שמות ב, כד	את בריתו את אברהם את יצחק ואת יעקב.
	3) וזכרתי את בריתי יעקב ואף את בריתי יצחק
ויקרא כו, מב	ואף את בריתי אברהם אזכר והארץ אזכר.

מקור	כתובים
תהילים קיא, ד	1) זכר עשה לנפלאותיו חנון ורחון ה'.
תהילים קיא, ה	2) טרף נתן ליראיו יזכר לעולם בריתו.

3) ויזכר להם בריתו וינחם כרוב חסדיו.   תהילים קו, מה

מקור	נביאים
ירמיה ב, ב	1) הלוך וקראת באזני ירושלים לאמר כה אמר ה' זכרתי לך חסד נעוריך אהבת כלולותיך לכתך אחרי במדבר בארץ לא זרועה.
יחזקאל טז, ס	2) וזכרתי אני את בריתי אותך בימי נעוריך והקימותי לך ברית עולם.
ירמיה לא, ט	3) הבן יקיר לי אפרים אם ילד שעשועים כי מדי דברי בו זכור אזכרנו עוד על כן המו מעי לו רחם ארחמנו נאם ה'.

מקור	תורה
ויקרא כו, מה	4) וזכרתי להם ברית ראשונים אשר הוצאתי אותם מארץ מצרים לעיני הגוים להיות להם לאלקים אני ה'.

פסוקי שופרות

מקור	תורה
שמות יט, טז	1) ויהי ביום השלישי בהיות הבקר ויהי קולות וברקים וענן כבד על ההר וקול שופר חזק מאד ויחרד כל העם אשר במחנה.
	2) ויהי קול שופר הולך וחזק מאד משה ידבר

והאלקים יעננו בקול.
3) וכל העם ראים את הקולות ואת הלפידים ואת קול השופר ואת ההר עשן וירא העם וינעו ויעמדו מרחוק. שמות כ, טו

שמות יט, יט

כתובים	מקור
1) עלה אלקים בתרועה ה' בקול שופר.	תהילים מז, ו
2) בחצוצרות וקול שופר הריעו לפני המלך ה'.	תהילים צח, ו
3) תקעו בחודש שופר בכסא ליום חגנו	תהילים פא, ד
כי חוק לישראל הוא משפט לאלקי יעקב.	תהילים פא, ה
4) הללו-יה הללו וגו' הללוהו בתקע שופר.	תהילים קנ

נביאים	מקור
1) כל יושבי תבל ושוכני ארץ כנשא נס הרים תראו וכתקע שופר תשמעו.	ישעיה יח, ג
2) והיה ביום ההוא יתקע בשופר גדול ובאו האובדים בארץ אשור והנדחים בארץ מצרים והשתחוו לה' בהר הקודש בירושלים.	ישעיה כז, יג
3) וה' עליהם יראה ויצא כברק חצו וה' אלקים בשופר יתקע והלך בסערות תימן ה' צבאות יגן עליהם.	זכריה ט, יד-טו

תורה	מקור
4) וביום שמחתכם ובמועדיכם ובראשי חדשיכם ותקעתם בחצוצרות על עולותיכם ועל זבחי שלמיכם והיו לכם לזכרון לפני ה' אלקיכם אני ה' אלקיכם.	במדבר י, י

Why Are the Kesuvim Verses From Tehillim?

I
Why does the Rambam mention the Book of Psalms?

The Rambam in Hilchos Shofar (פרק ג הלכה ח) states:

"שלש ברכות אמצעיות אלה של ראש השנה...שהן מלכיות זכרונות ושופרות מעכבות זו את זו. וצריך לומר בכל ברכה מהן עשרה פסוקים מעין הברכה. שלשה מן התורה. ושלשה מ<u>ספר תהילים</u>. ושלשה מן הנביאים...ואם אמר פסוק אחד מן התורה ואחד מן <u>הכתובים</u> ואחד מן הנביאים יצא..."

"These three intermediate blessings on Rosh Hashanah... Malchiyus, Zichronos, and Shofros are all dependent on each other... In each of these blessings one is required to recite three verses from Torah, three from the <u>Book of Psalms</u>, and three from the Prophets.

Should a person recite only one verse from the Torah, one from the Writings, and one from the Prophets, he fulfills his obligation."

This statement of the Rambam raises several questions:

1) Why, when the Rambam cites the need for pasukim from Kesuvim, does he say specifically that the verses must be from the Book of Psalms, "מספר תהילים"? Why not simply say "מן הכתובים". For what purpose did he choose to mention Sefer Tehillim, even though these verses represent Kesuvim?

2) Why does the Rambam change his words when he tells us that we must cite verses from the Kesuvim? In the first instance, he writes: "Three verses from the *Book of Psalms*". Yet later, when he states that one verse would be sufficient, he says: "one verse from the *Kesuvim*". Why did he change his terminology from the more specific "verses from the Book of Psalms" to a "verse from Kesuvim"?

Rav Yosef Dov Soloveitchik suggests the reason why the Rambam specifies "ספר תהילים" instead of "כתובים". We find in Sefer Shmuel II 23:1 that King David is described as the "sweet singer of Yisrael", "נעים זמירות ישראל". Rashi explains this to mean that we are not to sing any other hymns in the Holy Temple but those of David, "אין משוררים במקדש אלא שירותיו וזמירותיו".

This means that we have here not a description of King David, but rather a halachic requirement stimulating is that when we offer song and praise in the Bais HaMikdash we must sing only the songs of David.

The Rambam extends this halacha to include even the songs of praise which are to be sung outside the Temple. In other words, we must always select songs from King David's Book of Psalms whenever we wish to sing songs of praise to Hashem. Thus the Rambam writes in מהל׳, פרק ז, תפלה, הלכה יב-יג:

"שבחו חכמים למי שקורא זמירות מספר תהילים בכל יום ויום וכו׳. ותקנו ברכה לפני הזמירות והוא ברוך שאמר, וברכה לאחריהם והיא ישתבח. ויש מקומות שנהגו בהן לקרות בכל יום אחר שמברכין ישתבח שירת הים."

"Our Sages praised those who recite songs from the Book of Psalms every day... It has become customary to read verses before and after them. They instituted a blessing before the songs, 'Baruch She'Amar'...and a blessing after concluding them, 'Yishtabach'... There are places where they are accustomed to recite the 'Song of the Sea' each day after they recite 'Yishtabach'."

Although this custom is not the one we follow, yet we can appreciate the explanation why those who recite the שירת הים do so only after reciting ישתבח. For these praises recited until שירת הים constitute the פסוקי דזמרה, which come from the Book of Psalms. This was in keeping with Rashi's explanation that when we sing songs of praise, we choose them from the Book of Psalms. Thus we do not include even verses from the Torah in this section of פסוקי דזמרה.

Only after we say the concluding beracha of the פסוקי דזמרה may we now read the שירת הים, which consist of verses from the Torah.

HaRav Soloveitchik concludes that since the verses which make up the מלכיות זכרונות ושופרות are considered to be praises, the fact that we are required to read ten of them is derived from Psalm 150 ("הללו א-ל בקדשו") where "ten praises" are mentioned: "עשרה הלולים". Therefore, we choose for our praise verses from the Book of Psalms. And even though we can quote verses from the Torah and the Prophets, we quote verses from Tehillim, and thus we fulfill the verse which says that we must select the "songs of David", "הבוחר בשירי זמרה".

We might say, however, that this requirement of choosing verses from the Psalms is only called for at the outset, לכתחילה, and if one nevertheless were to choose a verse from the other books of Kesuvim, one would also have fulfilled the obligation of praise required here. And if this is true, then we can now understand why the wording was changed by the Rambam. For he first writes that we are to choose "three verses from the Book of <u>Psalms</u>". And later, that "if he recites one verse from <u>Kesuvim</u>, this suffices."

In light of our previous discussion, we can understand that the Rambam is speaking of what is preferable in halachic terms. According to his opinion, what is *most desirable* (לכתחילה) is that there should be three verses and quotations from the Book of Psalms. Later on, however, he speaks of what is *acceptable* after the fact, "בדיעבד". And he says that if one did not recite three verses, then one verse would be sufficient for him to have fulfilled his obligation. And just as one verse is acceptable, we may now understand why even the quotation of a verse from somewhere other than the Book of Psalms is also acceptable, as long as it comes from the Writings, כתובים. This explains the change in the Rambam's terminology from "ספר תהילים" to "כתובים".

"There is No One Besides You" (מלכיות)

I
The Griz HaLevi's question

The Griz HaLevi asks the following pertinent question:

"למה בשמונה עשרה אלוקי אברהם היא מלכיות, דכל ברכה צריך לי' שם ומלכות, ואלוקי אברהם הוא במקום מלך, עיין תוס' ברכות (מ'ב'), ובשמונה עשרה של ראש השנה לא מספיק אלוקי אברהם, ומאי שנא מלכיות של שמונה עשרה של כל השנה מראש השנה." — "מסורה", חוברת יג, אדר תשנז, עמ' ה.

The halacha requires a beracha to contain the following two elements: 1) the name of Hashem, and 2) an allusion to His being Sovereign over the whole world — מלך העולם. Therefore, in the first beracha of the Shemoneh Esreh, it is the phrase of "אלוקי אברהם" that stands in place of the key word "מלך העולם" (for it was Avraham Aveinu who declared to the world that Hashem is the universal King). This constitutes the required "מלכות", which is called for in this beracha at the beginning of the Shemoneh Esreh. If so, asks the Griz HaLevi, why does this phrase, "אלוקי אברהם", which is a verse from the Torah, not fulfill the requirement of מלכיות in the Mussaf prayer, and why must we search for another verse to fulfill this requirement of mentioning verses of מלכיות?

We might suggest a possible answer to the Griz Halevi's question, based on the following insight of Rav Yosef Dov Soloveitchik to the episode recorded at the beginning of the Book of Shmuel I, 1:4. He comments as follows on the pasuk from the chapter we read on the second day of Rosh Hashanah:

"ויהי היום ויזבח אלקנה ונתן לפנינה אשתו ולכל בניה מנות ולחנה יתן מנה אחת אפים וגו'"

"And it was on that day that Elkanah slaughtered peace offerings, and he gave portions to Peninah his wife and to all of her children. And to Hannah he gave a choice portion."

We must take note of the statement here, "ויהי היום", "And it was on that day". What day are we talking about? We must understand that throughout the period that Hannah was unable to bear children, Elkanah certainly must have followed the practice of our patriarch Yitzchak and our matriarch Rivkah, who also did not have children for many years. During that time, we are told, Yitzchak would stand in one corner and pray and Rivkah would stand in another corner and pray. And so we may assume that Elkanah undoubtedly stood in a corner and prayed while Hannah prayed in another corner. With this in mind, we can understand the meaning here of "ויהי היום". Until this time Elkanah, by his constant prayers, showed that he had faith that he and Hannah would eventually bear children. Now, however, he declared:

"למה תבכי ולמה לא תאכלי ולמה ירע לבבך הלא אנכי טוב לך מעשרה בנים..."

"Hannah, why do you weep? And why do you not eat? And why is your heart sad? Am I not better to you than ten sons?"

At this point he revealed that he was reconciled to the fact that they would never have children, and therefore he made this emotional declaration that it did not matter whether or not they had children, for his love for her was greater than that for even ten children. When Channah heard this declaration and understood that he was being reconciled to their childless fate, she was devastated. For she realized that Elkanah would now no longer pray for help from Heaven to have children. She felt deserted and alone, and in her bitter state of mind she prayed and cried out to Hashem like a person who knows that the situation is hopeless, such that only Hashem Himself can help "אין עוד מלבדו", "There is no one besides Him." This declaration of Hannah's constitutes true מלכיות.

This insight was also expressed by Rav Yaakov Yitzchak, the *"Yud HaKodesh"*, who explained the prayer of "ואנחנו לא נדע מה לעשות כי עליך עינינו", "We know not what to do, but our eyes are upon you", which tells us that salvation comes about when man reaches that state of mind in which all is lost and none can help but Hashem.

In light of this insight we can now attempt to answer the question raised by the Griz HaLevi as to why "אלוקי אברהם" does not suffice as a fulfillment of the expression of מלכיות. For to fulfill this requirement a beracha must contain a declaration that Hashem is the Supreme King, מלך העולם. Thus the statement of "אלוקי אברהם" should suffice, for it was Avraham Aveinu who declared to the world that Hashem is the Supreme King. However, the requirement of מלכיות in the Mussaf prayer of Rosh Hashanah requires something else — "אין עוד מלבדו" — a declaration that there is no one else besides Hashem and that our help can come from no other source. This further indicates that our Heavenly King will bring about our redemption and He will be universally recognized as the King of kings.

This explains the prayer of Aleinu, in which there seems to be a redundant statement. For we say:

"שהוא נוטה שמים ויסד ארץ ומושב יקרו בשמים ממעל, ושכינת עזו בגבהי מרומים, הוא אל-הינו אין עוד."

"He stretches out Heaven and establishes earth's foundation; the seat of His glory is in the Heavens above and His powerful presence is in the loftiest heights. *He is our God and there is none other.*"

And then we continue and say:

"אמת מלכנו, אפס זולתו, ככתוב בתורתו: וידעת היום והשבת אל לבבך, כי ה' הוא האלקים בשמים ממעל ועל הארץ מתחת, אין עוד."

"True is our God, there is nothing besides Him, as it is written in His Torah: You are to know this day and take to your heart, that Hashem is the only God, in Heaven above and on the earth below — *there is none other.*"

And one might ask, why is there a separate, seemingly repetitious statement of "אין עוד", "there is none other"? Why are the above attributes not joined in one statement and concluded with the declaration of "אין עוד", instead of dividing the praises here into two statements, each ending with the same words, "אין עוד"?

In light of our previous discussion, we might suggest that the reason for the first statement of "אין עוד" shows recognition that there is but one God and Creator; however, when we say: "אפס זולתו", "there is none besides Him", we are in essence declaring "אין עוד מלבדו", "there is no one else to help us but Hashem". Thus, the second "אין עוד" adds an important element to our understanding of the greatness and exclusive sovereignty of Hashem.

מלכיות Its Place in the "ה' ימלוך לעולם ועד"

I
The order of the verses

As previously mentioned, of the ten verses required in the מלכיות זכרונות ושופרות from Kisvei HaKodesh, four come from the Torah. These include the first three pasukim and the last of the ten. This leads Chazal, in Mesechtas Rosh Hashanah 32b, to raise the following question:

"אלא מלכיות תלת הוא דהוין,
"ה' אלקיו עמו ותרועת מלך בו" (במדבר, כג, כא)
"ויהי בישורון מלך" (דברים לג, ה)
"ה' ימלוך לעולם ועד" (שמות טו, יח)"

"The Kingship verses in the Torah are only three:

1) "The Lord his God is with him and the shouting for the king is among them". (Bamidbar 23:21)

2) "And He was a King in Yeshurun". (Devarim 33:5)

3) "Hashem shall reign forever and ever". (Shemos 15:18)

The sequence quoted here is not the order we follow in the *Machzor*, for in our actual prayers we follow the order of the Torah:

1) First we quote from Shemos 15:18: "ה' ימלוך לעולם ועד".

2) Then, Bamidbar 23:21: "לא הביט און ביעקב וגו' ה' אלקיו עמו".

3) And finally, from Devarim 33:5: "ויהי בישורון מלך".

Thus, maintains Rav Hai Gaon, as quoted in the commentary of the Ran here (עמ' ט מדפי הרי"ף):

"וכתב רבינו האי ז"ל נהיגי למימר מלכיות של תורה כסדרן בתורה, ה' ימלוך לעולם ועד, לא הביט און, ויהי בישורון מלך, ואע"ג דהכא אמרינן, מלכיות תלתא הוא דהוין: ,לא הביט און' ,ויהי בישורון מלך' ,וה' ימלוך' לא קפיד לאדכורינהו כסדרן דפשיטא דכסדרן אמרינן להו".

"Rav Hai Gaon writes: Our custom is to recite the Malchiyus verses of the Torah in the order they appear in the Torah; and although the sequence quoted here does not follow that order, we must say that the Gemara was not so particular here in following that order, for it was understood that we are to follow the sequence of the verses as they appear in the Torah."

Yet the (במדבר כג:כא ד"ה ותרועת מלך בו) "משך חכמה" is of the opinion that the Gemara in Rosh Hashanah did not mention these pasukim at random, not paying attention to their sequence, but rather, on the contrary, we must follow their sequence here as cited in Rosh Hashanah 32b:

"ותרועת מלך בו"

"ויהי בישורון מלך"

"ה' ימלוך לעולם ועד"

And here we need not pay attention to the chronological order of the Torah. The rationale for this, according to Rav Meir Simcha, is that we follow the sequence of the pasuk of:

"ה' מלך, ה' מלך, ה' ימלוך לעולם ועד."

Thus, we begin with the present: "ה' מלך". And we follow that with the past: "ה' מלך". And finally, we indicate the future: "ה' ימלוך לעולם ועד".

The reason we follow this particular order is because man always first focuses his attention on the present moment, for it is here that he finds himself in his life. Next he turns his attention to the past and only later to the future. Thus, "תרועת מלך בו", which represents the present, precedes the pasuk of "ויהי בישורון מלך" — the past, and this pasuk precedes the pasuk of "ה' ימלוך לעולם ועד" which, although mentioned first in the Torah, is placed last here, since it speaks of the future:

"והטעם, שהוא מושג במצב הנוכח המבט המוחשי [תפיסת הקב"ה על ידי בשר ודם היא בהירה וטובה ביותר בהוה, כלומר כאשר האדם עוסק בדברים המוחשים, והבנתו אינה בנויה על הזכרונות מן העבר או מדמיונות

לקראת העתיד]. ומזה יש לו דין קדימה על העבר, שאינו רק בכוח הזוכר המציין במוח מה שכבר היה. והעבר שקודם להעתיד אשר אינו מוגדר בהשכל בציור מדוקדק ואמיתי כהעבר רק משוער, ועיקרו בכוח המדמה - וזה ברור מצד השגתינו..."

[However, Hashem's perception is different and therefore in the pasukim of the Prophets we say:

אני ראשון — זה העבר

ואני אחרון — זה העתיד.

And we conclude with the present, הוה, of which the pasuk reads: "ומבלעדי אין אלקים".]

II

The order of our prayers

The order of our prayers in the Machzor is based on the opinion of Rav Hai Gaon, and consequently we follow the sequence of the pasukim from the Torah rather than the sequence of present, past and future. And we can defend this sequence of Rav Hai Gaon by pointing out that, as we previously explained, we begin by quoting the verses of the מלכיות זכרונות ושופרות, first those from the Torah, next, those from the Writings, and only then from the Prophets. The question here is obvious. Why quote the verses from the Writings before those of the Prophets, for isn't the sanctity of the Books of the Prophets greater than that of the verses from the Writings?

A possible answer is suggested by קרבן נתנאל , cited in "והמה [כתובים] פרק ב' דר"ה עמ' לח מדפי הרא"ש. There we read: מוקדמין בזמן שהוה ויהי', מה שאין כן פסוקי דנביאים שעדיין לא נתקיימו עד אחרית הימים..."

We here follow the sequence of the name of Hashem of "היה, הוה, ויהי'", past, present and future. And so, Torah is first, for it speaks of the past; the Writings follow, for they deal with the present, and finally come the Prophets, which deal with the future.

We might say that the past, present and future sequence affects only the order of the Torah, Writings and Prophets; yet in relation to the order within the Torah itself we might say that the decisive factor is indeed the chronological order. For we first recite, "ה' ימלוך וגו'", a quotation from Shemos, and then we say the subsequent verses found later in the Torah.

And yet, we might ask why indeed the Gemara did not follow the sequence of the parshios of the Torah. Why did it not place "ה' ימלוך וגו'", which is the pasuk we begin with, at the end? We might suggest an answer based on the following. The Shulchan Aruch, Orach Chaim (סימן תקצא) and the Mishnah Berurah (loc. cit. ס"ק ד') cite the law that if one did not follow the sequence of מלכיות זכרונות ושופרות and, for example, recited the verses of זכרונות before those of מלכיות, one did not succeed in fulfilling his obligation to mention these themes, and he is required to repeat them. Consequently, one might think that within the pasukim of מלכיות זכרונות ושופרות if one were to mix up the order of the pasukim, one would not have fulfilled the Mitzva of mentioning them, but this is not the case. In fact, the Gemara quotes these pasukim out of order to show that the pasukim themselves do not require a fixed order, and one has fulfilled his obligation even if he does not follow the correct sequence.

III

Why we follow the order of the Torah

We might then ask, if this is what we are being taught here, that order is not crucial, why then do we follow the order of the Torah here in the מלכיות? To answer this we might point out the following:

1) We are being taught that we *may* change the order, but this does not mean that we *must* change the order.

2) In order to accommodate the chronological order, we do follow the order of the Torah, and as far as the

The Commentators' Machzor Companion

חידוש, היתר, the permission granted to change the order, we applied it to the pasukim of the Writings throughout the מלכיות זכרונות ושופרות.

The verses from the Writings of the מלכיות are:

1) Psalm 22 — "כי לה׳ המלוכה ומושל בגוים"

2) Psalm 93 — "ה׳ מלך גאות לבש"

3) Psalm 24 — "שאו שערים ראשיכם"

Thus we see that we do not follow the normal order of Psalms here.

And similarly, in the זכרונות, we find this order:

1) Psalm 111:14 — "זכר עשה לנפלאותיו"

2) Psalm 111:5 — "יזכור לעולם בריתו"

3) Psalm 106:45 — "ויזכור להם בריתו"

Again, we see that we do not follow the normal order of the chapters of Psalms.

Finally, in the שופרות, the order is:

1) Psalm 47 — "ה׳ בקול שופר"

2) Psalm 98 — "בחצוצרות וקול שופר"

3) Psalm 81 — "תקעו בחדש שופר"

Here, too, the order is not followed.

The reason the order of Psalms was not followed was due to these considerations. See "מלכיות זכרונות ושופרות", (שמעתין 114, תשנ"ז ובספר הזכרון להרב משה ליפשיץ, עמ' 69)

The pasuk cited first in the verses from the Torah for the מלכיות reads: "ה' ימלוך לעולם". This verse combines the two key words that allude to מלכיות, the concept of kingship, ימלוך and ה'. This pattern and word-combination are followed in the pasukim from the Writings:

1) Psalm 22 — "כי לה' המלוכה"

2) Psalm 93 — "ה' מלך גאות לבש"

The third pasuk here, "שאו שערים", is from Psalm 24 and does not contain this sequence of ה' and מלך. Therefore, even though this Psalm (24) should precede Psalm 93, we do not follow the chronological order.

In the זכרונות, the pasukim from the Torah contain two key words: ויזכור and בריתו These are from Kesuvim:

1) Psalm 111:5 — "יזכור לעולם בריתו"

2) Psalm 106:45 — "ויזכר להם בריתו"

The verses from the Writings contain both key words and therefore they are placed next to each other; for had we followed the chronological order here, we could not have accomplished this combination. For then the order would have been:

1) Psalm 106 — "ויזכר להם בריתו"

2) Psalm 111:4 — "זכר עשה לנפלאותיו"

This does not contain the word "בריתו", and then:

3) "טרף נתן ליראיו, יזכור לעולם בריתו"

In the שופרות: The pasukim from the Torah contain the key words קול and שופר. Thus the pasukim from the Writings are:

1) Psalm 47:6 — "עלה אלקים בתרועה, ה' בקול שופר"

2) Psalm 98:6 — "בחצוצרות וקול שופר"

3) Psalm 81:4 — "תקעו בחדש שופר"

Thus only the first two pasukim contain the combination of קול and שופר, and thus they are placed next to each other, even though the order is not followed.

How, then, can we change the order of the Psalms to accommodate this pattern? The answer is that we have a היתר, permission, not to follow the sequence, and if there is a good reason to change the order, we *may* do so. Therefore, in the pasukim from the Torah there is no reason to change the order, and so we do not. However, in the pasukim from the Writings there is a valid reason, and therefore we are allowed to change the order.

"ויהי בישורון מלך"

I

Who was King: Hashem or Moshe?

As we have previously mentioned, one of the verses of מלכיות reads: "ויהי בישורון מלך בהתאסף ראשי עם יחד שבטי ישראל" (דברים לג,ה).

In this pasuk, the word "מלך" alludes to Hashem, as Rashi tells us: "ויהי: הקב"ה. בישורון מלך: תמיד עול מלכותו עליהם".

Yet we know from various sources that Moshe Rabbenu was a king, and the source of this information is this very pasuk: "ויהי בישורון מלך", and "מלך" here refers to Moshe Rabbenu. This is mentioned several times in the following Midrash:

"ויאמר הנני, הנני לכהונה ולמלכות. א"ל הקב"ה אל תקרב הלום, כלומר לא יהיו בניך מקריבין שכבר מתוקנת הכהונה לאהרן אחיך. "הלום" זו מלכות, כמה דתימא (שמואל-ב, ז, יח) כי הביאותני עד הלום כו'. א"ל הקב"ה כבר מתוקן המלכות לדוד, אעפ"כ זכה משה לשתיהן...מלכות דכתיב (דברים לג,ה) "ויהי בישורון מלך..." (מדרש שמות רבה סוף פרשה ב')

"And he said: Here I am, here I am for the priesthood and royalty. Hashem said to him: 'Draw not nigh thither, that is, your sons will not offer up sacrifices, for priesthood has already been allotted to your brother Aaron. "Halom" refers to kingship, for it says: That thou hast brought me thus far — halom (II Samuel, VII, 8)... Thus Hashem said to him: Kingship is already assigned to David. Yet even so, Moshe obtained both — priesthood, which he administered during the seven days of concentration; and kingship, as it says: 'And he [Moshe] was a king in Yeshurun."

"ויעש להם בתים" ומה היו הבתים — בית הכהונה ובית המלכות. יוכבד נטלה כהונה ומלכות, אהרן — כהן גדול, משה — מלך: ויהי בישורון מלך [מלך זו משה]. (שמות רבה מח,ד.)

"That He built them houses. This means that they established priestly and royal families. Yocheved took both priesthood and royalty. Priesthood — Aaron, her son, served as High Priest; and royalty, that Moshe, her other son, served as king, as it says: 'and there was in Yeshurun a king'."

"מהי ,תובל למלך' (תהילים מה,טו) זה משה שנקרא מלך, שנ' 'ויהי בישורון מלך'. (שם פרשה נב, א.)

"And what is the meaning of 'she shall be led unto the king'? This refers to Moshe who was called a king, as it is written, 'and he was a king in Yeshurun'."

"רב נחמן אמר מלך זה משה דכתיב, ויהי בישורון מלך' (— מדרש ויקרא רבה לא, ד.)"

"Rav Nachman said: 'the king' applies to Moshe, of whom it is written, 'and there was a king in Yeshurun'."

The Commentators' Machzor Companion

And so writes the אבן עזרא in his commentary to Bereishis 36:31.

"ואלה המלכים אשר מלכו בארץ אדום לפני מלך מלך לבני ישראל... והאמת שפי' לפני מלך מלך, על משה מלך ישראל וכן כתיב ויהי בישורון מלך."

And so writes the Ramban in his commentary to Devarim, 33:5. And the Rambam in Hilchos Bais Habechira 6:11 writes:

"אין מוסיפין על העיר...אלא על פי מלך...ומשה רבינו מלך היה."

Thus the following questions arise:

1) We have an apparent contradiction here in regard to the pasuk of "ויהי בישורון מלך". According to some sources we find that "מלך" refers to Hashem and yet in other sources it refers to Moshe Rabbenu.

2) The Rambam himself cites the verse of "ויהי בישורון מלך" as being one of the pasukim of the מלכיות (see רמב"ם הלכות בית הבחירה פ"ו) and yet he writes in (פ"ג מהל' שופר, ה"ט הל' ו) that Moshe Rabbenu was a king and cites the source for this as being this pasuk of "ויהי בישורון מלך".

II

Was Moshe king?

Before attempting to resolve these difficulties, we might ask if indeed we view Moshe Rabbenu as a king in Israel.

1) The Torah tells us that by virtue of the blessing given by Yaakov Aveinu, מלכות, kingship, belongs exclusively to the tribe of Yehudah, as the pasuk says: "לא יסור שבט מיהודה", "The scepter of kingship shall never be removed from Judah." How, then could Moshe Rabbenu accept upon himself the role of kingship when this would be an infraction of the above law?

2) The Midrash (מדרש רבה אמור פ' כו) bemoans the fact that "מלך ראשון שיעמוד על בניך ידקר בחרב", the very first king appointed for Bnai Yisrael was destined to be killed by the sword. This incident alludes to King Saul, שאול המלך, who died by the sword. We see clearly from this source that he was referred to as the *first* king of Yisrael. But how is this possible if Moshe Rabbenu was also considered to be a king of Yisrael?

3) We are told in Mesechtas Sanhedrin 20b: "שלש מצוות נצטוו ישראל בכניסתן לארץ להעמיד להם מלך...", that Bnai Yisrael were commanded when they first entered Eretz

Yisrael to appoint a king. Thus we see that the concept of מלכות, kingship, was initiated only after Bnai Yisrael entered Eretz Yisrael, and so, since Moshe Rabbenu never entered Eretz Yisrael, how could he be recognized as a king?

4) There is a halacha which states that a king is not allowed to relinquish the honor due him: "מלך שמחל כבודו אין כבודו מחול". How, then, ask the commentators, did Moshe Rabbenu serve as an attendant to Yisro and the other guests at the meal he offered them when they arrived in the camp of Yisrael, as described in Sefer Shemos? For it would certainly seem unfitting for a king to serve as a waiter, and such a demeaning action would not be allowed.

III
Moshe was appointed king by Hashem

To answer all the above questions as well as the previous questions raised regarding the pasuk of "ויהי בישורון מלך" we might suggest the following solution.

The Mitzva of appointing a king is based on the pasuk of "שום תשים עליך מלך". The appointment of a king in Yisrael, as we are taught by our Chazal, lies in the hands of the people. The people must request or demand the appointment of a king. This, as the Ramban points out in his commentary on this pasuk, is based on the key word "ואמרת", and *"you* shall say".

In light of this, we can now understand that Saul was indeed viewed as "the first king of Yisrael". For it was in his days that Bnai Yisrael requested that a king be appointed over them. They asked the Prophet Samuel, שמואל הנביא, to appoint a king for them. Thus Saul was the first king appointed according to the dictates of the Torah. However, the appointment of Moshe Rabbenu was not by virtue of a request by the people. It was rather Hashem Himself Who "appointed" Moshe Rabbenu as king over Yisrael. With this in mind, we can resolve all our apparent difficulties.

1) One is not to usurp or assume the role of king in Yisrael, since kingship belongs to שבט יהודה, the tribe of Yehudah. But this applies only to a king who was appointed by the people. Moshe Rabbenu, however, as well as Yehoshua, were appointed by Hashem Himself, and therefore they committed no infraction related to the Mitzva of kingship which belongs to the descendants of Yehudah.

2) Moshe Rabbenu is not considered to be the first king of Yisrael, whereas Saul indeed was, by virtue of the Mitzva of "שום תשים עליך מלך".

3) The very first Mitzva upon entering Eretz Yisrael was to appoint a king, based on the dictate of "שום תשים

עליך מלך". Moshe Rabbenu, however, was king as a temporary measure, "הוראת שעה". This was dictated by Hashem Himself.

4) The law forbidding a king to be forgiving is intended to preserve his dignity as a royal personage and to maintain the awe he must evoke in the eyes of the people. This is the intention behind the double expression, "שום תשים", to make sure that the respect and fear one must have for the king remains always intact. A king who had been appointed by the will of the people cannot allow anyone to show even the slightest disrespect for him, for this would jeopardize his authority, which was vested in him by the people. Moshe Rabbenu, on the other hand, who was appointed king by Hashem and not by the people, did not need to be fearful that his authority would be challenged, and therefore he could afford to overlook disrespect and to show mercy to one who did not display the proper respect for him. This explains how he was able to wait on Yisro on the occasion described in Sefer Shemos.

With this explanation, we can now understand how there is no contradiction concerning the pasuk of "ויהי בישורון מלך". Although this pasuk certainly alludes to Moshe Rabbenu as king of Yisrael, yet at the same time it refers to Hashem. For, as explained above, Moshe Rabbenu's appointment as king of Yisrael was not by the request of the people, but rather by the command of Hashem. Consequently, the very fact that Hashem has the authority and His appointment was recognized by all demonstrates that Hashem Himself is the King of all kings. Thus we can justifiably recite the pasuk of "ויהי בישורון מלך" in the מלכיות, which proclaims that Hashem is מלך and that מלכיות, all sovereignty, belongs to Him.

"ותרועת מלך בו"

I
The Mitzva of shofar

One of the verses of the מלכיות reads as follows:
"לא הביט און ביעקב, ולא ראה עמל בישראל, ה' אלוקיו עמו, ותרועת מלך בו" במדבר כג:כא

"He gazes at no iniquity in Yaakov and sees no evil schemes in Yisrael; Hashem, his God, is with him and homage to the king is within him."

This pasuk contains one of the berachos with which the wicked Bilaam blessed Bnai Yisrael. Therefore the sefer "ברוך שאמר" asks here why do we include among our verses of מלכיות one of the sayings of a person as wicked as Bilaam, who was not even a Jew?

The גרי"ז הלוי asks here what did the wicked Bilaam see that was unique about the nation of Yisrael? The pasuk here articulates the uniqueness of the Jewish people, when it says: "תרועת מלך בו". The Ramban in his commentary to this verse explains this to allude to the sounding of the shofar. In other words, Bilaam praised the Mitzva of shofar. But we might ask, what did he see here in the Mitzva of shofar that was so unique; and greater than any other? The גרי"ז הלוי answers: above and beyond the Mitzva of shofar, contained within it is the concept of prayer, "תפלה וזעקה". This is based on what is written in the Torah:

"על הצר הצורר אתכם והרעתם בחצצרת ונזכרתם לפני ה' אלוקיכם ונושעתם מאויביכם." בהעלותך י', ט.

"...against the oppressor that oppresses you, then you shall blow the trumpets and you will be remembered before Hashem, and you will be delivered from your enemies." And so the Rambam writes at the beginning of Hilchos Ta'anis: "מצות עשה מן התורה לצעוק ולהריע".

"It is a positive Mitzva to cry out and to sound trumpets in the event of any difficulty that arises which affects the community."

Here we are told that we are to "לצעוק", cry out, which denotes prayer; yet the pasuk previously cited only speaks of "להריע", to sound the shofar, or trumpets. Thus we see that the essence of shofar is a *cry of prayer*. This is also indicated in the makeup of the beracha with which we conclude the order of the שופרות.

"כי אתה שומע קול שופר ומאזין תרועת עמו ישראל ברחמים."

"For you *hear* the sound of the shofar and you *hearken* to the teruah (shofar sound) of His people Yisrael with mercy."

Thus we see that sounding the shofar is not just the fulfillment of the Mitzva of sounding the shofar; but also that Hashem *hear* and *give ear* in His *mercy,* all of which alludes to the concept of prayer.

Prayer belongs to all nations, as indicated in the prayer of King Solomon when he dedicated the Bais HaMikdash: "וגם אל הנכרי אשר לא מעמך ישראל הוא...ובא והתפלל" מלכים א, ח, מא-מב.

"And also to the stranger who is not of Your people Yisrael...and he will come and pray towards this house." And yet we see from here that prayer by means of sounding the shofar is not related to any nation other than Yisrael.

This then is what the pasuk alludes to — Bilaam praised the Jewish people, for they alone possess the ability to pray with the sound of the shofar.

This approach seems to raise the following questions:

1) Why point out the Mitzva of shofar when there are many other Mitzvos which are unique to Bnai Yisrael as well, such as the Mitzvos of succah, lulav, etc.? Why focus exclusively on that of shofar?

2) If indeed prayer is the lot of all nations and the shofar is an integral part of prayer, why do they also not possess this gift of the sounding of the shofar?

Related to this Mitzva of sounding the shofar we might ask why when we sound the shofar on Rosh Hashanah we are so full of awe and inspiration? After all, the Mitzva of sounding the shofar is a Mitzva like any other, and we do not find that when we fulfill any other Mitzva, such as that of succah or lulav, we experience this type of intense emotion. What is it about the shofar that calls for such a profound response?

II

The Mitzva of prayer

To answer these questions we might suggest the following.

There is a basic difference between the Rambam and the Ramban regarding the Mitzva of Prayer. The Rambam regarded tefillah as a חיוב מן התורה, a Divine command dictated by the Torah. He derived this view from the verse in Devarim (11:13) which says: "ולעבדו בכל לבבכם", "And serve Him with all your hearts." The words "serve Him" imply worship through prayer. The Ramban, however, did not acknowledge that Tefillah was a biblically ordained commandment. Rather, he writes in השגת הרמב״ן to the Sefer HaMitzvos, מצוה ה, where the Rambam writes:

"It is a Mitzva to pray and it is one of the Merciful Attributes of the Creator that He hears and responds when we call unto Him."

The Ramban, however, insisted that prayer is rabbinically ordained and he cited many Talmudic sources to support this view. However, even the Ramban conceded that in a moment of great distress, בעת צרה, the Mitzva of prayer is biblically required, מן התורה. He writes as follows:

"ואכן אולי יהי' מדרשם בתפלה עיקר מן התורה נמנה אותו במנינו של הרב ונאמר שהיא מצוה לעת הצרות שנאמין שהוא יתברך ויתעלה שומע תפלה והוא המציל מן הצרות בתפלה וזעקה."

"It is a Mitzva to plead fervently with Hashem through prayer and shofar blasts whenever the community is faced with great distress...for it is a Mitzva to affirm in moments of distress our belief that the Holy One listens to prayers and intervenes to grant aid."

On the surface, we could say that according to the Ramban prayer at a moment of distress requires two elements: 1) supplication, and 2) calling out, "זעקה", with the sounding of the shofar. And although we normally view the sounding of the shofar as a separate entity, apart from tefillah, yet we can see how shofar is here considered to be an integral part of prayer. It is a silent prayer without words, as previously pointed out by the גרי"ז הלוי. This, however, raises several questions.

1) Why, at a time of distress does the Ramban require the sounding of the shofar, silent prayer, as an accompaniment to regular supplication in words?

2) The Rambam also agrees with the need to sound the shofar at a time of distress, as he confirms at the beginning of Hilchos Taanis, where he writes, "It is a positive commandment to cry out and to sound trumpets in the event of any difficulty that arises which affects the community."

Why, then, if the shofar alludes to silent prayer, does he not require the sounding of the shofar in our daily prayers?

As we have mentioned, according to the Rambam there are two distinct kinds of prayer.

1) תפלה מן התורה, prayer as a means of serving Hashem, and not to ask anything from Him. Although we hope that our petition will be answered, that is not our

prime concern; rather our motive here is to subjugate ourselves to His Will.

2) תפלה מדרבנן, This type of prayer was instituted by our Sages as a means of petitioning Hashem for Mercy in fulfilling our needs.

The Ramban also agrees that the purpose of prayer from the Torah is "to affirm in moments of distress our belief that the Holy One listens to prayer and intervenes to grant aid."

Thus we could say that the call for silent prayer by the sounding of the shofar, which, as we have discussed, is to be viewed as an integral part of prayer, indicates that *even though we are speechless* due to our great distress, yet we still believe in the power of prayer and wish to serve our Creator wholeheartedly. Thus by sounding the shofar we affirm our commitment to and belief in Hashem.

And so we could say that the Ramban believes that we pray only מן התורה, at moments of distress, when we are speechless and unable to verbalize our emotions. Thus, we use the shofar to cry out for us. The Rambam also agrees that when we are in distress and unable to speak we sound the shofar to articulate our emotions. However, in normal daily situations, there is no need for the silent prayer of the shofar, and we pray in our own words to verbalize our requests and our commitment to Hashem.

With this in mind, we can perhaps now understand why Bilaam praised Klal Yisrael for their use of the shofar. For it meant that the Jew commits himself to the Almighty and affirms his deep faith in his most troubled moments. They pray both with words and in silence and are steadfast in their faith. This type of prayer is unique to the Jewish people. For even though the other nations of the world were also given the gift of prayer, yet their prayer is primarily to petition for their needs, תפלה משום רחמים. Only Bnai Yisrael pray primarily to affirm their faith.

This also explains why we use a pasuk uttered by an enemy of Yisrael — for who but our enemies know the distress and suffering of the Jewish people, for they are often responsible for it. They have brought us to our knees and made us speechless; yet not even their evil designs can deter us from our belief and determination to serve Hashem and affirm our belief in Him that he will eventually bring us salvation. This is the secret of the shofar — that even though we are speechless with suffering, we still offer the silent prayer of the shofar.

This, then, is the message of the shofar, and it explains why when we sound the shofar on Rosh Hashanah we are so emotionally moved. For we are now saying that although today is the Day of Judgement and our very lives hang in the balance, yet even though we are speechless, we are able to cry out with the sound of the shofar and reaffirm our commitment to the Holy One, Blessed be He.

III
Shofar: symbol of commitment to Hashem

This explanation can help us understand the words of Chazal, who tell us that when we recite the verses of the מלכיות, we are to accompany them with the sounding of the shofar. "אמרו לפני מלכיות — ובמה, בשופר".

This suggests that even when we find ourselves speechless because of our precarious situation in the world, yet we do not hesitate to declare that Hashem is our King, and the Master of the world.

This also could suggest a possible answer to the question posed by the פרי צדיק as to why, when Rosh Hashanah occurs on a Shabbos, we still recite the blessings of the shofar: "כי אתה שומע קול שופר", "You hear the sound of the shofar", even though we do not actually blow the shofar if Rosh Hashanah falls on a Shabbos day. The answer would be that the concept of shofar alludes to our commitment to Hashem under all circumstances. Thus by honoring the sanctity of Shabbos by not blowing the shofar we demonstrate our obedience to Hashem's Will, for He has prohibited us from blowing the shofar on this day. This absolute commitment to Hashem is the essence of what shofar represents. And so when we say, in our blessing of the shofar, that Hashem hears the sound of the shofar, "כי אתה שומע קול שופר", we allude to our total commitment to Him and His to us.

The Unusual Place of "Shema Yisrael" in Malchiyus

I
The tenth pasuk

As we have mentioned, according to the Midrash in Rosh Hashanah 4/6 there are no fewer than ten pasukim from Tanach, Torah, Prophets and Writings in the מלכיות זכרונות ושופרות. Three each are from Tanach, and the tenth pasuk is from another verse in the Torah itself, and according to our custom it is said "סמוך לחתימתן", just prior to the ending beracha. For example, in the זכרונות we conclude as follows:

"וקים לנו ה' אלוקינו את הדבר שהבטחתנו בתורתך...כאמור, וזכרתי להם ברית ראשונים אשר הוצאתי אותם מארץ מצרים...כי זוכר כל הנשכחות אתה הוא מעולם...ועקידת יצחק וזרעו היום ברחמים תזכור ברוך אתה ה' זוכר הברית."

Thus the tenth pasuk (ויקרא כו, מה): "וזכרתי להם וכו'" comes just before the concluding beracha of "סמוך לחתימתן". And so we find in the שופרות:

"כאמור וביום שמחתכם, ובמועדיכם ובראשי חדשיכם ותקעתם בחצצרות...."

כי אתה שומע קול שופר, ומאזין תרועה, ואין דומה לך. ברוך אתה ה' שומע קול תרועת עמו ישראל ברחמים."

Here, too, the tenth concluding pasuk (במדבר י') "וביום שמחתכם" is placed סמוך לחתימתן.

Yet in the מלכיות we find an unusual situation. The tenth pasuk from the Torah here in the מלכיות is "שמע ישראל וגו'"; and then we begin a completely new paragraph directed exclusively to the theme of the holiness of the day, קדושת היום:

"ובתורתך כתוב לאמר: שמע ישראל ה' אלוקינו ה' אחד. אלקינו ואלוקי אבותינו, מלוך על כל העולם כלו בכבודך...קדשנו במצותיך...כי אתה אלקים אמת ודברך אמת וקים לעד. ברוך אתה ה' מלך על כל הארץ, מקדש ישראל ויום הזכרון."

Therefore we must ask, why is there a difference here, and why is the "שמע ישראל" also not placed סמוך לחתימתן in the מלכיות?

The Avudraham, who touches upon this question, answers in the following way. Since the ending beracha of "מלך על כל הארץ, מקדש ישראל ויום הזכרון", which is קדושת היום, alludes only to the קדושת היום and not to the theme of מלכיות, therefore we conclude the tenth pasuk of malchiyus prior to beginning the section of the קדושת היום, for there is no possible justification for placing the שמע ישראל in an adjacent position, סמוך לחתימתן.

"והטעם שאין עושין כן במלכיות מפני שברכה של מלכיות [מלך ישראל] אינו חותם בענין מלכיות אלא בקדושת היום. ולפיכך אומר בפסוק אחרון של תורה בסוף המלכיות מיד, לא להניחו עד סמוך לחתימתן שאינו מענין המלכיות. אבל בזכרונות ושופרות מניחו עד סמוך לחתימה..."

Thus, according to the Avudraham, we see that the שמע ישראל is recited immediately after the completion of the pasukim, and before the recitation of the beracha for the קדושת היום, for the beracha of "מלך ישראל" is exclusively the ending beracha of the קדושת היום and not that of the מלכיות.

And so it appears that this is also the approach of the שבלי הלקט, who writes in סימן רצ:

"ואחר סדר מלכיות חוזרים לסדר קדושת היום, מלוך על כל העולם וכו' והשאינו וכו' וחותמין כסדר שחרית מלך על כל הארץ מקדש ישראל ויום הזכרון..."

According to the שבלי הלקט the ending beracha in the מלכיות of "מלך על כל הארץ" is a result of the fact that it refers to the קדושת היום. And so we see that this ending beracha is recited because of its relation to the קדושת היום rather than its relation to מלכיות.

However, HaRav Yosef Dov Soloveitchik, in addressing the question touched upon here by the

Avudraham, offers a similar answer and adds a new insight. Since the paragraph concerning the קדושת היום, which is: "אר"א מלוך על כל העולם כלו בכבודך" is recited in all the Rosh Hashanah prayers, Minchah, Ma'ariv and Shacharis, and there we do not include the pasukim of the מלכיות; therefore, in order to keep the Mussaf prayers of the קדושת היום similar to the others, we do not insert the שמע ישראל here, but rather add it before the section which speaks of the קדושת היום.

"אמנם במלכיות הפסוק העשירי נזכר תיכף ומיד אחר תשעת הפסוקים האחרים ולא באמצע הבקשה. והטעם לזה, דחתימה זו נאמרת גם בשאר התפלות [ובתוך חתימת ברכת קדושת היום] שאין בהן הזכרת בפסוקים כלל, ומכיון שלא רצו לשנות בנוסח החתימה במוסף, ע"כ הקדימו את הפסוק העשירי דמלכיות להאמר קודם התחלת החתימה, אבל באמת פסוק זה שייך הוא לחתימה..."

Thus, according to HaRav Soloveitchik, the beracha of "מלך על כל הארץ" is indeed the concluding beracha of the מלכיות as well as of the קדושת היום.

II
Kingship: the essence of the day

A practical difference then emerges between these two approaches. The שערי תשובה, סימן תקפה, סעיף קטן,ד raises the following question. If one omitted the beracha of "מלך על כל הארץ" from the Shacharis prayer in the קדושת היום, he nevertheless managed to fulfill his obligation of mentioning the theme of קדושת היום, since he did conclude his previous beracha with the words "מקדש ישראל ויום הזכרון". However, if he omitted the "מלך על כל הארץ" in the Mussaf prayer, he would have to repeat his Amidah there. Even though this should be a logical conclusion, the שערי תשובה wonders why the Mussaf prayer does not follow the same law as that of Shacharis. Since the Avudraham maintains that the beracha of "מלך על כל הארץ" is recited only because of its connection to the קדושת היום and to the theme of מלכיות; therefore it should follow that the Mussaf prayer should follow the same law as Shacharis; insofar as the prayer need not be repeated, since the קדושת היום was alluded to in the beracha of "מקדש ישראל ויום הזכרון". However, according to Rav Soloveitchik's approach, the beracha of "מלך על כל הארץ" also serves as a valid concluding beracha of the מלכיות. And so, if one omitted the key words of "מלך על כל הארץ" then there would be an obligation to repeat the entire Amidah here in the Mussaf.

Rav Chaim Brisker argues here with the decision of the שערי תשובה and maintains that one would have to repeat the Amidah even in Shacharis if one omitted to say "מלך על כל הארץ".

Rav Chaim's rationale here is that the essence of the קדושת היום is מלכיות, "כי זהו עצם תיאור קדושת היום גופא". And so, when one mentions the word "מלך" in the concluding beracha, he is actually describing the essence of the day's holiness, which is מלכיות. This means that if one fails to mention in the beracha "מלך על כל הארץ", one has also failed to mention the קדושת היום, and he must therefore repeat his Amidah. This view regards "מלך על כל הארץ", in both Shacharis and Mussaf, as an integral part of the קדושת היום and failure to mention it calls for repetition.

This way of thinking of Rav Chaim's seems to coincide with the opinion of the מאירי (בחיבור התשובה שער ב,פ"ב):

"ואע"פ שמעיקר ההלכה לא נאמרה חתימה זו [מלך על כל הארץ] אלא במוסף בברכת מלכיות הנכללת עם קדושת היום שצריך לחתום בה בברכת מלכיות וראוי לחתום בה מלך כל הארץ כענין מלכיות וכו', ונמצא אם כן שבשאר החתימות שבתפילת ערבית שחרית ומנחה וקידוש היום לא היה צריך לחתום אלא מקדש ישראל ויום הזכרון, אעפ"כ פשט המנהג לחתום בכל החתימות, מלך על כל הארץ מקדש ישראל ויום הזכרון', מצד אמרם תמיד תמליכוני עליכם בראש השנה, אמרו לפני מלכיות כדי שתמליכוני עליכם. כי הראות המלוכה הוא כשבת המלך על כסא המשפט, ביום זה וכל תפלות ביום על דרך זה..."

The Meiri addresses the question why in all the prayers of the day, including Kiddush, the ending beracha includes the phrase "מלך על כל הארץ", for only in the Mussaf prayer does it seem logical to include the theme of kingship; for there we join the theme of kingship with that of the holiness of the day, קדושת היום. In the other prayers of the day, however, the theme of kingship is not explicitly mentioned, and therefore why not simply conclude the berachos of the קדושת היום by saying "מקדש ישראל ויום הזכרון"? He answers that even though the theme of kingship is not explicitly stated, and the verses of kingship are not repeated, yet the idea of kingship is still the essential element of this day and an integral idea behind all the prayers of this day on which we coronate Hashem and accept Him as our King. This seems to verify Rav Chaim's approach.

However, the sefer שלמי חגיגה has a different view of the meaning here of "מלך על כל הארץ", in the beracha of קדושת היום:

"ונראה לעניות דעתי דמי שטעה ולא חתם אלא, מקדש ישראל ויום הזכרון' לבד, ולא אמר מלך על כל הארץ, דיצא ואין צריך לחזור, דלא מצינו לרז"ל שהקפידו להזכיר מלכות אלא דוקא בהמלך הקדוש, והמלך המשפט. שם בא הרמז וההורות נתן שמראה מלכותו להיום הזה על בני העולם ששופט אותם בימים אלו. אבל בברכה זו נראה שאין להקפיד כלל, שהרי הזכרת מלכות בברכה זו אינה באה על הכוונה הנזכרת לומר כי הימים האלה נזכרים כל באי עולם לבוא אל המלך אל כסא מלכותו ליתן דין וחשבון. אלא

מלכות שבברכה זו אינו אלא שבח בעלמא בכל מקום שאנו אומרים שבחיו יתברך, ובכלל מזכירין אותו בשם מלך.

וכך דייק קצת עיניך תראנה כי שם מלך בכאן אינו על הוראת פרטות הימים האלה, כי אם אדרבא הוא על שם העתיד בביאת המשיח, וכמו שכתב הרד"א ז"ל [האבודרהם] מפני שאנו אומרים, מלוך על כל העולם כולו, על זה אמר, ודברך אמת וקיים לעד ושהבטחתנו בעתידת הגאולה כמו שכתוב, והיתה לה' המלוכה...

וזהו שחותמין אחר כך, מלך על כל הארץ וכו' עכ"ל וכיון שכן נראה לי דליכא קפידא בכאן אם בדיעבד לא אמר, מלך על כל הארץ, כיון שהזכיר וחתם בקדושת היום דהיינו מקדש ישראל ויום הזכרון...״

The word "מלך" here, contends the שלמי חגיגה, does not allude to the theme of מלכיות, but rather denotes praise, as in other instances when we wish to praise the Almighty, we use the term "מלך". Therefore "מלך" is not an integral part of the קדושת היום, but rather an additional praise added here, and therefore, if one failed to mention this concept of "מלך" here in the קדושת היום but did mention it in the phrase "מקדש ישראל ויום הזכרון", one has nevertheless managed to fulfill his obligation in regard to the קדושת היום, and thus he need not repeat the prayer.

To conclude:

1) According to the Avudraham (as interpreted by the שערי תשובה), "מלך על כל הארץ" is a beracha that is related only

to the concept of קדושת היום, and therefore both Shacharis and Mussaf have the same law regarding one who fails to mention "מלך על כל הארץ"; which is that the prayer does not have to be repeated.

2) According to Rav Yosef Dov Soloveitchik, in the Mussaf prayer, "מלך על כל הארץ" is indeed an integral part of the ברכת מלכיות, and failure to mention it calls for a repetition of the prayer.

3) According to Rav Chaim Brisker, even in Shacharis, failure to mention "מלך על כל הארץ" requires that the prayer be repeated.

4) According to the שלמי חגיגה, if one failed to say "מלך על כל הארץ" in the קדושת היום one need not repeat the prayer either at Shacharis or at Mussaf.

III
The holiness of the day: the essence of Malchyius

In light of the above, we would venture to explain the following. There is a difference of opinion as to where exactly to place the section of מלכיות in the Mussaf prayers. ר' יוחנן בן נורי maintains it should be joined with קדושת היום. The question could be asked, why the need to couple it at all? Why couldn't the מלכיות call for a separate beracha?

The answer to this question can be readily answered based on what we discussed previously (according to Rav Chaim Brisker) that since the essence of קדושת היום is מלכיות; then it would be more logical to join them together rather than to make two separate berachos, which would be redundant.

However, if this is the rationale for joining מלכיות and קדושת השם, then one can justifiably ask the following. We find in the Gemara of Rosh Hashanah 32a:

"והיכן אומרת לקדושת היום?

תניא רבי אומר [קדושת היום] עם המלכות אומרת. מה מצינו בכל מקום ברביעית אף כאן ברביעית. רבן שמעון בן גמליאל אומר עם הזכרונות אומרת מה מצינו בכל מקום באמצע אף כאן באמצע."

"Where is the blessing of the sanctification of the day to be said?

It has been taught: Rebbe says, it should be said with the Malchiyus verses. For just as on all the festivals we find that it becomes fourth in the order of the blessings, so here too it should come fourth. Rabban Shimon ben Gamliel says, it should be said with the Zichronos verses. Just as we find on all other occasions it is said in the middle [it is the fourth of the seven blessings], so here too it should be in the middle [fifth out of the nine blessings of the Rosh Hashanah Amidah prayers]."

But if we say that the essence of קדושת היום is מלכיות then why did רבי give the reason that the קדושת היום should be placed with the מלכיות because מלכיות is the fourth beracha and קדושת היום is also the fourth beracha (in the Shabbos and Yom Tov prayers)? Why didn't he simply say that since the מלכיות is the essence of קדושת היום it belongs with the מלכיות? The answer would have to be that the קדושת היום is also the essence of the זכרונות, the Remembrances, and therefore he had to find a different rationale for placing the קדושת היום with the מלכיות.

Based on the above, we can now also appreciate and understand the structure of the קדושת היום prayers recited throughout the day.

או"א מלוך על כל העולם בכבודך, והנשא על כל הארץ ביקרך, והופע בהדר גאון עזך על כל יושבי תבל ארצך...ה' אלוקי ישראל, מלך ומלכותו בכל משלה...

Our petition here is that Hashem reign over His world; and one wonders how this petition of מלכיות belongs here in the section of קדושת היום (of Shacharis, etc.) which describes the uniqueness of the day and its sanctity? However, in light of Rav Chaim's explanation that מלכיות is the essence of the קדושת היום we can understand the relevance of "מלוך על כל הארץ" here. For by saying this prayer we are spelling out the essence of the קדושת היום, which is the concept of kingship, מלכיות.

מלך ישראל וגואלו

I

Hashem as King over all nations

One of the pasukim of מלכיות from the Prophets is the following: "כה אמר ה', מלך ישראל וגואלו, ה' צבאות, אני ראשון ואני אחרון ומבלעדי אין אלהים".

"So said Hashem, the King of Yisrael and its Redeemer, the Host of legions: I am the first and I am the last, and besides Me there is no other god."

This prompts the שם משמואל to ask a question. The Gemara in Rosh Hashanah 32b states that, according to Rav Yehudah, the pasuk of "זמרו למלכנו זמרו", "Sing praises unto our King" (from Psalms 47:7) can not be included in the pasukim of מלכיות, for it does not proclaim Hashem *King* over all the world. And only such a declaration is acceptable to warrant inclusion among the verses of מלכיות. For if only one nation is mentioned, it is not enough, but rather He must be seen as Sovereign over *all* nations. Thus here, where we read "זמרו למלכנו", "Sing unto our King", since this alludes only to Klal Yisrael, the pasuk does not qualify for inclusion among the verses of the מלכיות. How then, asks the שם משמואל, can we include the pasuk of "מלך ישראל וגואלו", "the King of Yisrael and his Redeemer", for here Hashem is depicted as only the King of Yisrael, and the other nations of the world are nowhere mentioned?

He also points out the source for this requirement that the verses of מלכיות depend on all the nations of the world being declared under the sovereignty of Hashem. This source is the concept of "כדי שתמליכוני עליכם", that Bnai Yisrael is recognized as being ruled by Hashem. From this we can see that a declaration that proclaims Hashem King over Yisrael suffices for that verse to be included in the מלכיות. Why, then, do we rule out the pasuk of "זמרו למלכנו זמרו", because it only mentions Bnai Yisrael and not the other nations of the world?

The שם משמואל answers this by pointing out that the purpose of requiring the statement that Hashem is "מלך העולם", King over the entire world, is that we want all the nations of the world to acknowledge that Hashem is the God of Yisrael, as we say in our Rosh Hashanah prayers:

"ויאמר כל אשר נשמה באפו ה' אלוקי ישראל מלך"

Therefore the call for "שתליכוני עליכם" is that מלכיות requires that the world recognize this fact. Therefore, any pasuk that does not indicate this universal recognition of his Sovereignty is not included in the verses of מלכיות. Consequently, if we say here "מלך ישראל וגאלו", that Hashem is the redeemer of Yisrael, it is understood that if Hashem

Himself will redeem Yisrael, we need no longer fear the other nations of the world or their designs against us.

"דהא דאנו אומרים הפסוק מלך ישראל וגואלו, דבגאולת ישראל מהם לעתיד שוב אין חשש עוד שיעמדו לשטן על דרכנו א"כ שפיר די בהזכרת מלכיות על ישראל בלחודייהו, ויתקימו בישראל כל היעודים הטובים ויהיו ישראל מאירים לכל העולם אכי"ר ב"ב."

II
Salvation more important than kingship

Rav Yosef Dov Soloveitchik, in answer to these questions of the שם משמואל, contends that indeed the מלכיות of "מלך ישראל וגואלו" is not from these particular words but from the subsequent statement of "ומבעלדי אין אלהים", "And besides Me there is no other god." And even though it is not explicitly mentioned here that Hashem is King, still the allusion to assuming the yoke of Heaven, "קבלת עול מלכות" is enough to justify that this pasuk be included among the verses of מלכיות, even though the word "מלך" is nowhere to be found in this statement. This approach is based on a statement of the מאירי in his commentary:

"ורשאי להזכירם [שמע] במקום מלכיות שהאחדות הוא קבלת עול מלכותו ושוללות הממשלה מכל אחר."

We might suggest a similar approach to that of the שם משמואל based on an insight offered elsewhere by HaRav Yosef Dov Soloveitchik. He delineates for us the distinction between the terms "גאולה" and "הצלה". All the miracles performed on our behalf and all the wars won by means of miracles which relieved us from oppression are referred to by the term "הצלה". There are two exceptions, though — the Exodus from Egypt and the Ultimate Redemption. These two incidents are referred to by the term "גאולה". For in both cases the effect of the salvation is permanent. The Exodus changed the character of the Jew forever; and the Ultimate Redemption will also have a transformational effect on Klal Yisrael as well as on the rest of mankind. In these two instances of גאולה, the salvation comes about solely by Divine Intervention. This is explicitly stated in the Haggadah of Pesach, where we read: "אני ולא מלאך, אני ולא שליח, אני ולא אחר". Whereas each salvation had its human hero, in these two redemptions, it must be attributed to Hashem alone. It is for this reason that we do not mention the name of Moshe Rabbenu in the Haggadah.

Thus, when we say here "מלך ישראל וגואלו", we are alluding to the Ultimate Redemption, when all of mankind will recognize and accept the Kingdom of Hashem and will allow Bnai Yisrael to serve Him without hindrance. Therefore the key word here, apart from the word "מלך" is that of "גאולה". And it is this description of Hashem's intention to bring about the Ultimate Redemption that justifies this pasuk being included among the verses of מלכיות. For it alludes to the two key factors in this redemptive process — acceptance of Hashem's Sovereignty, מלכות, and the Ultimate Redemption, גאולה.

שאו שערים: One Verse or Four?

I
Why are there more than three verses from the Writings?

As we previously discussed, the Gemara in Rosh Hashanah tells us that we are required to recite ten verses in the מלכיות זכרונות ושופרות — three each from the Torah, the Writings and the Prophets, and a concluding tenth verse, preferably from the Torah. But when we examine the verses recited from the Writings, we find a problem, for it seems that we have more than three.

<u>פסוקי כתובים:</u>

1) כי לה' המלוכה ומושל בגוים — תהילים כב, כט

2) ה' מלך גאות לבש, לבש ה' עוז התאזר וגו' — תהילים צג,א

3) שאו שערים ראשיכם והנשאו פתחי עולם ויבא מלך הכבוד — תהילים כד,ז

4) מי זה מלך הכבוד ה' עזוז וגבור ה' גבור מלחמה — תהילים כד,ח

5) שאו שערים ראשיכם ושאו פתחי עולם ויבוא מלך הכבוד — תהילים כד,ט

6) מי הוא זה מלך הכבוד ה' צבאות הוא מלך הכבוד סלה — תהילים כד,י

The Commentators' Machzor Companion

However, even if we combine the "שאו שערים" with the "מי זה מלך" in both pasukim of "שאו", we still find that we have more than the three required pasukim. Why is this so?

The issue of how many pasukim we are to count here in this chapter (24) of Psalms is discussed in the Gemara of Rosh Hashanah 32b:

"שאו שערים ראשיכם והנשאו פתחי עולם ויבוא מלך הכבוד. מי (הוא) זה מלך הכבוד ה' עזוז וגבור מלחמה. (ז-ח)

שאו שערים ראשיכם ושאו פתחי עולם ויבא מלך הכבוד מי הוא זה מלך הכבוד ה' צבאות הוא מלך הכבוד. (ט-י)

ראשונה שתים דברי ר' יוסי. ר' יהודה אומר: ראשונה אחת שניה שתים."

"The first ("שאו", verses 7-8) contain two mentions of kingship. And the second ("שאו", verses 9-10) three. So says Rav Yossi. Rav Yehudah, however, says that the first contains one and the second, two."

Rav Yehudah arrives at the sum of "one" and "two", as Rashi explains, because he does not include the verse of "Who is the King of glory" — "מי הוא זה מלך הכבוד". And, as the Meiri explains: "שאינו אלא בלשון שאלה", this pasuk is not a statement but rather a question, and therefore it is not to be counted as one of the verses of מלכיות.

The Tur in סימן תקצ״א agrees with Rav Yossi.

"שאו שערים ראשיכם קדמאה עולה במקום ב' שיש בו ב״פ (ב' פעמים) 'מלך'. ובתראה עולה במקום ג' שיש בו ג״פ 'מלך'.

The Rif and the Rambam do not discuss this issue at all, and the question is obvious: why doesn't this question concern them?

II

The Rosh versus the Bais Yosef

We have here a difference of opinion between the Rosh and the Bais Yosef as to exactly what are the practical consequences of this difference of opinion between Rav Yossi and Rav Yehudah. The Rosh writes as follows:

"ונפקא מינה במחלוקת זו מי שרוצה לצמצם בעשרה מלכיות. אבל לענין התוספות שידע לכמה מלכיות יעלו הפסוקים כדי שלא יוסיף על עשרה מלכיות, לענין זה לא נחלקו דאין פותחין מעשרה, אבל אם בא להוסיף הרשות בידו, ואין לומר כיון שיצא ידי חובתו בעשרה התוספות הוי כמו הפסק באמצע הברכות, דהכי איתקין דאם רצה יוסיף והוי הכל בכלל הברכה."

It would seem that the practical consequence of this difference of opinion regarding the counting of verses here is that if one would be particular to recite exactly ten verses, then it is important for that person to know the exact number here. However, this is not so, for if one really wishes to add more than ten verses he may do so, for we are only concerned that one not say less than ten verses, but if one wishes to say more, this does not cause any problem.

And so, according to the Rosh, if one were to recite, for example, the last "שאו", which, according to Rav Yossi contains three expressions of מלכיות, there is no need to mention any other pasuk. And consequently, if the Tur decides as does Rav Yossi, we have a further question: By reciting all the verses of "שאו", we will find that we have many more than the three required expressions of מלכיות. And if we answer that indeed we are not particular about the number ten here, for if one wishes to add verses to it he may, then, as the Rosh points out, we may still ask why only here in the מלכיות do we add verses, and nowhere else?

The Bais Yosef, in סימן תקצ״א explains the practical difference here regarding the counting of verses. He writes as follows:

"ויש לתמוה דבמאי פליגי דמשמע דלא נפקא לן מידי במחלוקת זה דהא משמע די׳ פסוקים אנו צריכין לומר שבכל אחד מהם מוזכר מלכות ומה לי אם יהיה נזכר בפסוק אחד מלכות פעם אחת או שיהיה נזכר כמה פעמים.

ומדחזינן דפליג בהני קראי נראה דלאו אמניין קראי קפדינן, אלא אמניין הזכרת מלכיות וזכרונות ושופרות.

ולישנא דמתני' הכי דייק דקתני, אין פוחתין מי' פסוקי מלכיות וי' פסוקי זכרונות וי' פסוקי שופרות' אלמא דלאו במניין קראי תליא מילתא אלא במניין המלכויות והזכרונות והשופרות. ואף על פי שרבינו [הטור] כתב אין פותחין מי' פסוקים שמלכות בכל אחד מהם וגם הרמב"ם כתב וצריך לומר בכל ברכה מהן י' פסוקים מעין הברכה. י"ל דלאו דוקא נקטי פסוקים אלא משום דברובן אין בכל פסוק אלא מלכות אחת או זכרון אחד או שופר אחד נקטיה הכי אבל אין הכי נמי דאי משתכח קרא דאית ביה תרי זימני או תלתא מלכויות עולה במקום שנים או שלשה, וה"ה לזכרונות ולשופרות כנ"ל."

The Bais Yosef questions the issue here of whether we have one or two expressions of kingship in the pasuk; for what is important is that there is a mention of kingship; thus if we have even two expressions of kingship, we nevertheless count them as one (for a pasuk can contain more than one mention of kingship). And so, we must conclude that the issue here does not concern ten *verses*, but rather ten *references* of kingship. Proof of this is that the Mishnah does not say that we mention "ten verses" but rather "we do not mention kingship less than ten times," which is to be understood as ten references, and therefore the issue here between Rav Yossi and Rav Yehudah is how many references to kingship we find here.

The Bais Yosef dismisses the fact that the Rambam writes that "ten verses are required" and contends that what he meant here were not actual "verses" but rather "references" to the idea of kingship. And yet it seems that the Rambam does in fact call for "verses" and not "references", and thus it seems that the Bais Yosef is correct in his belief that what is important here is the counting of verses, according to the opinion of Rav Yossi and Rav Yehudah. What, then, does the Rambam really mean?

III
References to kingship

The Maharsha here asks a pointed question. All that was required here was to cite the pasuk of "מי זה מלך". For this is really the issue here, and Rav Yossi considers this to be a verse of kingship; whereas Rav Yehudah does not. Why, though, must we cite all the verses of "שאו שערים"? He answers that if we were to cite only the pasuk of "מי זה מלך", then even Rav Yehudah would agree that this constitutes a verse of kingship. And it is only after we recite the first pasuk of "שאו שערים וגו'" that we follow this with a recitation of the pasuk of "מי הוא זה מלך הכבוד". According to Rav Yehudah, this pasuk is not to be counted, for its purpose is only descriptive, to explain "Who is the King", which was mentioned in the first verse and is therefore not to be counted as a separate expression of kingship. "ומיהו ק"ק לר'

יהודה דמי הוא זה מלך לא קחשיב ממנינא בין בראשונה בין בשנייה לא הוי לי' למפלגי אלא במי הוא זה מלך הכבוד וגו' דלאו ממנינא די' מלכויות הן, ומה להם להזכיר דהיו שתים או שלש או אחד ושלש עם המלכיות דכתיבי בהנהו קראי. וי"ל דמי הוא זה מלך הכבוד וגו' לחוד דודאי דהני נמי ממנין מלכויות היא אפילו לר' יהודה אם אמרו בשאר פסוקי מלכיות דכתיבי בכתובים אלא באמרו וירא מלך הכבוד ואומר בתריה מי הוא זה מלך וגו' הוה לי' פירושא דיבא מלך הכבוד שהוזכרו לעיל ומש"ה לאו ממנינא הוא דר"ל דמלך הכבוד שהזכיר לא תימא דהיינו שלמה שבא לפתוח השערים כמפורש במסכת מכות..."

[However, the Bais Yosef contends that all that is required is "references" and not "verses", and as proof he cites the fact that two expression of kingship are counted from the last pasuk of "מי זה מלך הכבוד", "ה' צבאות הוא מלך", הכבוד סלה". From this we can see that we do not count pasukim (for here we have one pasuk and yet we count it as two expressions of kingship) but rather "references". The last sentence is important, for it shows that we have here two references; and this emphasizes the fact that it is the reference that counts. For had he not mentioned this pasuk, we might have thought that the issue here is "verses" and not "references"].

The Sfas Emes disagrees, however, and contends that had one mentioned the first pasuk of "שאו שערים וגו'" alone, this would indeed not be counted as a pasuk at all. For in this pasuk only "מלך" is mentioned, without stating that Hashem is that מלך. For only when we have the second pasuk, "מי הוא זה מלך הכבוד", do we know that the מלך referred to in the first pasuk is Hashem.

From this we see that according to both the Maharsha and the Sfas Emes it is only when we combine the pasukim that we obtain a complete allusion to kingship. Therefore we might suggest that this is the reason we do not here have two separate pasukim (according to the Bais Yosef), in the first "שאו שערים", but rather together they constitute only one. And yet, the second "שאו שערים" is still problematic, since, according to Rav Yossi, there are three references to kingship here, and according to Rav Yehudah, there are only two. Once again, we might ask why there are more than three references to kingship?

IV

Verses, not references, are of prime importance

Rav Yosef Dov Soloveitchik (see p.181 of the sefer "נוראת הרב", שני שעורים בעניני ר"ה מאת הרב סולובייציק ז"ל,

published by my nephew, הרב ברוך שרייבר נ"י,) attempts to explain the position of the Rambam here that "verses" are to be counted, as he states in Hilchos Shofar, (פ"ג ה"ח): "וצריך לומר עשרה פסוקים מעין הברכה". This conforms to our custom of reciting all these pasukim from Psalm 24 ("שאו "שערים וגו"). The תוספתא בר"ה tells us: "רבי יוסי אומר אומרין כל אחד ואחד בפנ"ע [בפני עצמו]...ר' יהודה אומר: אומרין כולם כאחד".

Unlike our Gemara, which interpreted this disagreement as to whether the first two verses of that chapter are counted as two or three separate expressions of kingship, the Tosefta implies that this difference of opinion should focus on whether or not the entire chapter was considered to constitute only one verse, since together they all comprise a single chapter. The text of the prayer which we find in our Machzor conforms to the view of Rav Yehudah, as modified by the Tosefta, that the entire chapter is to be counted as a single reference to the concept of kingship, and this is why we recite the entire chapter.

There still remains a puzzling question here, which is:

1) Why did the Rambam choose the Tosefta over the Gemara in Rosh Hashanah?

2) What about the proof offered by the Bais Yosef that "references" are counted and not "verses", based on Rav

Yossi's reckoning of two expressions of kingship from a single pasuk?

In the commentary of Rabbenu Hananel to our Gemara in Rosh Hashanah, we find: "שאו שערים ראשיכם וגו' ראשונה שתים, שניה שלש דברי ר' יוסי. ר' יהודה אומר אחת."

"Rav Yossi counted two and three kingships from these verses, whereas Rav Yehudah counted one."

With this in mind, we might say that Rav Yossi considers "references" (as the Bais Yosef contends); whereas Rav Yehudah considers "verses" (as it appears from the Tosefta). And so we might contend that this was the text of the Rambam.

1) This leads us to accept Rav Yehudah's view, and consider "verses" to be primary. This is why the Rambam does not mention the issue of the number of expressions of kingship here.

2) And we do not add verses in excess of the three which are required.

V
The Meiri's view

We can take another look at the proof of the Bais Yosef that from the Gemara in Rosh Hashanah we deduce the principle that it is references and not verses which are to be counted, based on Rav Yossi's reckoning of two counts of kingship from one verse. If we look at this from the point of view of the Meiri, we will see that his approach differs from that of the other Rishonim, in that he considers the verses to be of primary importance. In his sefer (מאמר ב' פרק ג') "חבור התשובה", the Meiri contends that there is a difference of opinion between Rav Yossi and Rav Yehudah regarding whether when we have two verses adjacent to each other we are to count the second verse as one or as two.

"ונחלקו בגמרא ר' יהודה ור' יוסי במקראות סמוכים אם הם עולים לאחד או לשנים. והוא שאמרו ז"ל בגמרא: שאו שערים ויבא מלך הכבוד מי זה מלך הכבוד, ומקראות הסמוכים להם שהם, שאו שערים ראשיכם ומי הוא זה מלך הכבוד. ראשונה עולה לשנים, ושניה לשלש. ר"ל [רצה לומר] שהמקראות השנים משלימים לשלש, דברי ר' יוסי. ר' יהודה אומר ראשונה אחת, שניה שתים. פרוש שמקרא שני ר"ל מי זה מלך הכבוד, אינו עולה כלל לא בראשונה ולא בשני, שמצורף הוא לראשון, ובראשון הוא נחשב."

Rav Yossi maintains that in the first section of verses we are to count two expressions of kingship: 1) "שאו שערים"

and 2) "מי זה מלך". And the final pasukim, since they immediately follow the first two, are counted only as one. Thus we have here *three* verses of kingship. And so the words of the Gemara, "ושניה שלש", which refer to the second set of pasukim, is not to be understood to indicate that we have here three expressions of kingship, but rather there is a third verse which refers to kingship, even though the word "מלך" is mentioned three times in two different pasukim.

Rav Yehudah, however, is of the opinion that the word "מלך", which is mentioned both in the first set of pasukim and in the second set, is not to be counted at all; and so we have:

One expression of kingship in the first section: "שאו שערים ויבא מלך הכבוד".

And two in the second section:

1) "שאו שערים"

2) "מי זה...הוא מלך הכבוד"

Thus, if this second verse is considered an expression of kingship, then we have a difference of opinion as to whether the second set is to be counted as one or as two expressions of kingship. Rav Yossi regards it as one, whereas Rav Yehudah sees it as two. This represents a different view from the usual explanation.

Consequently, we see from the Meiri that we should focus on "verses" rather than on "references". And he does not accept the proof from the Gemara which is usually given to support this contention.

The שבלי הלקט in סימן רצ׳ has a similar view and argues that we should focus on the verses placed next to each other. He explains this by saying that all the verses in Psalm 24 are to be viewed as one pasuk, since they are all contained within one psalm. Therefore, according to this way of thinking, we have no extra verses, but rather all three verses are considered as one, and this means that we have three verses from the Writings for all of Psalm 24. He writes as follows:

"הני קראי דכתובים דסמיכי אהדדי כל תרי ותרי חשיב כאחד, כגון במלכויות ,שאו' ו,שאו' תרווייהו חשיב לחד. הואיל דסמיכי אהדדי במזמור לדוד לה' הארץ ומלאה."

The Commentators' Machzor Companion

The Controversy Over the Pasuk "וביום שמחתכם"

I
Trumpet and shofar

The Rosh in Mesechtas Rosh Hashanah (פרק ד סימן ג) tells us: "ויש מרננים על מה שאנו משלימים בשופרות בהאי קרא וביום שמחתכם ובמועדיכם, שכתוב בו ותקעתם בחצוצרות ואין כתוב בו שופר".

In the section of Shofros the tenth pasuk from the Torah is: "או"א תקע בשופר גדול לחרותינו...כמצוה עלינו בתורתך...וביום שמחתכם ובמועדיכם ובראשי חדשיכם, ותקעתם בחצצרות על עולותיכם...ונזכרתם לפני ה' אלוקיכם. ברוך אתה ה' שומע קול תרועת עמך ישראל ברחמים".

Thus the tenth pasuk of the Shofros section is this pasuk of "וביום שמחתכם". The complaint was made that this pasuk merely mentions "חצצרות", "trumpets", and nowhere is the word "shofar" explicitly stated. Thus we might think that this pasuk should not be included as one of the ten verses in the Shofros section.

The Rosh defends the inclusion of this verse here by giving several reasons why it should be included, even though the key word, "שופר" is not mentioned. The Rosh reads:

"כתב ראב"ה משום דאנו רגילין להוסיף והרי הזכיר עשרה פסוקים ואם השלים בנביא יצא ואותו פסוק קבעוהו בתפלה שהוא דבר רצוי ורחמים."

The ראב"ה contends that since we have already mentioned the required ten pasukim, for we added to the pasukim of the Writings, therefore the pasuk of וביום" "שמחתכם does not need to serve here as the concluding tenth pasuk. But rather the tenth pasuk is the one quoted from the Prophets, which the halacha allows. Rather, וביום" "שמחתכם is said here because it is considered an integral part of the beracha, since its theme is appeasement and a petition for Hashem's mercy.

"והרמב"ן היה אומר, לא הביט און ביעקב, אע"פ שכבר אמרו עם המלכיות, הא אמר ר' יוסי: אומרים עם המלכיות ואומרים עם השופרות."

The Ramban would prefer to substitute here the pasuk of "לא הביט און ביעקב", although this pasuk is also recited as one of the verses used for מלכיות. However, Rav Yossi maintained that this pasuk could be used for both מלכיות and שופרות, for both words "מלך" and "שופר" are mentioned in it, and the halacha follows his opinion.

"רבינו יונה היה אומר: יום תרועה יהי' לכם."

Rabbenu Yona substituted here the pasuk of יום" "תרועה יהי' לכם instead of "וביום שמחתכם".

However, the Rosh himself says:

"ואני אומר שאין לשנות מטבע ברכות שנהגו בימות הראשונים. וכי היכי דתרועה בלא שופר מקרי שופר הה"נ ותקיעה, ומשום דכתיב חצוצרות בקרא לא גריעי וכן משמע בירושלמי שהיו משלימין בו שופרות."

The Rosh defends the inclusion of this verse for the following reasons.

1) We may not change the structure of the berachos which were established as custom by previous generations.

2) Even though the key word, "שופר", is not mentioned in this pasuk, yet just as we say that the expression "תרועה" alludes to shofar, so, too, does the word "תקיעה" also allude to shofar, and in this pasuk we find the word "ותקעתם", which is considered as if the word "שופר" was written. The addition of the word "חצוצרות" here does not interfere with this interpretation.

3) The Yerushalmi mentions the practice of concluding the שופרות with this pasuk of "וביום שמחתכם".

The Ritva, however, maintains that because "חצוצרות" is written here, this is a clear indication that shofar is not meant at all, and he cites an interesting proof for this. In Rosh Hashanah 29a, the Gemara states:

"ת"ר הכל חייבים בתקיעת שופר כהנים ולוים וישראלים... פשיטא אי הני לא מחייבי מאן מחייבי. כהנים איצטריכא ליה, ס"ד אמינא הואיל וכתיב

יום תרועה יהי' לכם, מאן דליתיה אלא בתקיעה דחד יומא הוא דמחייב והני כהנים הואיל ואיתנהו בתקיעות דכל השנה דכתיב ותקעתם בחצוצרות על עולותיכם אימא לא ליחייבו, קמ"ל. מי דמי התם חצוצרות והכא שופר."

    The Mishna tells us that all are obligated in the Mitzva of Shofar. "All" includes kohanim, for the Torah commands, "It shall be for you a day of sounding the Shofar". Thus only those who hear the shofar once a year are included; however, I might think that kohanim, who hear the trumpets each day, are not included in this Mitzva. Therefore, we are told that even kohanim are obligated in this Mitzva. To this the Gemara comments: what has the sounding of the trumpets to do with the shofar? For here the Torah says "sound the trumpets" and on Rosh Hashanah it says, "sound the shofar".

    Thus, points out the Ritva, "שופר" and "חצוצרות" are not synonymous. And he concludes as follows:

"מהא שמעינן דתקיעה דפסוק של חצוצרות אין לחושבו במקום שופר כלל, ומשום הכי טועה האומר פסוק אחרון של שופרות קרא דוביום שמחתכם אלא אומר במקומו ובחודש השביעי וכו'."

    We learn from here that we are not to include the pasuk of "וביום שמחתכם", since shofar is not mentioned here and we are to substitute a different pasuk.

The Rashba also rejects the selection of "וביום שמחתכם", as follows: "ואותן שנהגו לומר בסוף השופרות, ותקעתם בחצוצרות טעות הוא, ואף על גב דבכל מקום שיש חצוצרות יש שופר, מכל מקום אנן קרא דמזכיר בו שופר בעי' והא ליכא..."

Although it is true that the shofar always accompanied the sounding of the trumpets, the sounding of the shofar is alluded to as well, yet what is necessary is to have the word "shofar" clearly spelled out; for a mere allusion does not suffice for it to be included in the ten verses of Shofros.

II
The tenth pasuk: petition and prayer

The שלטי הגבורים points out yet another question here in selecting the pasuk of "וביום שמחתכם". For whereas the tenth pasuk of the מלכיות, the "שמע ישראל", is said in conjunction with the preceding nine pasukim, here in the שופרות the tenth pasuk, the one from the Torah, is added just before the concluding beracha, סמוך לחתימתן, separately and apart from the other nine pasukim. This is incorrect, contends the שלטי גבורים, as does the Ramban. And this way of thinking relates also to the זכרונות, where the tenth pasuk, the one from the Torah, is set apart from the other nine. In the מלכיות, though, the tenth pasuk is recited immediately after completing the nine pasukim, before reciting the concluding beracha.

"כתב אבי"ה יש משלימין למנין עשרה פסוקים של זכרונות 'וזכרתי לכם ברית ראשונים' וכן, וביום שמחתכם' לפי שאינן סמוכין לשאר המקראות כמו של מלכיות שאומר מיד, ובתורתך כתוב לאמר, שמע ישראל'..."

To justify the selection of "וביום שמחתכם וזכרתי לכם ברית וגו'", an answer is offered to the above question:

"ומה שהרחיקם לפי שהפסוק נופל על לשון התפלה."

The tenth pasuk of both שופרות and זכרונות reflect a petition, and therefore it is included as part of the concluding beracha. This is true in the order of the זכרונות, where we conclude by saying: "וקיים לנו...את הדבר שהבטחתנו בתורתך...וזכרתי להם ברית ראשונים".

And in the שופרות the tenth pasuk also reflects a prayer: "ושם נעשה לפניך את קרבנות חובותינו...כאמור וביום שמחתכם...והיו לכם לזכרון".

However, in the מלכיות the tenth pasuk, that of the שמע ישראל, does not reflect a petition, and therefore it is not included in the beracha.

We might suggest that this approach is based on the following. The Sifri comments on the pasuk of:

"וביום שמחתכם...ותקעתם בחצוצרות...והיו לכם לזכרון לפני ה' אלוקיכם אני ה' אלוקיכם."

In Bamidbar 10:10 he makes the following comments:

ותקעתם בחצוצרות — הרי שופרות

והיו לכם לזכרון — זה זכרונות

אני ה' אלוקיכם — זה מלכיות

אם כן מה ראו חכמים לומר מלכיות תחלה ואחריכם זכרונות ושופרות? אלא המליכוהו עליך תחלה ואחר כך בקש רחמים מלפניו כדי שתזכור לך. ובמה בשופר של חרות."

It would seem that according to the source for the requirement to cite verses of Kingship, Remembrance and Shofar, the order should be reversed. Why, then, do we follow the sequence we do? The answer is that we first set Hashem as Master and King over us; and then we proceed to petition for His mercy. This is all accomplished by means of the shofar.

Thus we see that we first declare His sovereignty, מלכיות, and then petition for זכרון, to be remembered with mercy in conjunction with the sounding of the shofar. Thus the declaration of מלכיות is made together with the other pasukim which are also considered to be declarations that we accept the yoke of Heaven, עול מלכות. After that, we petition by means of זכרונות and שופרות; and in this way we place the concluding verses of these two sections just before the concluding beracha.

III

The Rashba versus the Rosh

As we have mentioned, the Rashba objects to the selection of "וביום שמחתכם ותקעתם בחצוצרות", because even though this pasuk alludes to the shofar, since the trumpets were always accompanied by the sounding of the shofar, yet because the actual word "shofar" is not included in the verse, he does not accept this pasuk as the tenth verse of the section of שופרות. Yet the Rosh does accept this pasuk as the proper one to be included in the verses of the שופרות, even in the absence of the word "shofar".

Perhaps we can say that his opinion is based on the following considerations.

In the Gemara of Rosh Hashanah 32b, there is a difference of opinion between Rav Yossi and Rav Yehudah as to whether the שמע can serve as a pasuk for the מלכיות. Rav Yossi contends that it can; whereas Rav Yehudah rejects this pasuk, because the word "מלך" is not spelled out explicitly, even though the essence of the pasuk does indeed include the notion of מלכיות.

Rav Yossi, however, maintains that it is sufficient that the concept is alluded to even though it is not explicitly spelled out here. Consequently, the halacha follows Rav

Yossi and states that the שמע can serve as one of the verses of the מלכיות. And so we adopt the theory that allusion is sufficient and the concept need not be explicit. And so, in the שופרות the words "וביום שמחתכם" qualify as the tenth verse of שופרות.

And the reason this pasuk of "וביום שמחתכם" was chosen rather than any other pasuk, even though it does not really solve our problem, is explained by many commentators. According to the Sifri, this pasuk serves as the source which requires us to recite the verses of מלכיות זכרונות ושופרות. Therefore it is fitting to quote this section among the verses of the שופרות.

HaRav Mordechai Zacks, ז"ל, offers a beautiful explanation of this (in his sefer "מילי דמרדכי" עמ' נא). The Torah required that all animal sacrifices be accompanied by the sounding of trumpets. The Midrash tells us that in all the sacrifices offered on the Altar the word "והקרבתם", "and you shall offer", was used. However, regarding the sacrifice of Rosh Hashanah this term is not used, but rather "ועשיתם", "and they shall make". The reason for this special term is that on Rosh Hashanah man is called upon to "offer himself" as a sacrifice: "ועשיתם, שיעשה אדם עצמו כקרבן".

By doing this we call attention to the sacrifice of Yitzchak, the Akeida, which stands in our stead. Thus it is certainly most fitting to quote the pasukim of "וביום

"שמחתכם ותקעתם בחצוצורות, to show that it is as though the trumpets are accompanying the sacrifice of the day, which represents the sacrifice of man himself, just as it also accompanies the sacrifices of the entire year.

The Order of the Verses:
מלכיות זכרונות ושופרות

I
Why not follow chronological order?

The verses of the Torah recited in the מלכיות זכרונות ושופרות (מז"ש) are arranged in order of their appearance in the Torah. The verses from the Prophets also follow their written order in both the מלכיות and the שופרות. However, in the זכרונות they do not. For there we begin with a quotation from the Book of Yirmeyahu, followed by a verse from the Prophet Yehezkail, and then we conclude with another verse from Yirmeyahu. Why do we change from Yirmeyahu to Yehezkail and then go back to Yirmeyahu? Why not follow the usual chronological order, first Yirmeyahu and then Yehezkail? In the Writings the verses do not follow chronological order in all the sections here of the מלכיות זכרונות ושופרות. Why do we suddenly deviate and quote verses out of order in the Writings? Why not follow the chronology of verses as they appear in the Book of Psalms, from which all the verses quoted here derive?

The reason the verses from the Writings are quoted out of order can be answered in the following way. (See the introduction of the sefer of HaGaon Rav Betzalel Hacohen of Vilna to the "קונטרס זבחי תרועה", reprinted in the "ספר הזכרון לרבי משה ליפשיץ", עמ' תש"פ, and see also the article of הרב מאיר זיכל in the following journal: ('שמעתין, תשנ"ד,גליון מס, 114, עמ' 67-69.)

A. The order of verses from the Writings in the מלכיות are as follows:

1) "כי לה' המלוכה ומושל בגויים" — תהילים כד, כט

2) "ה' מלך גאות לבש וגו'" — תהילים צב,א

3) "שאו שערים ראשיכם...ויבא מלך הכבוד" — תהילים כד,ז-י

1) "For the sovereignty is Hashem's" — Psalms 22:29

2) "Hashem will have reigned, He will have donned grandeur" — Psalms 93:1

3) "Raise up your heads, O Gates...so that the King of Glory may enter" — Psalms 24:7-10

We might have thought that the proper order should rather be:

1) "כי לה' המלוכה וגו'" — תהילים כב

2) "שאו שערים וגו'" — תהילים כד

3) "ה' מלך גאות לבש וגו'" — תהילים צג

But this particular order is established, based on the following insight. The first pasuk from the Torah in the מלכיות requires a mention of "ה' ימלוך לעולם ועד". For here we have the combination of the words ה' and מלך (מלכות), which reflect the ideas of "Hashem" and "kingship". Thus in the Writings the first two verses cited (from Psalms 22 and 93) also include these two words adjacent to each other.

1) "כי לה' המלוכה" — תהילים כב
2) "ה' מלך" — תהילים צג

And although in the "שאו שערים" both key words are also quoted, yet they do not appear adjacent to each other.

And this is why we quote Psalms 22 and 93 and then Psalm 24, although this is not the proper chronological order. However, because of the consideration explained here we follow this particular order.

B. The verses in the זכרונות are as follows:

1) "זכר עשה לנפלאותיו וגו'" — תהילים קיא,ד
2) "טרף נתן ליראיו יזכור לעולם בריתו" — תהילים קיא,ה
3) "ויזכור להם בריתו וגו'" — תהילים ק"ו, מה

1) "He made a memorial for His wonders..." — Psalms 111:4

2) "He provided food for those who fear Him,

He eternally remembers His covenant" — Psalms 111:5

3) "He remembered His covenant for them" — Psalms 106:45

Here again, we follow the pattern set down in the verses of the Torah. For the pasukim from the Torah are as follows:

"וישמע...ויזכר...את בריתו" — שמות ב, כד

"וזכרתי את ברית יעקב" — ויקרא כו, מב

Here we stress that Hashem *remembered* (ויזכור) His Covenant, ("ברית"). The key words here are "ויזכור" and "ברית". Thus, in the Writings, the pasukim emerge as follows:

We place Psalm 111:5 next to Psalm 106:45, for in both pasukim we find the key words:

פסוק ב': "טרף נתן...יזכור...בריתו" — 111:5

פסוק ג': "ויזכור...בריתו..." — 106:45

We follow this arrangement, for had we started with verse 106:45 (which is first in the chronological ordering of the chapters of Psalms mentioned here), then we would lose the benefit of placing those pasukim ajacent to each other which contain the key words, "ויזכור" and "בריתו". For since the pasuk of "זכר עשה לנפלאותיו" (Psalm 111:4) would be placed next and afterward Psalm 111:5: "טרף וגו'", we would lose the proximity of these two pasukim which contain both key words.

But why couldn't we just place Psalm 111:4 at the end, and then we could have the two pasukim containing the key words ויזכור and בריתו, as the first and second? The answer might be that although we do not follow the order of the psalms, yet since these two psalms are adjacent to each other, it would not seem right to let a later verse (111:5 — "טרף") precede an earlier verse (111:4 — "זכר עשה לנפלאותיו").

C. Again, here in the שופרות, we follow the order of the Torah. Thus the order we follow is this:

1) "ויהי ביום השלישי...וקול שופר חזק מאד" — שמות יט,טז

2) "ויהי קול שופר הולך וחזק מאד" — שמות יט

3) "וכל העם רואים...ואת קול השופר..." שמות כ, טו

The pasukim from the Writings here are:

1) "עלה אלקים בתרועה ה' בקול שופר" — תהילים מז,ו

2) "בחצצרות וקול שופר..." — תהילים צח,ו

3) "תקעו בחדש שופר..." — תהילים פא, ד-ה

1) "Hashem has ascended with a blast, Hashem with the sound of the shofar" — Psalm 47:6

2) "With trumpets and shofar sound..." — Psalm 98:6

3) "Blow the shofar at the moon's renewal..." — Psalm 81:4-5

Here verse 3 should have preceded verse 2. However, since the pasukim of the Torah contain the key words, "קול שופר" we begin with Psalm 47:6: "עלה אלקים...ה' בקול שופר" together with Psalm 98:6: "בחצצרות וקול שופר", and then we conclude with Psalm 81 which, although it comes from an earlier verse, does not contain these key words of "קול שופר".

II
Revealing the Divine Presence

There is still another question which remains here to be answered regarding the verses from the Writings of the שופרות. After the previously mentioned three verses, we quote another verse:

"הללו-יה הללו א-ל בקדשו...הללוהו בתקע בשופר" — תהילים קנ,ג-ו

"Halleluyah, praise Hashem in His Sanctuary...Praise Him with the blast of the Shofar..." — Psalm 150:3-6

Why do we have here four verses from the Writings? Several answers have been offered, maintaining that this verse is really not part of the ten required verses and was recited out of other considerations.

1) The שבלי הלקט (in ר"ה סימן רצ) writes:

"הללוהו בתקע שופר לא חשיב בחשבון י' שופרות שאין אומרין עשרה הלולים אלא לפי שכנגדן קבעו חכמים עשרה מלכויות, עשרה זכרונות, עשרה שופרות כדיאתא במסכת ראש השנה ולא הוין ממנין עשרה."

"This verse is not to be counted as one of the *ten verses*, since only ten are to be recited. However, since the source for quoting ten verses is derived from this section, as taught to us in Rosh Hashanah 32a, therefore it is most proper that we cite these verses in our liturgy."

2) HaRav Yosef Dov Soloveitchik offers the insight that the theme of שופרות is related to גילוי שכינה, revealing the Divine Presence. For whenever we blow the shofar, the Divine Presence appears in our midst. Shofar heralds the arrival of Hashem, the King, "ותרועת מלך בו", and we are told that the Majesty of Hashem arrives with the shofar. Thus we cite the three aforementioned verses which articulate this concept. And then, suddenly we begin to sing the whole psalm of "הללו-יה הללו א-ל בקדשו". But why do we need to quote this seemingly superfluous chapter of Psalms? The נוסח of this הללו-יה changes dramatically, and we sing the same exhilirating melody as "מלך עליון". To explain this we might say that once we state that there is a revelation of the Divine Presence, גילוי שכינה, then we precipitate חובת שירה, praise similar to that which was found in the Bais HaMikdash, and this is why we sing the shirah of הללו-יה to Hashem, which is the same shirah that was sung in the Bais HaMikdash. This expression of shirah is not part of

שופרות; rather once we state in the שופרות that תקיעת שופר is symbolic of גילוי שכינה and that the קדושת ראש השנה actually expresses גילוי שכינה, then we realize that we are in the presence of Hashem and we must sing His praises, "הללו-יה הללו א-ל בקדשו" (see pages 68-69 of "נוראות הרב").

To prove this contention that "הללו-יה הללו א-ל בקדשו" is not viewed as part of the ten verses we can see that many machzorim do not add the word, "ונאמר", "and so it is said", which usually prefaces a citation from Kisvei HaKodesh. But since "ונאמר" is not added here (although it does appear in some machzorim), this proves that this verse was not said as part of the required ten verses.

III

Hashem as father and mother

We may now return to our original question as to why in the verses from the Prophets we change from Yirmeyahu to Yehezkail and then back to Yirmeyahu. One possible reason is that they share a common expression.

In Yirmeyahu 2:2 we read: "זכרתי לך חסד נעוריך", and in Yehezkail 16:60: "וזכרתי אני את בריתי אותך בימי נעוריך...". The key word "נעוריך" appears in both of these verses and therefore they are placed adjacent to each other. The second quotation from Yirmeyahu (31:19), however, does not contain this key word, but rather: "הבן יקיר לי אפרים".

"מסורה", חוברת י"ג, see) HaRav Yosef Dov Soloveitchik
185-86 'אדר, תשנ"ז, ונוראת הרב', עמ) writes as follows:

"והתירץ בזה, דבפסוק הראשון מירמיה וכן ביחזקאל ה' זוכר לנו החסד והברית של ימי נעורינו — המצוות שעשינו כשהייינו נערים. אבל בהפסוק, הבן יקיר לי אפרים' ה' חושב אותנו כמו שאנחנו עדיין נערים וילדים עכשיו, ומשו"ה מזכיר אפרים הצעיר ובאמת הקב"ה נוהג בנו כאב וגם כאם. ואצל האם הבן נשאר תמיד כילד שלה אפי' לאחר שנתגדל, וזהו הבן יקיר לי אפרים' (עכשיו) על כן המו מעי לו רחם ארחמנו נאום ה'.'"

"We are corrupt criminals and unworthy of salvation. But Hashem remembers us as a child — innocent and worthy. Hashem's recollection of the criminal as a young boy transforms His anger into love and understanding. This is the message of the first verse of Yirmeyahu and that of Yehezkail. The final verse of Yirmeyahu says "הבן יקיר לי אפרים", you are *still* a child and worthy of love and salvation. A child cannot be corrupt. This is the difference between a father's love and that of a mother. A father remembers a child when he was young and this memory arouses the father's love and compassion for the child. The memory of youth placates the father's anger. A mother always regards her children as *children*. So in the first two verses, Hashem is a father, and the pasuk says that we ask Hashem to remember our actions performed when we were young and therefore to forgive us. The final verse sees Hashem as a mother. It reads: "כי מדי דברי בו זכור אזכרנו". The word "זכור" used here does not mean to remember. It means I have compassion for him; I am aware of him. Whenever I speak of him I am *aware* of him because I love him. The pasuk mentions Ephraim, since he was the youngest child and a mother always regards her youngest as a child, and she remembers her youngest child more than the others."

The Issue of אדיר המלוכה

I
The laws of berachos on yom tov

We have discussed the difference of opinion which exists among the Rishonim as to whether the verses of מלכיות זכרונות ושופרות are to be recited in all the Amidah prayers of the day or only at Mussaf. As we have seen, the Ramban, in his מלחמות, cited at the end of Mesechtas Rosh Hashanah, brings proof that we add the verses of מלכיות זכרונות ושופרות only in the Amidah of Mussaf. He writes as follows:

"ועוד מצאתי בירושלמי: ר' אבהו בשם ר"א בכל מקום עבר והזכיר אדיר המלוכה לא יצא, חוץ מן הא-ל הקדוש של ר"ה ובלבד במוסף ואתיא כר' יוחנן בן נורי. פירוש, בכל ימות השנה אם חתם בברוך אדיר המלוכה לא יצא, חוץ מא-ל הקדוש של ר"ה, שהוא כולל מלכיות עם קדושת השם לדברי ריב"נ שאע"פ שיש לו לחתום בקדושת השם אם חתם במלכיות יצא, שהרי שניהם נכללים בברכה אחת לריב"נ, ובלבד במוסף, אלמא דבמוסף הוא שאומר זכרונות ושופרות וכולל מלכיות עם קדושת השם אבל ערבית שחרית ומנחה אינו אומר מלכיות זכרונות ושופרות."

"Rav Avahu in the name of R' Elazar states that if one would, instead of saying 'הא-ל הקדוש' say 'אדיר המלוכה', 'Mighty in Majesty', one would have not fulfilled his obligation to conclude the beracha of קדושת השם, except on Rosh Hashanah. For there, since he joins the verses of kingship with the Kedushas Hashem, according to Rav Yochanan ben Nuri, both verses are alluded to in this concluding beracha. This is true only according to R' Yochanan ben Nuri and only in the Mussaf prayer.

Thus we see that the verses of מלכיות וכו' were recited only during the Mussaf prayer and not in any of the other daily prayers."

Based on this Ramban, the Achronim derive a new application regarding the laws of berachos. The Shulchan Aruch in או"ח סימן תפ"ז, rules that if Yom Tov falls on a Shabbos, the concluding beracha in the section of the קדושת היום should read: "מקדש השבת וישראל והזמנים". We join the themes of Shabbos and Yom Tov in the concluding beracha. In relation to this ruling we find a difference of opinion between the נשמת אדם and the ביאור הלכה. Although both agree that if one forgets to mention Yom Tov here in the beracha of קדושת היום but did mention Shabbos, one is considered to have indeed fulfilled his obligation. However, if one forgot to mention Shabbos but did mention Yom Tov, the נשמת אדם maintains that he has fulfilled his obligation (is יוצא) regarding the beracha of קדושת היום. On the other hand, the ביאור הלכה contends that in such a situation, one is not יוצא. The נשמת אדם gives proof for his opinion by citing the ירושלמי which states that if one is obligated to mention two themes and he only mentions one, then he is יוצא. Examples given include the obligation to mention Yom Tov and Shabbos or Rosh Chodesh and Shabbos. If one mentions only Yom Tov, in the first instance, or Rosh Chodesh, in the second, but not Shabbos, then one has fulfilled his obligation, in keeping with the opinion of רבן יוחנן בן נורי that his primary obligation is to mention the קדושת השם, which is the main beracha here. And yet one must also mention the theme of מלכיות, even though it constitutes a secondary theme. The ירושלמי states here that if one said "אדיר המלוכה", which alludes to מלכיות, this is acceptable and he has fulfilled his obligation, although he did not mention the Kedushas Hashem, "הא-ל הקדוש". From this we see that if one mentioned only the secondary theme and not the central theme of the beracha, he has still managed to fulfill his obligation. And so the נשמת אדם contends that if one mentioned Yom Tov but not Shabbos, he is still יוצא.

"ואסתייע זה מן הירושלמי דהיכי דהברכה כולל שני דברים וסיים בשל אחת יצא דהרי איתא התם ר' אבהו בשם ר' אלעזר בכל מקום עבר והזכיר אדיר המלוכה לא יצא חוץ מן הא-ל הקדוש של ראש השנה ובלבד במוסף ואתיא כריב"נ. ופירש משום דלריב"נ צריך לכלול מלכיות בקדושת השם, ולכן אף אם חתם בסוף רק בא"י [ברוך אתה ה'] אדיר המלוכה, יצא,

אף שלא הזכיר קדושת השם בחתימה. הרי דברכה שכוללת שני דברים וחתם באחת ואפילו במה שאינו מעיקר הברכה [כגון הכא שעיקר הברכה הוא קדושת השם ומלכיות נכלל בה] יצא בדיעבד."

The ביאור הלכה, however, contends that the ירושלמי here must be interpreted differently. What is meant is a case where one did mention both המלך הקדוש and אדיר המלוכה. The issue here is that all year round he concluded with the normal ending, מטבע הברכה. If he departed from this during the year, then he is not יוצא. However, on Rosh Hashanah he is considered to have fulfilled his obligation with the addition of אדיר המלוכה, since this beracha reflects the theme of the day. This, as we have previously discussed, is the opinion of Rav Yochanan ben Nuri, and it is not considered to be a change in the acceptable conclusion of the blessing, ששינה ממטבע הברכות. The ביאור הלכה writes:

"נלע"ד דמיירי דחתם בקדושת השם רק שהזכיר גם אדיר המלוכה...דבכל השנה לא יצא ששינה ממטבע לבד במוסף של ר"ה לריב"נ...אם עבר ואמר בא"י אדיר המלוכה הא-ל הקדוש יצא שגם זה הוא מענין הברכה לדידיה..."

This position of the נשמת אדם raises the following questions:

1) The ביאור הלכה asks, if the issue here is as the נשמת אדם maintains — that only אדיר המלוכה was said and not also המלך הקדוש — why then does the ירושלמי state that "all

year round אדיר המלוכה does not suffice as the concluding beracha", when this should be obvious?

"לענ"ד קשה לי טובא לפירוש זה [של הנשמת אדם] דא"כ מאי קמ"ל דבכל מקום אם עבר והזכיר בא"י אדיר המלוכה לא יצא, פשיטא דהא לא חתם בקדושת השם כלל..."

2) HaRav Yaakov Yoffen שליט"א, raises the question whether the issue here is as the נשמת אדם maintains — that the mention of a secondary theme is sufficient to justify the concluding beracha — then, even according to Rabbi Akiva we could apply the same principle. For, according to Rabbi Akiva, we join the קדושת היום with מלכיות. And if, for example, we were to say "אדיר המלוכה" instead of "מלך על כל הארץ מקדש ישראל ויום הזכרון", this should be sufficient for קדושת היום, since we mentioned the theme of מלכיות when we said "אדיר המלוכה", even though this is a secondary theme. Why then, did the ירושלמי mention only רבן יוחנן בן נורי and not also Rabbi Akiva?

II
The sanctity of the day and kingship

We can answer these questions based on the following two insights:

1) If in the concluding beracha of קדושת היום in Shacharis one fails to mention the phrase: "מלך על כל הארץ",

then one is considered to have fulfilled his obligation of concluding the beracha with only the theme of קדושת היום, when we say "מקדש ישראל ויום הזכרון", since we do not recite verses of מלכיות at Shacharis. Or perhaps this is not the case?

The שערי תשובה סימן תקפ״ב maintains that one did in fact fulfill the requirement by mentioning only the theme of קדושת היום. However, Rav Chaim Brisker contends that one is not יוצא if he failed also to mention the phrase of "מלך על כל הארץ" in the Shacharis prayer. Rav Chaim maintains that the essence of קדושת היום, the sanctity of the day, is מלכיות, which declares Hashem King over all creation. Thus, the failure to add "מלך על כל הארץ" means that the required beracha was not said here.

If we accept this, then we could expand the rationale of Rav Chaim to apply to Rabban Yochanan ben Nuri, who joins the מלכיות with קדושת השם, and we could say that the essence of the מלכיות is the theme of קדושת השם. (We have shown earlier that this is exactly the reason Rabban Yochanah ben Nuri joined these two themes.) And so, we can now understand that מלכיות is viewed as a petition for קדושת השם, the sanctification of the Holy Name.

2) In the Gemara in Berachos 12b, Rav Elazar states that although it is preferable to recite המלך הקדוש as the

concluding beracha of the קדושת השם, yet if one said "הא-ל הקדוש", he is still יוצא. For הא-ל הקדוש is equivalent to המלך הקדוש, based on the pasuk in Isaiah 5:16: "ויגבה ה' צבאות במשפט והא-ל הקדוש נקדש בצדקה", "But the Lord of Hosts is exalted through justice, and the Holy God is sanctified through righteousness." When is Hashem exalted through justice? In the ten days between Rosh Hashanah and Yom Kippur, and nonetheless the verse reads, "the Holy God", "הא-ל הקדוש".

And so we may say that if the essence of מלכיות is קדושת השם, as Rabban Yochanan ben Nuri believes, then when we say אדיר המלוכה, we are asserting the kingship of Hashem, המלך הקדוש. This means that the ירושלמי does not address the question of mentioning a secondary theme and thereby fulfilling one's obligation for a primary theme. But rather the focus is on the theme of the day, מלכיות, which, according to Rabban Yochanan ben Nuri, corresponds to the sanctification of the Holy Name, קדושת השם. And by reciting אדיר המלוכה it is as if one said המלך הקדוש. It is worth noting that the author of this statement of "אדיר המלוכה" is the same ר' אלעזר who contends in Mesechtas Berachos that הא-ל הקדוש is in essence המלך הקדוש, based on the pasuk of "והא-ל הקדוש נקדש בצדקה".

With this background, we can now attempt to answer our two previous questions:

1) Why was it necessary for the ירושלמי to mention that the phrase "אדיר המלך" does not suffice as the concluding beracha of הא-ל הקדוש in the קדושת השם all year round, when this should be obvious? In light of our explanation, we might now understand that since "אדיר המלוכה" may be viewed as if one said הא-ל הקדוש or המלך הקדוש, then we might think that all year round one could fulfill one's obligation by saying "אדיר המלוכה". To dispel this illusion, it is necessary to clarify the situation by explaining that only during the period of the Ten Days of Repentance between Rosh Hashanah and Yom Kippur is it possible to equate אדיר המלוכה with קדושת השם in order to be יוצא with a recitation of "אדיר המלוכה". During the rest of the year, however, this statement is taken at face value, and one cannot fulfill the requirement of mentioning קדושת השם with מלכיות.

2) Why did the ירושלמי find that the issue of אדיר המלוכה is related to the opinion of Rabban Yochanan ben Nuri but not to Rabbi Akiva's opinion, when it could also have included Rabbi Akiva's opinion? For instead of saying "מלך על כל הארץ מקדש ישראל ויום הזכרון", the appropriate concluding beracha, we could simply have said "אדיר המלוכה", since this,

too, alludes to the theme of מלכיות. Therefore, even though "מקדש ישראל ויום הזכרון" was not said, one would still be יוצא, since he mentioned מלכיות.

The answer to this question must be that we can distinguish between the positions of Rabban Yochanan ben Nuri and Rabbi Akiva. Rabban Yochanan contends that all that is required is a beracha that alludes to the קדושת השם. And since he perceives the beracha of "אדיר המלוכה" to be equivalent to an expression of מלכיות, its recitation would suffice to fulfill this requirement of קדושת השם.

According to Rabbi Akiva, however, even though משפט (מלכיות) is the essence of the day's sanctity, there is yet another aspect to the sanctity of the day of Rosh Hashanah, and that is the prohibition against doing any work, איסור מלאכה, which is common to all the holidays. Thus we have dual aspects of the קדושת היום of Rosh Hashanah.

1) מלכיות (משפט is the essence of מלכיות and characteristic of the day)

2) קדושת היום is the same as all the other holidays with its obligation to abstain from work, איסור מלאכה

Consequently, if one were to conclude the beracha of קדושת היום of מלכיות with the phrase "אדיר המלוכה", he would have fulfilled his obligation regarding מלכיות as related to the קדושת היום. However, by reciting "אדיר המלוכה", he would not fulfill his obligation regarding the other aspect of קדושת היום, that of איסור מלאכה. Thus, one would be יוצא only by joining "אדיר המלוכה" with "הזכרון ויום ישראל מקדש". This explains why the ירושלמי addresses the issue of "אדיר המלוכה" alone, and he applies the opinion of Rabban Yochanan ben Nuri, because it presents the situation where one said "אדיר המלוכה", without any other accompanying statement (לפי הנשמת אדם).

זכרונות

I
Hashem knows past, present and future

In the Zichronos we read: "אתה זוכר מעשה עולם...ואין נסתר מנגד עיניך...צופה ומביט עד סוף כל הדורות...".

"You remember the deeds done in the universe ... before You all hidden things are revealed...and you see to the very end of all generations."

We say here that Hashem remembers the past, that nothing in the present is hidden from Him, and that He is aware of everything that will happen in the future.

On Rosh Hashanah every human being is judged as to whether he will live or die and what will be his circumstances in life. If so, why speak of the past and the future here? Rav Yosef Dov Soloveitchik (see נוראת הרב עמ' 98-99) suggests an answer when he says:

"A person is judged not just by his deeds in the present dimension of time, but also by the deeds of his forefathers. God takes into consideration the conditions and circumstances of the past which had their impact upon him. He also weighs the deeds of man vis-a-vis the future, what that man means to the future millenium. In other words, the individual is judged as the link between those who were already here and are no more, and those who are not yet here. God judges both in retrospect and in anticipation."

II
What is the book of death?

The Gemara in ערכין י,ב tells of a dialogue between the angels and the Holy One, Blessed be He:

"אמרו מלאכי השרת לפני הקב"ה מפני מה אין ישראל אומרים שירה לפניך בראש השנה וביום הכפורים? אמר להם: אפשר מלך יושב על כסא הדין וספרי חיים וספרי מתים פתוחים לפניו וישראל אומרים שירה לפני..."

"The ministering angels said before the Holy One, Blessed be He: Why do not Bnai Yisrael sing a song before You on the New Year and the Day of Atonement? He answered them: Would that be possible, that the King sits on the throne of Judgement with the books of life and death open before Me, and Yisrael sings a song before Me?"

What does the "Book of Death" allude to? Does it mean that those who are to die this year have their names inscribed in a book called "ספר מתים", or does this book contain the names of all those already deceased? Each possibility has its difficulties. For if we contend that this book contains the names of those who are destined to die, why do we need a separate book, as long as their names do not appear in this year's Book of Life, ספר החיים?

In support of this view the חכמי מוסר describe how the decree of death is issued. We might think that the person destined to die this year is under sentence of a proclamation which contains his name. But the truth is, we live by virtue of Hashem's will, which proclaims from moment to moment, "Live, live, live". The moment Hashem stops willing a particular creature to live, he dies immediately.

And if we were to say, on the other hand, that the book of death contains the names of those already deceased, what need is there for a book with this information, for one does not usually keep a record of "dead accounts".

Chazal tell us in Bava Basra 16:a:

"ירמיה כתב ספרו וספר מלכים...עזרא כתב ספרו ויחס של דברי הימים עד לו..."

"Jeremiah wrote his book and the Book of Kings...Ezra wrote his book and the Book of Chronicles..."

These statements have implications apart from who authored which books of the Tanach. For example, we are well aware that King Menashe was a wicked person who did more than anyone else to perpetuate idol worship in Yisrael. Yet we are told that he repented of his evil ways. This fact is recorded in the Book of Chronicles II 33:12-17. However, even though his story is told in the Book of Kings, the fact that he repented is not mentioned there. Why not?

The answer given is that even though a person eventually passes from this world, yet his deeds continue to have an effect on future generations. The accounting which a person receives after his death takes into consideration the influence his actions may have had on others. Even though he might have repented, still his evil influence might continue to have spiritual consequences. This is certainly true of King Menashe. This is why in the Book of Kings, which details the period of the First Bais HaMikdash, we read how his influence continued to cause others to worship idols. His repentance is not recorded here since it did not have any effect on the spiritual climate of his time. However, Chazal tell us that in the time of Ezra the evil inclination for idol worship was eradicated by the Sages (see יומא ס,גא). This meant that the evil influence of Menashe was also nullified and now he could be considered a person who had repented, and his act of returning to the true path could be appreciated and accorded merit.

(See the sefer "תולדות יהושע" על פרקי אבות מהרב ר' יהושע העליר, עמ' 36, ובהערה שם, ובספר "פחד יצחק" לר' יצחק למפרונטי, אות ת ערך תשובה עמ' קע"ד, מובא בספר "הגיוני הלכה" ח"ב, מהרב יצחק מירסקי, עמ' 161).

With this explanation in mind, we can now appreciate:

1) The meaning and importance of what constitutes the "ספר המתים", which refers to those who once lived in this world and are no longer here. Yet, as we have explained, they too still have to stand in judgement to determine their influence on present and future generations. This explains why their names must be recorded in a sefer.

2) The deeper implication of the statement that Jeremiah wrote the Book of Kings. For Jeremiah lived in the period when idol worship was still practiced in Yisrael, and therefore he could not mention the fact of the repentance of Menashe, as we have explained. Yet since Ezra wrote the Book of Chronicles at a time when idol worship ceased from the world, the repentance of Menashe could now be recorded, since his influence on future generations had dissipated.

III

We do not say Hallel for an ongoing process

We can gain a deeper insight into the words of Chazal in מסכת ערכין that Yisrael does not say Hallel on Rosh Hashanah when the books of life and death stand open before Hashem, based on the following.

Our commentators ask why we have no sefer dedicated to the holiday of Channukah. The Bnai Yissachar suggests an answer to this question by saying that the Books of the Tanach, כתבי הקודש, are concerned with what transpired in the past and its message for us in the present or prophecies which are to be realized in the future (נבואה שהוצרכה לדורות נכתבה). However, prophecies which are ongoing are not recorded. Thus the reason the miracle of Channukah is not recorded in a book of the Tanach because the miracle of the oil alludes to the beginning of the period of Redemption, אתחלתא דגאולה, which is an ongoing process and will culminate in the Ultimate Redemption.

We could apply this same idea to the concept of Hallel. Hallel is always recited to commemorate something which happened in the past. For example, when we remember the miracle of the Exodus from Egypt we are required to say Hallel. However, an ongoing process does not call for Hallel. This is what the Gemara means when it explains that the "Book of Death" remains open. For the influence of those who have already lived and are no longer in this world is an ongoing process, whose effects are felt for countless generations. Thus this day of Judgement, Rosh Hashanah, is not an end in itself but it is rather an integral part of an on-going process of judgement. This, then, is another reason we do not say Hallel on Rosh Hashanah.

My son, Rabbi Yaakov Sender, נ"י, raised the following question. If this is so, why do we say Hallel on Channukah, for isn't the miracle of Channukah considered to be an ongoing process, which will one day culminate in the Ultimate Redemption, אתחלתא דגאולה? My answer to this is that, according to the עמק ברכה, we say Hallel on Channukah to commemorate the *military victory which took place in the past*, and not for the sake of the miracle of the oil, which is the beginning of the ongoing process of the Ultimate Redemption.

The Verses of Zichronos

I

Does "visitation" equal "remembrance"?

In the Gemara in Rosh Hashanah 32b we find a difference of opinion between Rav Yossi and Rav Yehudah.

פקדונות הרי הן כזכרונות, כגון 'וה' פקד את שרה' (בראשית כא): וכגון 'פקוד פקדתי אתכם' (שמות ג) דברי ר' יוסי, ר' יהודה אומר אינן כזכרונות.

"Visitation" (פקוד) is equivalent to "remembrance" (זכרונות), as in the verse in Bereishis 21:1, where we read: "And Hashem *visited* Sarah"; or "I have surely *visited* (remembered) you," (Shemos 3:16). This is the view of Rav Yossi. Rav Yehudah, on the other hand, holds that "visitation" is not equivalent to "remembrance".

There also seems to be a difference of opinion between the Tur and the Rambam regarding how we are to determine the halacha here. The Tur maintains that although the halacha is determined according to the opinion of Rav Yossi, yet the common practice is to follow the opinion of Rav Yehudah, which is that "פקדונות" are not considered to be "זכרונות". He states this view in סימן תקצא:

וה' פקד את שרה' עולה במקום זכרונות...דברי ר' יוסי. ר' יהודה אומר אינו כזכרונות. והלכה כר' יוסי ומכל מקום נהגו כר' יהודה.

" 'And Hashem visited Sarah'. Here visitation is equivalent to remembrance...so says Rav Yossi. Rav Yehudah says that it is not like remembrance. And the halacha follows the opinion of Rav Yossi, although the custom is according to the opinion of Rav Yehudah."

The Rambam, in Hilchos Shofar 3:9 writes as follows:

"ופקדונות אינן כזכרונות."

"Visitation *is not* equivalent to "remembrance".

The Rambam seems to simply reject the verses of "פקדונות", since the halacha is determined according to the opinion of Rav Yehudah. It is important to clarify the thinking behind each of these opinions, and also the following questions need to be answered.

1) In Eruvim 46b we find the halachic principle that whenever Rav Yossi and Rav Yehudah disagree, Rav Yossi's opinion is accepted: "ר' יוסי ור' יהודה הלכה כר' יוסי". Why, then, does the Rambam accept the halachic opinion of Rav Yehudah here as the decisive one?

2) And indeed, if, as the Tur contends, the law is halachically decided according to the opinion of Rav Yossi, how can this be set aside by mere "custom" and the

opinion of Rav Yehudah accepted instead? For the halacha tells us that if one wishes to be stringent (מחמיר), in the manner of Shammai, this is not permitted. How, then, can we follow the more stringent opinion of Rav Yehudah here, when the halacha follows the more lenient opinion of Rav Yossi?

There are several possible answers to these questions.

1) The Bais Yosef contends that since we have many verses in the Torah in which the key word is "זכרון", and everyone agrees that a verse which includes this word is to be preferred over other verses, we may reject any other word or phrase, even if its meaning is similar. And to answer the question of how we can accept a more stringent opinion when the halacha directs us to be more lenient, Rav Gustman, זצ"ל, offers the following solution. The reason we do not adopt a stringent view is because if we were to do so, this would constitute an affront to the opinion which the halacha determined we should follow. However, if we can follow the more stringent view without any disrespect to the lenient view, then we are permitted to do this. Consequently, in this situation, since there are many verses which contain the key word "זכרון", we are not causing any affront to the view of Rav Yossi, for one could say that the reason we do not include the key word "פקוד" is

because there is no need for this, since we have a sufficient number of verses to choose from already. Therefore, if we accept Rav Yehudah's view, this does not imply that we are rejecting Rav Yossi's contention that we can use verses of "זכרונות" if we wished to do so.

2) The רלב"ח (cited here in the commentary of the פרישה) suggests that even Rav Yossi admits that it is *preferable* to use the verses of "זכרונות", even though he does allow the verses of "פקדונות". Therefore, as we have pointed out, we are not rejecting Rav Yossi's opinion when we accept that of Rav Yehudah, since that opinion is actually included within his broader one.

"ולי נראה לומר שאפילו רבי יוסי אפשר דמודה דלכתחלה עדיף טפי להזכיר זכרונות בהדיה" (מהרלב"ח).

Here, too, we will attempt to clarify each of these answers. And in conclusion, we may cite another apparent conflict of opinion among the Rishonim.

The Tur maintains that "פקדונות" can count for or take the place of "remembrances": "פקדונות...עולה במקום זכרונות".

The ר"ח, on the other hand, tells us, in ר"ה לב, ב, that "פקדונות" can be quoted *together with* "זכרונות":

"ואם בא להזכירו 'עם' הזכרונות".

The Tur, however, contends that it can be quoted not together with, but only *in place of* זכרונות. We will attempt to discover the basis for the difference between these two approaches.

II

Equivalent or only similar in meaning?

The following insights will help us clarify our previous questions. What did Rav Yossi mean when he said that: "פקדונות הרי הן כזכרונות"? Did he mean that both "פקדונות" and "זכרונות" are exactly equivalent in meaning: היינו הם; or did he mean rather that they have similar meanings which allude to the same concept?

If we accept the second possibility, that they are similar but not equal in meaning, then this would imply that Rav Yossi takes an approach similar to his way of reading the pasuk "שמע ישראל", where he maintains that this is an appropriate foundation for the verses of מלכיות, although it does not contain the key word, "מלך". But the reason it can be used is that it expresses the same concept, that of kingship. This is comparable to the situation here, too, for although we require the key word "זכרון", yet "פקדונות" is considered equivalent, for they both express the same concept.

In light of this explanation, we might conjecture that the Tur, whose text reads: "עולה במקום זכרונות", that one can *take the place* of the other, means that "פקדונות" and "זכרונות" are considered to be exactly the same. This raises the question: if this is the case, why do we follow the opinion of Rav Yehudah that we are to reject "פקדונות", when the halacha follows the opinion of Rav Yossi?

To answer this we can apply the rationale of the רלב״ח, that even Rav Yossi admits that לכתחילה, at the outset, we should prefer not to utilize the verses of "פקדונות", and therefore we generally adopt the custom of not utilizing these verses if at all possible.

The Rambam is of the opinion that "פקדונות" are not to be considered exactly the same as "זכרונות", yet since the theme of both is the same, we can join verses of "פקדונות" together with (עם) verses of "זכרונות". But this leaves us with the same question: if the halacha follows the opinion of Rav Yossi, why do we adopt the view of Rav Yehudah and say, "פקדונות אינן כזכרונות"? To answer this, we can apply the thinking of the Bais Yosef that since we have numerous verses available which contain the key word "זכרון", we need not use the verses of "פקדונות". However, regarding the verses required as a foundation for the מלכיות, we may indeed adopt the pasuk of "שמע ישראל" as a legitimate verse on which to base מלכיות, even at the outset. For, as the Gemara tells us in relation to the verses of the מלכיות, we have only three verses available that contain the key word "מלך". Therefore, we are forced to adopt this pasuk, even though it does not contain the key word, since the theme of the pasuk is the same.

III

Thought before action: does Hashem ever forget?

Just before the recitation of the Akeidah, we recite the following supplication:

"או"א...זכרנו בזכרון טוב לפניך, ופקדנו בפקדת ישועה ורחמים משמי שמי קדם..."

"Hashem, the God of our forefathers, remember us with a favorable remembrance before You and recall us with a recollection of salvation and mercy..."

What is the difference between "זכרון" and "פקידה", don't both allude to "remembrance"? (See קונטרס פרי טוב מהרב יעקב חיים סופר, עמ' ה).

The מהרש"א, in his commentary on Mesechtas Rosh Hashanah 32b, explains the rationale of Rav Yehudah in rejecting the equation of "זכרון" and "פקידה". He writes that

"זכירה" alludes to something constant, תמיד; whereas "פקידה" refers to a specific event that occurred at a particular time, "ענין מה לזמן מה".

The Malbim, on the other hand, defines the discrepancy differently. "זכרון — היינו כאשר במחשבה עולה הדבר", that the matter entered one's mind; and "ופקדון — היינו כשהזכרון יוצא לפועל במעשה", that which was thought about was brought to fruition. Therefore we pray, "זכרנו בזכרון טוב לפניך", that Hashem should regard us with a favorable memory, and "ופקדנו בפקודת ישועה ורחמים", that He should then show us salvation and mercy.

However, Rav Yaakov Sofer (op. cit.) asks: if this is so, why does the prayer of "יעלה ויבוא", according to נוסח ספרד, read as follows: "יעלה ויבוא...וכו' ויפקד ויזכר", "May there rise, come, etc....*be considered* and be remembered." For if "זכרון" alludes to thought and "פקידה" to action, then the order should have been reversed, and we should say: "ויזכר ויפקד". In addition, at the end of this prayer we say, "זכרנו ה' לטובה ופקדנו בו לברכה". Here the order is first זכרון and then פקידה. How do we account for this change from what was said at the beginning?

To answer these difficulties, we might suggest the following. How can we petition Hashem to "remember", when we know that He never "forgets" anything, even momentarily? The answer must be that when we petition the Almighty on Rosh Hashanah, we are asking Him to act on His memory of past events and to bring to the forefront those events from the past. Thus we might suggest that the words "זכרון ופקידה" allude to a distinction between past and present. When we refer to the present and the future, we ask Hashem to first consider our immediate petitions and to act upon these "new" thoughts. Thus here we can see a difference between "זכרון ופקידה". For now we can employ the distinction of the Malbim, that זכרון refers to thoughts that "enter one's mind", and פקידה to "acting on those thoughts". However, when we call for זכרונות on Rosh Hashanah, we refer to that which transpired in the past, and so "זכרון" and "פקידה" in this case are indeed the same.

Thus we can see that "יעלה ויבוא" is added in the Avodah section of our prayers, and therefore, when we come to recite this petition of "יעלה ויבוא", we are asking that Hashem reinstate our Bais HaMikdash, which already existed in the past. And so, in this case, both זכרון and פקודה are equivalent. However, at the end of this prayer we petition that He remember us at present, which, as we have explained, means that He should regard us with favorable thoughts and also "פקדנו", bring our prayers to fruition. In this case, זכרון comes before ופקדנו.

Kol Nidre

I
Why begin with Kol Nidre?

Just before sunset on the eve of Yom Kippur, we begin the Yom Kippur prayer service by reciting "כל נדרי". This has become one of the most familiar prayers in our liturgy, and it is well-known even among non-Jews. We approach this prayer with great solemnity, and it is considered one of the most important prayers of the Jewish year. The significance of this prayer and the fact that we recite it just before sunset on the eve of Yom Kippur lead to the following questions.

1) Kol Nidre absolves us of all oaths sworn during the year and not fulfilled. But weren't we absolved of all our vows, oaths and promises (נדרים) just a few days earlier on Rosh Hashanah, when we recited "התרת נדרים"? The purpose of that prayer was also to nullify vows. Isn't it superfluous to say Kol Nidre now to be absolved of all our vows and promises once again?

2) Kol Nidre ushers in Yom Kippur, the most solemn day of the year. But why do we inaugurate it with such a seemingly marginal prayer, which serves the practical

purpose of absolving the congregation of their unfulfilled vows. Wouldn't it have been appropriate to begin this most solemn of days with something more profound? Indeed, many recite the moving prayer of "תפלת זכה" just before the beginning of Yom Kippur. This prayer contains all the fitting words and emotions with which one should approach this day — words of remorse and regret for one's sins of the past year. Why, then, do we begin with Kol Nidre?

II

Two versions of Kol Nidre

Rav Yosef Dov Soloveitchik explains the meaning and purpose of Kol Nidre and why it is fitting that it serve as the opening prayer of Yom Kippur.

There are two versions of Kol Nidre, one by Rav Amram Gaon and the other by Rabbenu Tam. Rav Amram Gaon's text reads as follows:

"מיום כפורים שעבר עד יום הכפורים הזה הבא עלינו".

"All vows...from last Yom Kippur until the present Yom Kippur are to be retroactively nullified."

We nullify the vow rather than doing teshuvah for not fulfilling it (or letting the day of Yom Kippur itself atone for it through its power to absolve all sins), since teshuvah involves two prerequisites:

1) Regret over the past: חרטה

2) Resolving to avoid repetition of the sin in the future: קבלה

The essence of חרטה is a sense of shame, בושה. One is unable to look at oneself in the mirror without feeling ashamed. In the first chapter, the first halacha, of Hilchos Teshuvah, the Rambam discusses the formulation of Vidui (The Confession):

"והרי נחמתי ובושתי במעשי" "and I regret and am *ashamed* of my deeds..."

Since חרטה requires בושה, it is not enough for the penitent merely to seek atonement, כפרה. He also must feel that he is morally defiled and wishes to uproot his past sins. This applies to all his sins, apart from any oaths or vows he might have violated. Other than praying for atonement on Yom Kippur, one cannot erase one's desecration of the Shabbos, חילול שבת, for example, or the eating of non-kosher food, אכילת טריפה. However, it is possible to annul one's vows retroactively before one sins by not honoring them. Thus we are required to annul all vows, and when we do this we demonstrate that we feel a sense of shame about our sins and wish to repent. Without this feeling of shame, our teshuvah would not be effective, for it would be lacking a crucial component.

Rabbenu Tam changed the text of Kol Nidre from the past to the future tense. His text reads:

"כל נדרי...מיום כפורים זה עד יום כפורים הבא עלינו לטובה."

"All vows...*which will take place* between this Yom Kippur and the next Yom Kippur."

Whereas the text of Rav Amram Gaon highlights the component of חרטה, relating to the past, that of Rabbenu Tam focuses on the element of קבלה, one's resolve for the future. In truth, a sense of repentance is better served by commiting oneself to the future than by dwelling on the mistakes of the past. The Rambam recognized this, and therefore he writes in the second chapter, first halacha, of Hilchos Teshuvah as follows:

"איזו היא תשובה גמורה, זה שבא לידו דבר שעבר בו...ואפשר בידו לעשותו ופירש ולא עשה מפני התשובה..."

To conclude, we can say that the reason we recite Kol Nidre at the beginning of Yom Kippur is to express a feeling of shame as an essential part of our regret for past sins. This is in accordance with Rav Amram Gaon's emphasis on the past in his version of the prayer. And Kol Nidre also takes us into the future, where we make a commitment to distance ourselves from sin. This focus on the קבלה aspect is reflected in Rabbenu Tam's version of Kol Nidre.

III
The significance of Kol Nidre

HaRav Shimon Schwab, ז״ל, makes an interesting observation. In the Torah we find that the chapter of Nedarim, which deals with the laws concerning vows, is placed just before the war between Yisrael and its enemy, Midian. One possible reason for placing it specifically here is that at a moment of crisis, it is typical of human nature that a person vows that if he is saved from danger, he will repay his good fortune in some way. Thus the Torah saw fit to detail the laws of Nedarim here, just before the declaration of war against Midian, so that Bnai Yisrael would be fully aware of the laws governing the making of vows, and they should be prepared for the consequences if these vows are not fulfilled.

We might further point out that since it is human nature to make vows at a time of crisis, there might be a tendency for one to make new vows now, at the critical moment just before the awesome Day of Atonement, when one is about to stand before the Highest Judge. Even though one's previous vows were annulled on the eve of Rosh Hashanah, one might want to renew them now in the hope of being judged favorably on Yom Kippur and receiving the Divine Mercy which awaits one. Kol Nidre is a firm reminder that what Hashem wants is not "empty promises" or "crocodile tears". He rather seeks words that truly emanate from the depths of the human heart and soul — true remorse and regret for past transgressions and a sincere desire to commit oneself to a future of righteous deeds.

From this we can understand that the ceremony of the nullification of vows is not primarily the result of fear that one might not fulfill them, but rather a sign that we are rejecting such vows because they do not reflect sincere teshuvah. A deep, genuine soul searching is what is required here, and Kol Nidre reminds us of our true priorities.

"ברוך שם כבוד מלכותו לעולם ועד":
Said Aloud on Yom Kippur

I
The source for this practice

During the rest of the year, this declaration, which follows the Shema, is recited silently. Only on Yom Kippur are we permitted to say these words aloud. The Gemara in Pesachim 56a is the source for the halacha that these words must be whispered all year.

"דאמר רשב"ל: 'ויקרא יעקב אל בניו ויאמר האספו ואגידה לכם' [בראשית מט] ביקש יעקב לגלות לבניו קץ הימים ונסתלקה ממנו שכינה. אמר שמא חס ושלום יש במטתי פסול כאברהם שיצא ממנו ישמעאל ואבי יצחק שיצא ממנו עשו. אמרו לו בניו שמע ישראל ה' אלקינו ה' אחד. אמרו כשם שאין בלבך אלא אחד כך אין בלבנו אלא אחד. באותה שעה פתח יעקב אבינו ואמר ברוך שם כבוד מלכותו לעולם ועד.

אמרי רבנן: היכי נעביד, נאמרוהו, לא אמרו משה רבינו. לא נאמרוהו, אמרו יעקב. התקינו שיהו אומרים אותו בחשאי. אמר רבי יצחק אמרי דבי רב אמי משל לבת מלך שהריחה ציקי קדירה. אם תאמר, יש לה גנאי. לא תאמר יש לה צער. התחילו עבדיה להביא לה בחשאי:

אמר רבי אבהו התקינו שיהו אומרים אותו בקול רם מפני תערומת המינין ובנהרדעא דליכא מיני עד השתא אמרי לה בחשאי."

"R' Shimon ben Lakish explained: and Yaakov called to his sons and said: Gather yourselves together that I may tell you what will be in the end of days. Yaakov wished to reveal to his sons the 'end of the days', whereupon the Divine Presence departed from him. Said he, Perhaps, Heaven forbid, there is among my children one who is not fit, like my grandfather Avraham from whom there issued Ishmael, like my father Yitzchak from whom there issued Esav. His sons then answered him: 'Hear O' Israel, the Lord our God is One'. Just as there is one God in your heart, so is there in our hearts only One. At that moment our father Yaakov opened his mouth and exclaimed: 'Blessed be the Name of His glorious Kingdom forever and ever.' Said the Sages: How shall we act? Shall we recite it [בשכמל"ו] aloud? But our teacher [Moshe Rabbenu] did not say it. Shall we not say it? But Yaakov our father said it? Hence they enacted that it should be said quietly.

R' Yitzchak said: the School of Rav Ammi said: This is to be compared to a king's daughter who smelled a spicy pudding and conceived a strong desire for it. If she reveals her desire, she suffers disgrace. If she does not reveal it, she suffers pain. So her servants began bringing it to her in secret.

R' Avuhu said: The Sages enacted this [בשכמל"ו] should be said aloud on account of the resentment of the heretics. But in Neharda, where there are no heretics thus far, they recite it quietly."

The source for the halacha that on Yom Kippur this declaration can be said aloud is a midrash in Parashas V'Eschanan quoted by the Tur in סימן תרי"ט:

"כשעלה משה לרקיע שמע מלאכי השרת שהיו מקלסין להקב"ה ברוך שם כבוד מלכותו לעולם ועד, והורידו לישראל. למה הדבר דומה: לאדם שגנב הורמין (פ' חפץ נאה) מתוך פלטרין של מלך ונתנו לאשתו, ואמר לה: אל תתקשטי בו אלא בצנעה, בתוך ביתך, לכן כל השנה אומרים אותו בלחש, וביום הכפורים אומרים אותו בפרהסיא לפי שאנו כמלאכים."

"When Moshe ascended to Heaven he heard the ministering angels saying to God: Blessed be the Name of His glorious Kingdom, forever and ever. This declaration Moshe brought down to Bnai Yisrael. This can be compared to a man who stole jewelry from the royal palace which he gave to his wife, telling her: Do not wear these in public, but only in the house. So, too, we recite it [בשכמל"ו] silently a whole year. But on the Day of Atonement, when Yisrael is as pure as the ministering angels, they recite it publicly. 'Blessed be the Name of His glorious Kingdom forever and ever.' "

II

Moshe "stole" it from the angels

The אליהו זוטא, in his commentary on the above-mentioned Tur, raises the following questions.

1) Why does the Tur need to quote the midrash as the source for saying בשכמל"ו silently during the rest of the year when he himself, in סימן סא cites a different reason, namely that "Moshe Rabbenu did not say it", from the Gemara in Pesachim 56a.

2) If we accept the rationale of this Gemara in Pesachim, as the Tur does in סימן סא, not only do we have the above mentioned difficulty, but it also would seem to indicate that even on Yom Kippur one still should say the בשכמל"ו silently, for the very reason that Moshe Rabbenu did not say it. Why, then, rely on the reason given in the midrash, which is that Moshe Rabbenu 'stole' it from the angels, and therefore on Yom Kippur, when we resemble angels (because we are engrossed in prayer all day and neither eat not drink) we can say it aloud?

Before attempting to answer these questions which the אליהו זוטא raises, we must ask: What was it that Moshe Rabbenu "stole" from the angels and brought down from Heaven to add to our earthly prayers? It seems from the midrash which the Tur quotes that Moshe brought words of praise which belonged exclusively to the angels and were never heard here below. However, we know from the above-quoted Gemara in Pesachim that Yaakov Aveinu's children heard these same words of praise when their father Yaakov made this declaration on his deathbed after they recited in unison the Shema Yisrael. What, then, was unique about Moshe's discovery?

The following insight by the נתיבות, in his sefer "נחלת יעקב על התורה" suggests an answer to the question why Moshe did not also say the בשכמל"ו aloud. Before the giving of Torah on Mount Sinai to Bnai Yisrael, our forefathers served Hashem by acknowledging that there was but one God in the world and that He was the Creator of everything in heaven and earth, אחדות הבורא. They glorified God's Name in this world by declaring that He was Master of the Universe. In turn, Bnai Yisrael experienced miracles beyond the laws of nature to assure their continued existence and Divine Protection. After Matan Torah, however, in addition to their required belief in one God, they were obligated to accept 613 Commandments. And so now this declaration of בשכמל"ו which articulated their acceptance of the yoke of heaven, קבלת עול מלכות, was no longer enough to show their commitment; they also had to take upon themselves the yoke of Torah and Mitzvos. This is the reason Moshe Rabbenu did not include this declaration of בשכמל"ו in his reading of the Shema.

Consequently, what Moshe brought down from heaven was a new concept of בשכמל"ו, which was that since the angels are not required to observe the 613 Mitzvos, and yet they proclaimed בשכמל"ו, this declaration does not only signify the acceptance of קבלת עול מלכות, but is rather a unique kind of praise to Hashem. This is the new form of praise that Moshe brought down from Heaven, and because he stole it from the angels, Bnai Yisrael had to recite בשכמל"ו silently. And so, when Yaakov Aveinu recited this declaration, he meant something different. For he was alluding to the קבלת עול מלכות; whereas the בשכמל"ו of Moshe Rabbenu alluded to a unique form of praise being offered to Hashem which comes straight from Heaven.

With this approach in mind, we can explain the Gemara in Pesachim in the following way. The Chachamim did not know whether or not to include the בשכמל"ו in our reading of the Shema, since Moshe Rabbenu did not include it. The reason Moshe did not include it was because after Matan Torah this declaration did not suffice to express the acceptance of the yoke of Heaven; for that now included much more — the observance of 613 Mitzvos. On the other hand, it would have been a problem as well to have completely ignored this declaration of בשכמל״ו, for Yaakov Aveinu did say it, and his declaration of praise should not be considered any less significant than that of the angels. And so we do say it, but silently, since the בשכמל״ו is now essentially praise rather than a declaration of קבלת עול מלכות. Thus we recite it silently, just as Moshe Rabbenu did. On Yom Kippur, though, when Bnai Ysrael are compared to angels, they are permitted to say it aloud.

Thus the Gemara in Pesachim was aware of the words of the midrash and is not to be taken as a separate reason for reciting בשכמל״ו silently; rather the Gemara complements the words of the midrash. This answers the questions of the אליהו זוטא regarding the seeming contradiction of the Tur's position.

III
Is it inferior to the Shema?

This clarification might help us resolve yet another apparent discrepancy regarding the position of the בשכמל״ו. From the standpoint of the Gemara in Pesachim, בשכמל״ו seems to be inferior to the declaration of the Shema itself. The Gemara compares its recitation to a princess who inhaled the aroma of a spicy pudding, "בת מלך שהריחה ציקי

"קדירה. If she reveals her desire she will suffer disgrace. From this we see that בשכמל״ו is considered to be inferior to the Shema. For it is likened to a "spicy pudding". However, the position seems to be reversed in the midrash, where בשכמל״ו is compared to a "jewel", "חפץ נאה", which only the angels may possess. How are we to reconcile this apparent contradiction?

We find a similar contradiction regarding the value of בשכמל״ו in the Maharal's sefer "נתיבות עולם" (נתיב העבודה, פרק ז). The Maharal writes as follows:

"וברכה זו [של בשכמל״ו] אינו ראוי רק למי שאינו גשמי, וראוי הברכה הזאת לעליונים אשר הם בלא גוף והם נבדלים..."

The Nefesh Hachaim, however, in שער ג', has another opinion:

"דלפי האמת אינו שבח כלל, כמו האם יחשב לשבח למלך בשר ודם לומר שהוא מולך על רבי רבבות נמלים ויתושים. והם מקבלים עליהם עול מלכותו ברצון. כל שכן וקל וחומר אין ערך כלל שהוא יתברך אשר אין ערוך לקדושתו ועוצם אחדותו הפשוט וכל העולמות כלא חשיבין קמאי, ודאי באמת אינו שבח כלל שנשבחוהו יתברך שהוא ברוך ומפואר בכבוד מלכותו על עולמות נבראים שכולם שפלים ולא חשיבין קמיה כלל.

רק שהוא יתברך במקום גדולתו תמצא ענוותנותו שגזרה רצונו לקבלו מאתנו לשבח, לזאת המשילוהו ז״ל לציקי קדירה, והתקינו על כל פנים לא נאמרהו אלא בחשאי."

According to the Nefesh Hachaim, the בשכמל"ו is to be considered like the spicy pudding, and therefore inferior to the Shema (See the sefer "פחד יצחק", יום כפורים, מאמר ה' עמ' עג-פ).

In light of our above discussion, however, we could say that בשכמל"ו is viewed as inferior to accepting the yoke of heaven, קבלת עול מלכות, with all its implications, for, as we have discussed, after the Torah was given on Mount Sinai the declaration of בשכמל"ו was no longer sufficient to signify one's acceptance of the yoke of Heaven. Rather the acceptance of Torah and Mitzvos are also required. On the other hand, in relation to the "קילוס ה'" ("praising Hashem"), the declaration of בשכמל"ו is considered a jewel from Heaven, which only the angels are capable of uttering. This means that the concluding statement in the Gemara compares the בשכמל"ו, when said in the context of קבלת עול מלכות, to a princess who must be silent about her desire for spicy pudding, just as we say the בשכמל"ו silently, to show that it is not sufficient to fulfill our obligation. And so we conclude that it should be said as Moshe Rabbenu said it, in a whisper, for it is praise which comes straight from Heaven and only the angels, who are not committed in Torah and Mitzvos, can say it aloud.

IV

Why we do not recite it aloud the rest of the year

The Rambam in פרק א' מהלכות קריאת-שמע הלכה ד' states:

"הקורא קריאת-שמע כשהוא גומר פסוק ראשון, אומר בלחש, ברוך שם כבוד מלכותו לעולם ועד'. וחוזר וקורא כדרכו, ואהבת את ה' אלה-יך עד סופה..."

"When reciting the Shema after completing the first verse, one says quietly, 'Blessed be the name of His glorious Kingdom forever.' He then continues to read the first section in his usual manner, 'And you shall love Hashem, your Lord'..."

The Brisker Rav, Rav Velvele, זצ"ל, questions the intention of the phrase, "he then continues to read in the usual manner." What does the Rambam mean here by this statement? What constitutes "כדרכו", in the usual manner, and what is considered "שלא כדרכו", not in the usual manner? The Brisker Rav answers that this statement of בשכמל"ו shares certain halachos with the laws pertaining to the reading of the first verse of the Kriyas Shema. Yet this halachic equivalence only pertains to such laws as having the proper intention, "כוונה והפסק", and the warning not to interrupt the reading of these statements. For both these requirements apply to the Mitzva of accepting the yoke of the kingdom of Heaven upon oneself, קבלת עול מלכות. However, since the בשכמל״ו is not a pasuk from the Torah, the law does not apply here that one must be very careful to pronounce each word and letter as written, לדקדק באותיותה.

Consequently, the Rambam informs us here that after we complete reciting the statement of בשכמל״ו, which, as we have just said, does not require that we concentrate on an exact reading of every word and letter, we return "to complete the other chapters of the Kriyas Shema", where we must once again concentrate on pronouncing the words exactly as they are written in the Torah.

We might suggest that the rationale behind this statement, that he then continues to read in the usual manner, is based on the following statements of the מהרש״א and the צל״ח. Both commentators explain the statement of the Gemara in Pesachim 56a, that "Moshe did not say it [בשכמל״ו]" to mean that the inclusion of this declaration in the Kriyas Shema constitutes an interruption, הפסק, in the reading of the Shema. Any interruption invalidates the Mitzva of reciting Kriyas Shema. Therefore, if one recites this declaration of בשכמל"ו silently, one would not invalidate a continuous reading of the Shema. The צל"ח explains this as follows:

"נאמרה, לא אמר משה: יש לדקדק ואטו שבח אחד יש לנו שאנו אומרים מה שלא אמרו משה, וכמה פיוטים שאנו אומרים שחברו הפייטנים, ולא יהי' יעקב אבינו כאחד הפייטנים שניחוש מלומר השבח ששיבח סבא קדישא ישראל סבא עבור שלא אמרו משה. לכן נלע"ד שעיקר הקפידה שנפסיק באמצע דברי משה בשבח שלא אמרו הוא, כמו בשכמל"ו, שאנו מפסיקין בו בין שמע לואהבת, בזה יש קפידא שלא אמרו משה...שוב מצאתי במהרש"א בח"א [בחידושי אגדות] שכתב ג"כ שעיקר קפידא משום הפסק באמצע דברי משה."

He explains here that in order to avoid a הפסק, an interruption, we read the Shema silently, בלחש. Therefore, after the Rambam mentions that we must read the בשכמל"ו silently, he then points out that when we return and continue reading the Shema as written in the Torah, then we must read it "in its usual manner", כדרכו, which means that we must read it clearly and loudly. For in order to show that the בשכמל"ו is not part of our reading from the Torah, we read it in a different manner. For if we were to read it in the same manner as we do the rest of the verses of the Kriyas Shema, then we would have no indication that it has a different source and would constitute an interruption in the required reading of the Shema. This means that the Rambam is suggesting that we return to our normal manner of reading, to tell us that we are required to read Shema differently. For otherwise we would have no indication that בשכמל״ו is not an integral part of the Torah based text of the Shema. And so, by reciting it in a whisper, we avoid the halachic problem of interrupting our required continuous reading.

V
Why it is not part of Malchyius

The Shema constitutes one of the pasukim of מלכיות, with its theme of Hashem as the Sovereign of the Universe. HaRav Shlomo Fisher, שליט״א, in the Torah journal, "ישורון", חלק ב, maintains that the Gemara in Pesachim 56a seems to indicate that whenever we mention the Shema we join the declaration of בשכמל״ו to it. Why, then, if we include the Shema in the verses of מלכיות, do we not include this declaration of בשכמל״ו as well?

We might suggest the following answer. The מהרש״ל, in his classic commentary on the sefer of the סמ״ג (מצוה ה') defines the ramifications of the Mitzva of belief in God, אמונה בה׳. There are two components to this Mitzva.

1) One must have faith in God based on what he has been taught by his forefathers. One's faith must therefore be rooted in the religion of one's ancestors.

2) One must become convinced on his own, by logical proof, of the truth of the Creator's existence.

"מצוות עשה להאמין...פירוש צריך שניהם, אמונה וקבלה. כי אמונה על דרך התולדה שמגודל בה כל ימי מנעוריו, ומ"מ אף שנשתקע באמונת שמים, אין יוצא בה על ידי חובתו. אלא כששמע וקבל בלבו הקבלה שהיא המופת על הראיה...וכן כתב בעל הנצחון, שאין אדם יוצא באמונה אא"כ למד ספר מדע. ומ"מ קשה לסמוך על המופת לבד אם לא שיהא אמונה תקועה בלבו מן התולדה, אז מספיק הראיה, אף שיש ספרים הרבה.

וסיוע לזה, שמע ישראל וגו' שאמרו בני יעקב לאביהם, כדאיתא בגמ'. וגם לבני יעקב היה האמונה על דרך התולדה מנעוריהם, אלא שהיה מסופק בהם, שלא ידע אם היה מופת להם מספיק לפי דעתם. לכך אמרו לו שמע ישראל', כשם שאין בלבך וכו' עכ"ל המהרש"ל."

The מהרש"ל here explains the intention of the Gemara in Pesachim 56a, that Yaakov Aveinu feared that his sons' belief in God was rooted primarily in the teachings of their father Yaakov and their grandfather, Yitzchak Aveinu. Yet perhaps they lacked faith in Hashem based on their own logical and philosophical reasoning. Thus, Yaakov's sons reassured him when they declared "שמע ישראל...אל-הינו", that Hashem was their God based on the fact that they had arrived at the truth of His existence on their own initiative.

Rav Fisher concludes that the Gemara explains that when Yaakov Aveinu heard their declaration of "שמע ישראל", his response of בשכמל"ו signified that although it was commendable for them to have come to their belief in God through their own intellectual reasoning, חקירה, yet this must be accompanied by belief which is rooted in tradition.

In light of this insight, we might answer the question posed by HaRav Fisher as to why we do not join the pasuk of שמע ישראל with the statement of בשכמל"ו in the verses of מלכיות, by saying that when we read the Kriyas Shema, we are only required to mention both שמע ישראל and בשכמל"ו in the morning and in the evening, as a statement of our acceptance of the yoke of Heaven, קבלת עול מלכות שמים. And we have seen that, according to the insight of the מהרש"ל, that acceptance of the yoke of Heaven requires belief in Hashem based on tradition, coupled with belief based on one's own logical and philosophical reasoning. Therefore, as explained by the מהרש"ל, both the Shema and the בשכמל"ו allude to these two aspects. However, in the verses of מלכיות, all that is required is an allusion to the concept of מלכיות — that Hashem is the Universal Sovereign, and this is accomplished by reciting the verses of the Shema.

Therefore the additional declaration of בשכמל"ו is not needed here and thus we do not recite it.

VI
When are we compared to angels?

HaRav Yehudah Leib Auerbach (father of HaRav Shlomo Zalman Auerbach) made the following observation. On the night of Yom Kippur, we enter the synagogue after a day of eating and drinking, which is required on erev Yom Kippur. However, not long after, we recite aloud the declaration of בשכמל"ו, for we are now compared to angels. And yet, on motzei Yom Kippur, after spending a whole day in prayer, fasting and teshuvah, in the Maariv prayer of that evening we no longer say the בשכמל"ו out loud. This seems strange, for it would appear that the opposite should have occurred. For on this night of Yom Kippur, when we just began fasting, we might have thought that we would not be viewed as having reached the level of angels. However, after an entire night and day of acting like angels, we might think that now we should be viewed as angels and be able to recite the declaration of בשכמל"ו aloud. And yet we find that the exact opposite is true.

To explain this, we could say that a person is not to be measured spiritually according to the way he stands before us physically, but rather he should be judged by the condition of his heart and mind. On Yom Kippur night, we look forward to a day of repentance, prayer and fasting, and thus we can be viewed here and now as angels. At the end of Yom Kippur, however, after an entire day of prayer and fasting, our minds are set on breaking the fast as soon as possible, and thus we can no longer be looked upon as angels, as we naturally return to a preoccupation with our physical needs.

The Nusach of the Yom Kippur Amidah

I
How is it different from the other holidays?

The Rambam describes the nusach of the Yom Kippur prayers in his "Order of the Prayers Throughout the Year", "סדר תפלות כל השנה", which is found at the end of "ספר אהבה". There he writes:

"ברכה אמצעית של צום יום הכפורים בערבית ושחרית ומנחה ונעילה אתה בחרתנו כו' ותתן לנו ה' אלקינו את יום הכפורים הזה ואת יום מקראי קדש הזה..."

"The middle section of the Amidah prayer on Yom Kippur reads: 'You have chosen us...and You gave us *this day of Atonement* and *this day of holy convocation*'..."

He distinguishes between Yom Kippur and the other holidays, when we say something different.

"ותתן לנו...את יום טוב מקראי קדש הזה את יום חג המצות."

"You gave us this holiday of holy convocation, this holiday of Matzos."

From this we can see that in relation to the other holidays the name of the particular holiday follows the statement of "מקראי קדש", "a holy convocation". This difference leads us to ask these questions:

1) Why on Yom Kippur does the name of the holiday precede the phrase "מקראי קדש"; whereas on all other holidays this phrase comes before the name of the particular yom tov?

2) Why on Yom Kippur is there a *vav* (ו) added to the word "ואת" ("ואת יום מקראי קדש הזה"); whereas on the other holidays there is no connecting vav and we read simply:

"את יום מקראי קדש הזה" ?

In the Yom Kippur Mussaf prayers we find another difference from all the other holidays. For on the other holidays we say: "יום טוב מקרא קדש הזה יום חג הפלוני הזה". "A holiday of convocation", and then the name of the particular holiday. In the Mussaf prayer on Yom Kippur, however, we do not mention the name of the holiday at all, but say rather: "ואת מוספי יום מקרא קדש הזה". How do we account for this difference?

II
The uniqueness of Yom Kippur

We might suggest an answer based on what we have discussed elsewhere (See *The Commentators' Pesach*, pp. 37-40) concerning the final beracha which includes the word "והזמנים". ("מקדש ישראל והזמנים"). On Yom Kippur this word is not mentioned in the concluding beracha. The reason we gave there was that there is a fundamental difference between Yom Kippur and the three pilgrimage festivals, שלש רגלים, Succos, Pesach and Shavuos. The unique nature of Yom Kippur is based on the principle of: "עיצומו של יום מכפר", that *the day itself* offers atonement, even if one failed to observe the particular Mitzvos of the day, such as fasting, confession and prayer. Thus the appropriate concluding blessing must contain a special mention of Yom Kippur, and no mention of "והזמנים" is required. Regarding the three pilgrimage festivals, on the other hand, the days themselves have no special significance intrinsic in themselves, apart from the special meaning we give them when we sanctify them. Thus, on these days, we stress in the concluding beracha these special times, "והזמנים", and we say that it is "at these times" that one should eat matzah, or sit in a succah, etc. We accentuate that it is the "זמן", the special time, that is important. This means that when we name a festival, such as "חג המצות", the intention behind this act is to stress that on this day we should do certain special Mitzvos. For instance, on the festival of Pesach we eat matzos and offer the Korban Pesach. The essence of the day is the performance of these particular Mitzvos, rather than that this day is intrinsically holy, in the same sense that Yom Kippur as a spiritual entity is intrinsically holy.

With this in mind, we can attempt to answer our above questions. But first we must define the phrase of "מקראי קדש". It refers to the holiday itself and our obligation to do a particular Mitzva on that day. Consequently, there is a vast difference between Yom Kippur and the other holidays, for Yom Kippur is itself a day of atonement, even if we do nothing to call forth that atonement. And so, the fact that it is Yom Kippur, a day which achieves atonement because of its intrinsic holiness, "מקראי קדש", calls for fasting, and we act out what the day itself requires of us. This is the reason the name of the holiday, Yom Kippur, precedes the phrase "מקראי קדש", for it is the day itself which brings forth the holiness of the day, the "מקראי קדש".

In relation to the other holidays, however, the "מקראי קדש" comes first, because it is how we conduct ourselves regarding the particular Mitzva of the day that gives the holiday its unique character, "חג המצות". And this is why we say "מקראי קדש" before the name of the holiday.

We can now also understand why the connecting *vav* is added on Yom Kippur and not on the other holidays. For on Yom Kippur the "מקראי קדש", which includes fasting and prayer, is an "addition" to the day. But it is the day itself which is central and its essence — atonement — comes about by its very nature. On the other holidays, though, the "מקראי קדש", and the name of the holiday are equal and therefore we do not need the connecting *vav*.

With this in mind, we can appreciate the difference in the makeup of the prayers on Yom Kippur as compared to the other holidays. The above discussion relates only to the section of the קדושת היום, when we say "אתה בחרתנו", with the stress on the holiday and its subsequent specific Mitzvos: "מקראי קדש את יום חג המצות הזה". In the Mussaf prayer, on the other hand, the focus is on the special sacrifice of the day. This is not a result of the intrinsic character of the day, but rather depends on the aspect of "מקראי קדש", which calls for a Korban Mussaf offering.

This argument is explained in the sefer "בית אהרן" by HaGaon Rav Aaron Kohen. The author points out that in Parashas Pinchas the sacrifical offerings are enumerated, the korbanos which are required on each holiday. Concerning Yom Kippur, the Torah states: "ובעשור לחדש השביעי הזה מקרא קדש ... והקרבתם". Here in this parasha where the various holiday sacrifices are discussed, "Yom Kippur" is not mentioned, but instead we read: "מקרא קדש". And so too in our Mussaf prayer on Yom Kippur we do not mention Yom Kippur either, but only "מקראי קדש". The reason for this, as we have explained, is that the sacrifices of the day do not result from its being "יום כפור", but rather because of the intrinsic holiness of the day, "מקראי קדש". On the other holidays the situation is different, and both the sacrifice of that holiday and its special Mitzvos are equivalent to the "מקראי קדש", and it has no intrinsic holiness apart from our actions in sanctifying the particular day. This is the reason both the holiday and "מקראי קדש" are mentioned in the Mussaf prayer on the other holidays.

The Seder of the Avodah

During the time of the Bais HaMikdash, the Kohen Gadol's offering of korbanos, סדר עבודה, was of central importance on Yom Kippur, the holiest day of the year. For with this offering, the Kohen Gadol made atonement, כפרה, on behalf of Klal Yisrael. In the Torah, Hashem assured us that this atonement would be accepted. After the Temple was destroyed, however, we no longer have the ability to offer this סדר עבודה, and so it is our recitation of what the Kohen Gadol used to do that "compensates" for this service, "ונשלמה פרים שפתינו". When we finish recounting this סדר עבודה we recite the piyut of "אשרי עין", in which we read:

"אבל עונות אבותינו החריבו נוה, וחטאתינו האריכו קצו, אבל זכרון דברים תהא סליחותינו."

"But the iniquities of our fathers destroyed our home, and our sins have prolonged its period of captivity, yet may the *remembrance* of these things bring us pardon."

To appreciate the order of the Avodah, סדר עבודה, we may outline here the number of animals required for the sacrifices, and secondly, the sequence of the service. We must also answer the following questions.

1) Why is the prescribed order so crucial that if it is not followed exactly it invalidates the entire service?

2) Why is the service of the day of Yom Kippur explained in two separate sedras — (ויקרא טז) אחרי מות and במדבר כט:ט — rather than in a single sedra?

I
The animal sacrifices

Before attempting to answer these questions, we must enumerate all the animals required as sacrifices on the day of Yom Kippur, as well as their proper sequence as stipulated in the Torah in במדבר כט:ט and in ויקרא טז.

The Animals:

Seventeen animals were offered on Yom Kippur:

1) Two daily burnt offerings
2) Ten sacrifices offered as Mussafim
3) Five sacrifices offered as part of the special Yom Kippur sacrifices, חובת היום

Two daily burnt offerings:

1) תמיד של שחר
2) תמיד של בין הערבים

"את הכבש אחד תעשה בבקר ואת הכבש השני תעשה בין הערבים.." (במדבר כח,ד).

The Commentators' Machzor Companion

"One lamb sacrifice you are to perform in the morning, and the second lamb sacrifice you are to perform in the afternoon..."

Ten Mussafim:

3) פר - The burnt offering of an ox

4) איל - The burnt offering of a ram

5-11) שבעה כבשים - Seven lambs

12) שעיר - He-goat sin offering, the blood is sprinkled on the outer altar

"והקרבתם עולה לה' לריח ניחוח: פר בן בקר אחד, איל אחד, כבשים בני שנה שבעה תמימים...שעיר עזים אחד חטאת..."

"You shall offer as a burnt offering one *bull*, one *ram*, and seven *sheep*...and one *goat* for atonement."

Five Special Yom Kippur Sacrifices:

13) פר של כהן גדול - Kohen Gadol's sin offering of an ox

14) שעיר לה' - He-goat for Hashem, sin offering

15) איל של כהן גדול - the Kohen Gadol's burnt offering of a ram

16) איל של העם - the people's burnt offering of a ram

According to the Mishna in Yoma 7:3, this is the same ram as mentioned in the Mussafim (4).

17) שעיר לעזאזל - The he-goat sent to Azazel

(See chart in Section II)

We have enumerated here fifteen animals, yet the Rambam in פרק א מהלכות עבודת יום הכפורים הלכה א writes as follows:

"ביום הצום מקריבין תמיד בשחר ותמיד בין הערבים כסדר כל יום ויום. מקריבין מוסף היום פר ואיל ושבעה כבשים כולן עולות. ושעיר חטאת הנעשה בחוץ והוא נאכל בערב.

ועוד מקריבין יתר על מוסף זה, פר בן בקר לחטאת והוא נשרף, ואיל לעולה ושניהם מכהן גדול. ואיל הבא משל צבור האמור בפרשת אחרי מות. והוא האיל האמור בחומש הפקודים בכלל המוסף והוא הנקרא איל העם.

ועוד מביאין משל צבור שני שעירי עזים, אחד קרב חטאת והוא נשרף, והשני שעיר המשתלח.

נמצאו כל הבהמות הקרבים ביום זה חמשה עשר: שני תמידים, ופר, ושני אילים, ושבעה כבשים כולן עולות. ושני שעירים חטאת אחד נעשה בחוץ ונאכל לערב, והשני נעשה בפנים ונשרף, ופר כהן גדול לחטאת והוא נשרף."

"On this fast day, they offered the morning and evening Tamid as well as the Mussaf, consisting of one bull, one ram and seven sheep, all of which were burnt offerings. They also took a goat as an atonement offering, upon the outer altar.

In addition to the Mussaf, the Kohen Gadol donated a bull as an atonement offering, which was burnt outside the

Bais HaMikdash; and a ram as a burnt offering. The community offered the ram referred to in Parashas Acharei Mos (16:5), and that is the ram mentioned in Bamidbar (29:8) as part of the standard Mussaf offering.

Finally, the community brought two goats, one of which was burnt outside the Bais HaMikdash, and the other which was sent into the wilderness.

Thus *fifteen* animals were offered on this day. *Two* sheep as a Tamid, *one* bull, *two* rams, and *seven* sheep as burnt offerings, one which was offered on the outer altar and eaten at night, and the other, was sprinkled on the inside altar and burnt.

Finally, the Kohen Gadol offered one bull as an atonement offering which was burnt."

This raises a question: The Torah enumerated *seventeen* animals to be offered on Yom Kippur; why, then, does the Rambam list only fifteen? We might suggest the following answer to this problem:

1) The שעיר לעזאזל, the goat sent into the wilderness, is not considered to be a sacrifice, for then it would appear as though we are offering a sacrifice to the devil, God forbid.

2) The people's ram which is a burnt offering, and the ram which is mentioned as part of the Mussaf sacrifice, are

the same. This accounts for the fact that only fifteen actual sacrifices were offered on this day, although we count seventeen animals.

II
The sequence of the Avodah

The Kohen Gadol who was designated to perform the Yom Kippur service wore two sets of priestly garments, בגדי כהונה. He wore eight gold garments, בגדי זהב, when he performed the daily service. And he wore four linen garments, בגדי לבן, when he entered the Holy of Holies, the קדשי קדשים, and performed there the special Yom Kippur service, חובת היום. Each time he changed his garments he was required to immerse himself, טבילה, and thus we have five immersions on this day, חמש טבילות.

<u>The First Immersion:</u>

The Kohen Gadol changed from his everyday clothes into the golden vestments, בגדי זהב, even though this first immersion was not for the purpose of changing priestly garments, but rather to allow him to enter the Bais HaMikdash. This immersion, which was rabbinically ordained, was referred to as the *first immersion*.

After this immersion, the Kohen Gadol would offer the daily burnt offering followed by the daily routine, which consisted of preparing the five lamps of the Menorah, offering the daily incense, preparing the remaining two lamps of the Menorah, burning the limbs of the Tamid, the daily meal offering, the wine libation, the ox, and seven lambs of the Korban Mussaf.

All this was done while the Kohen Gadol wore his golden vestments.

The Second Immersion:

He then changed into the linen vestments, בגדי לבן, in order to perform the special Yom Kippur service, חובת היום, which included the following:

1) First confession on the Kohen Gadol's ox offering

2) Drawing lots to select a he-goat for Hashem and one for Azazel

3) Second confession on the Kohen Gadol's ox offering

4) Slaughter of the Kohen Gadol's ox offering

5) The unique Yom Kippur service of the incense, which included scooping up the coal, scooping the incense into the ladle, burning the incense in the Holy of Holies.

This was the Kohen Gadol's first entrance into the Holy of Holies.

6) Sprinkling the blood of the Kohen Gadol's ox in the Holy of Holies.

This was his second entry into the Holy of Holies.

7) Slaughtering the he-goat for Hashem

8) Sprinkling the he-goat's blood in the Holy of Holies

9) Sprinkling the blood of the Kohen Gadol's ox on the curtain, the פרוכת, within the holy Temple, the היכל

10) Sprinkling the he-goat's blood on the פרוכת in the היכל

11) Mixing the blood of the ox and the he-goat

12) Sprinkling the mixture of bloods on the inner altar

13) Confession (וידוי) on the he-goat to Azazel and its presentation to the person designated to dispatch it to Azazel, איש עתי

14) Removing the entrails of the Kohen Gadol's ox and the he-goat and placing them in a special utensil

15) Preparing the limbs of the Kohen Gadol's ox and the he-goat for removal to the place of burning

16) Reading from the Torah by the Kohen Gadol

The Third Immersion:

The Kohen Gadol changes into the golden vestments

17) He sacrifices the he-goat offering of the Mussafim

18) Offering of the Kohen Gadol's ram

19) Offering of the people's ram, which is the same as the ram sacrificed as a burnt offering at Mussaf

The Commentators' Machzor Companion

20) Burning the entrails of the ox and the he-goat on the outer altar

Fourth Immersion:

The Kohen Gadol dons the linen garments.

21) Removal of the incense ladle and the shovel, כף ומחתה, with the burning coals. This was the Kohen Gadol's fourth and final entry into the Holy of Holies.

Fifth Immersion:

22) The daily afternoon burnt offering
23) Burning the afternoon incense
24) Lighting the menorah

III
The sources from the Torah

The sequence of the חובת היום is based on the following verses found in Vayikra 16 (Acharei Mos). Please follow the footnotes which follow for explanations of this service.

ויקרא פרק טז

(א) וידבר ה' אל משה אחרי מות שני בני אהרן בקרבתם לפני ה' וימתו:

(ב) וַיֹּאמֶר ה' אֶל מֹשֶׁה דַּבֵּר אֶל אַהֲרֹן אָחִיךָ וְאַל יָבֹא בְכָל עֵת אֶל הַקֹּדֶשׁ מִבֵּית לַפָּרֹכֶת אֶל פְּנֵי הַכַּפֹּרֶת אֲשֶׁר עַל הָאָרֹן וְלֹא יָמוּת כִּי בֶּעָנָן אֵרָאֶה עַל הַכַּפֹּרֶת:

(ג) בְּזֹאת יָבֹא אַהֲרֹן אֶל הַקֹּדֶשׁ בְּפַר בֶּן בָּקָר לְחַטָּאת וְאַיִל לְעֹלָה:

(ד) כְּתֹנֶת בַּד קֹדֶשׁ יִלְבָּשׁ וּמִכְנְסֵי בַד יִהְיוּ עַל בְּשָׂרוֹ וּבְאַבְנֵט בַּד יַחְגֹּר וּבְמִצְנֶפֶת בַּד יִצְנֹף בִּגְדֵי קֹדֶשׁ הֵם וְרָחַץ בַּמַּיִם אֶת בְּשָׂרוֹ וּלְבֵשָׁם:

(ה) וּמֵאֵת עֲדַת בְּנֵי יִשְׂרָאֵל יִקַּח שְׁנֵי שְׂעִירֵי עִזִּים לְחַטָּאת וְאַיִל אֶחָד לְעֹלָה:

(ו) וְהִקְרִיב אַהֲרֹן אֶת פַּר הַחַטָּאת אֲשֶׁר לוֹ וְכִפֶּר בַּעֲדוֹ וּבְעַד בֵּיתוֹ:[1]

(ז) וְלָקַח אֶת שְׁנֵי הַשְּׂעִירִם וְהֶעֱמִיד אֹתָם לִפְנֵי ה' פֶּתַח אֹהֶל מוֹעֵד:

(ח) וְנָתַן אַהֲרֹן עַל שְׁנֵי הַשְּׂעִירִם גּוֹרָלוֹת[2] גּוֹרָל אֶחָד לַה' וְגוֹרָל אֶחָד לַעֲזָאזֵל:

(ט) וְהִקְרִיב אַהֲרֹן אֶת הַשָּׂעִיר אֲשֶׁר עָלָה עָלָיו הַגּוֹרָל לַה' וְעָשָׂהוּ חַטָּאת:

(י) וְהַשָּׂעִיר אֲשֶׁר עָלָה עָלָיו הַגּוֹרָל לַעֲזָאזֵל יָעֳמַד חַי לִפְנֵי ה' לְכַפֵּר עָלָיו לְשַׁלַּח אֹתוֹ לַעֲזָאזֵל הַמִּדְבָּרָה:

(יא) וְהִקְרִיב אַהֲרֹן אֶת פַּר הַחַטָּאת אֲשֶׁר לוֹ וְכִפֶּר בַּעֲדוֹ וּבְעַד בֵּיתוֹ[3] וְשָׁחַט אֶת פַּר הַחַטָּאת אֲשֶׁר לוֹ:[4]

---

[1] Since the bull is slaughtered only later (16:11), after lots have been drawn, this pasuk is interpreted to mean "כפרת דברים", atonement through confession of sin (וידוי). Here the Kohen Gadol makes confession for himself and his household and thus attains atonement for himself and his family, "וכפר בעדו ובעד ביתו".

[2] The casting of lots, הגרלה, served to designate which of the he-goats was to be consecrated to Hashem, חטאת לה', and which sent to Azazel, חטאת לעזאזל.

[3] Although the Kohen Gadol had previously confessed, that confession did not suffice. For the law required that immediately after the Viduy (סמיכה), the ox must be slaughtered, "שתיכף לסמיכה שחיטה". After the first confession, lots were cast, which constituted an interruption, and this required a second

(יב) ולקח מלא המחתה גחלי אש מעל המזבח מלפני ה' ומלא חפניו קטרת סמים דקה והביא מבית לפרכת:

(יג) ונתן את הקטרת על האש לפני ה' וכסה ענן הקטרת את הכפרת אשר על העדות ולא ימות:[5]

(יד) ולקח מדם הפר והזה באצבעו על פני הכפרת קדמה ולפני הכפרת יזה שבע פעמים מן הדם באצבעו:[6]

והביא את דמו אל מבית[7] (טו) ושחט את שעיר החטאת אשר לעם והביא את דמו אל מבית לפרכת ועשה את דמו כאשר עשה לדם הפר והזה אתו על הכפרת ולפני הכפרת:[8]

(טז) וכפר על הקדש מטמאת בני ישראל ומפשעיהם לכל חטאתם וכן יעשה לאהל מועד[9] השכן אתם בתוך טמאתם:

---

confession. This had a new dimension (חידוש), in that this confession was on behalf of his brother kohanim, שבט כהנים.

[4] The reason he cast lots before slaughtering the ox and not much earlier was because the ox and the he-goat required a parallel service. What is obligatory for the ox was also obligatory for the he-goat. In the rest of the service, the offering of the he-goat was not to precede that of the ox. Therefore we must first cast lots to determine which goat was to serve which function. Once this is decided, we can proceed with the slaughter of the ox and then the appropriate he-goat.

[5] At this point he gave the blood to another kohen, who would stir the blood in order that it not congeal. He then offered incense in the Holy of Holies, for only after the room was covered with the smoke of the incense could he enter to sprinkle the blood of the ox.

[6] He then sprinkled the blood of the Kohen Gadol's ox. This sprinkling atoned for "טומאת מקדש וקדשיו", the accidental defilement of the Holy Temple and its contents (See pasuk 16).

[7] Now he performed the service of the he-goat as he had done for the ox.

[8] Its sprinkling also atoned for accidental defilement of the Temple, "טומאת מקדש וקדשיו".

(יז) וכל אדם לא יהיה באהל מועד בבאו לכפר בקדש עד צאתו וכפר בעדו ובעד ביתו ובעד כל קהל ישראל:

(יח) ויצא אל המזבח אשר לפני ה' וכפר עליו ולקח מדם הפר ומדם השעיר ונתן על קרנות המזבח סביב:

(יט) והזה עליו מן הדם באצבעו שבע פעמים וטהרו וקדשו מטמאת בני ישראל:[10]

(כ) וכלה מכפר את הקדש ואת אהל מועד ואת המזבח והקריב את השעיר החי:

(כא) וסמך אהרן את שתי <ידו> ידיו על ראש השעיר החי והתודה עליו את כל עונת בני ישראל ואת כל פשעיהם לכל חטאתם ונתן אתם על ראש השעיר ושלח ביד איש עתי המדברה:

(כב) ונשא השעיר עליו את כל עונתם אל ארץ גזרה ושלח את השעיר במדבר:

(כג) ובא אהרן אל אהל מועד ופשט את בגדי הבד אשר לבש בבאו אל הקדש והניחם שם:

(כד) ורחץ את בשרו במים במקום קדוש ולבש את בגדיו ויצא ועשה את עלתו ואת עלת העם וכפר בעדו ובעד העם:

(כה) ואת חלב החטאת יקטיר המזבחה:

(כו) והמשלח את השעיר לעזאזל יכבס בגדיו ורחץ את בשרו במים ואחרי כן יבוא אל המחנה:

---

[9] Based on this pasuk, Chazal tell us: "As he sprinkled in the Holy of Holies, so must he also sprinkle in the Hechal."

"כשם שמזה לפני ולפנים כך מזה בהיכל. מה לפני ולפנים אחת למעלה וכו' מדם הפר, ואחת למעלה וכו' מדם השעיר, כך מזה בהיכל." -- יומא נו,ב

[10] See footnote 6.

(כז) ואת פר החטאת ואת שעיר החטאת אשר הובא את דמם לכפר בקדש יוציא אל מחוץ למחנה ושרפו באש את ערתם ואת בשרם ואת פרשם:

(כח) והשרף אתם יכבס בגדיו ורחץ את בשרו במים ואחרי כן יבוא אל המחנה:

(כט) והיתה לכם לחקת עולם בחדש השביעי בעשור לחדש תענו את נפשתיכם וכל מלאכה לא תעשו האזרח והגר הגר בתוככם:

(ל) כי ביום הזה יכפר עליכם לטהר אתכם מכל חטאתיכם לפני ה' תטהרו:

(לא) שבת שבתון היא לכם ועניתם את נפשתיכם חקת עולם:

(לב) וכפר הכהן אשר ימשח אתו ואשר ימלא את ידו לכהן תחת אביו ולבש את בגדי הקדש:

(לג) וכפר את מקדש הקדש ואת אהל מועד ואת המזבח יכפר ועל הכהנים ועל כל עם הקהל יכפר:

(לד) והיתה זאת לכם לחקת עולם לכפר על בני ישראל מכל חטאתם אחת בשנה ויעש כאשר צוה ה' את משה:

V

The three parts of the Avodah

To understand the order of the Avodah of Yom Kippur, it is possible to simplify this order by breaking it down into three parts.

1) Preparing the Kohen Gadol to receive permission, היתר, to enter the Holy of Holies. This includes steps 1 through 6, in the previously enumerated stages of the Kohen Gadol's Yom Kippur service.

2) Attaining atonement for the unintentional sin of defiling the Bais HaMikdash and its utensils, "טומאת מקדש וקדשיו". This covers steps 6 through 13.

3) Attaining atonement for all the sins of Klal Yisrael. This is step 13.

From this breakdown it would seem that the special service of the day, חובת היום, was accomplished with the second immersion, after which the Kohen Gadol was no longer required to enter the Holy of Holies and don the four linen vestments, בגדי לבן. Consequently, he would now be able to remove the ladle and the pan, כף ומחתה, and he could have concluded the remaining aspects of the service which were to be performed while wearing the golden vestments. Following this sequence, we would have only three immersions, in contradiction to the tradition, הלכה למשה מסיני, which stipulates that there must be five immersions. In order to clarify this apparent confusion, the Gemara in Yoma 32a makes the following statement:

"תנו רבנן: 'ובא אהרן אל אוהל מועד' (ויקרא טז,כג). למה הוא בא? אינו בא אלא להוציא כף ומחתה. הפרשה כולה נאמרה על הסדר חוץ

מפסוק הזה. מאי טעמא? גמירי חמש טבילות ועשרה קדושין טובל כהן גדול ומקדש בו ביום, ואי כסדרן לא משכחת לה אלא שלש טבילות וששה קדושין."

"The Rabbis taught: the verse states that Aaron came to the Tent of Meeting (Ohel Moed). What was the purpose of that entry into the Ohel Moed? The Rabbis answer: This verse was interpreted as Aaron's removal of the spoon and pan of incense from the Holy of Holies. [The verse thus is interpreted to mean that Aaron entered the Holy of Holies, removed the spoon and the pan, and following that he removed the linen garments, immersed himself and donned the golden garments for the purpose of completing what was required of the remaining service.] The entire parsha is written in a sequential order detailing the Avodah in the order it was performed, with the exception of this verse. The Rabbis deduced that it was out of sequence, otherwise there would be only three immersions and six washings, and the Rabbis had a tradition that there were five immersions and ten washings."

Thus, as we have previously explained, after the Avodah performed in the Holy of Holies was completed, it seemed that the Kohen Gadol need not enter the Holy of Holies again. Therefore, the Torah inserted the pasuk of "ובא הכהן", to inform us that he must enter and remove the spoon and the pan. If we follow the flow of the verses and the sequence of the service as quoted in ויקרא טז, it would then appear that after sending the he-goat to Azazel in the wilderness to atone for the sins of Klal Yisrael, the Kohen Gadol removed the spoon and the pan *then and there*. If so, then we would have only *three* immersions, and in order to correct this misconception, we moved this pasuk and deferred the removal of the spoon and the pan until after the Avodah performed during the third immersion, while the Kohen Gadol was wearing the golden vestments. This meant that he once more put on linen garments, immersed himself and re-entered the Holy of Holies to remove the spoon and the pan, *only after* the service of 1) שעיר הנעשה בחוץ, the he-goat offering of the Mussafim performed on the outer altar; and 2) the offering of the two rams, איל העם, ואיל של כהן גדול. This, then, would constitute the fourth immersion. Afterwards he immersed himself a fifth time and put on golden garments, in order to complete the day's service with the lighting of the Menorah and the offering of the evening incense.

V

The ingenious approach of the Gra

The Gra suggests a way of resolving the apparent discrepancy between the requirement of only three immersions (as depicted in Parashas Acharei Mos), with the spoon and the pan being removed in the second immersion; and the Oral Tradition, הלכה למשה מסיני, which requires five immersions (and the spoon and the pan were not removed at the end of חובת היום, but rather at the time of the fourth immersion).

In the Midrash Vayikra Rabba, we find that every Kohen Gadol was allowed to enter the Holy of Holies whenever he wished, providing he followed exactly the prescribed order of service as delineated in Acharei Mos. Aaron HaKohen himself was allowed to enter whenever he wished, subject to this condition. In verses 2-3 we read: "Speak to Aaron, your brother. He should not always come into the Holy... בזאת יבא... With this [specified order] shall Aaron come into the Holy, with an oxalate." Nothing in this chapter suggests that this entry took place on Yom Kippur. On the contrary, only at the very end of the chapter (verses 29-34) is it stated that this service is to be performed annually on the day of Yom Kippur, and the Kohen Gadol who *succeeded* Aaron HaKohen may perform it *only* on that occasion.

"וכפר הכהן אשר משח אותו ואשר ימלא את ידו לכהן תחת אביו...".

Thus the limitation of entering only once a year, "אחת בשנה", applied only to Aaron's descendants. They are forbidden to enter all year long, even if they follow the prescribed procedure as described here in Acharei Mos. Aaron himself had the privilege of being able to enter at any time, בכל עת, providing he followed the prescribed procedure. Consequently, if he were to follow the procedure described here in Chapter 16, he would change his clothing only three times and he would have to remove the spoon and the pan in the exact sequence described here, which would be at the time of the second immersion. The requirement of five immersions, as established by tradition, therefore applied only to the later Kohanim Gadolim who came after Aaron and served only on Yom Kippur. This is how the Vilna Gaon reconciles the apparent contradiction between the Torah account in Vayikra and the Oral Tradition.

VI

Appreciating the Gra's solution

Despite the Gra's resolution of this contradiction between the necessity for three or five immersions, yet we might not be totally satisfied with this solution. For we can still ask why the Oral Tradition required five immersions? Why not be satisfied with the Torah's account, which applies to Aaron HaKohen in Vayikra 16? But this would leave us with only three immersions, and the spoon and the pan would have to be removed in step two instead of step four.

To answer this difficulty and appreciate the greatness of the Gra's solution, we may point out the following. As we have seen, the "people's ram", "איל העם", mentioned in Vayikra 16:24 and the ram as burnt offering counted with Mussafim in Bamidbar 29:8, are one and the same. This ram had a double role: 1) It was part of the order of the regular Mussafim service. And 2) it was an integral part of the special order of the Yom Kippur day Avodah.

In addition, we have attempted to explain the sequence that was followed during the third immersion.

1) The goat offering of the Mussafim: "שעיר הנעשה בחוץ"
2) The ram of the Kohen Gadol: "איל של כהן גדול"
3) The people's ram: "איל העם"

As we have seen, the people's ram was an integral part of the service of the day, חובת היום, and it was the reason the Kohen Gadol changed into golden vestments, because this service was performed not inside the Holy of Holies, but rather outside its confines, on the outer altar. But if so, why did the he-goat offering of the Mussafim precede the offering of the people's ram? Surely it would have been more logical to first complete the required service of the day, חובת היום, that which was performed

בפנים, within the Holy of Holies, and only then to continue with the offering of the people's ram, which was part of the required service of the day, but which took place בחוץ, in the outer chamber. *Only then* we might expect to continue with the Mussafim of Yom Tov. Why interrupt the normal sequence of חובת היום?

Both the burnt offering (עולות) of the people's ram and the Kohen Gadol's ram are considered gift offerings, דורון, for the law states (see זבחים ז,ב) that the חטאת are considered sacrifices of atonement, whereas burnt offerings are considered gift offerings which accompany the preceding sin offering, והעולות דורון. Consequently, it should follow that two עולות, the people's ram, איל העם, and the Kohen Gadol's ram, איל של כהן גדול, should follow the sin offerings, חטאת, which were sacrificed in the Holy of Holies (this included the Kohen Gadol's sin offering of an ox and the he-goat for Hashem, שעיר הנעשה בפנים ופר). For this reason, the people's ram and that of the Kohen Gadol should precede the Mussaf offering, שעיר הנעשה בחוץ.

Thus it becomes apparent that we should see the שעיר הנעשה בחוץ as an integral part of the prescribed day's Avodah, חובת היום. The rationale for this is that it too contributed to completing the purification of the Temple and its utensils, טומאת מקדש וקדשיו, for it atoned for unintentional defilement, "על יש בה ידיעה בתחילה ואין בה ידיעה בסוף", "to one who did not realize that he was impure when he entered, although he was previously aware of this." The שעיר of the Mussafim atoned for this type of sin, and complemented the sin offerings which were offered within, בפנים. Since it completed the purification of the Temple and its utensils, it should follow the חובת היום and precede the two gift offerings, איל העם ואיל של כהן גדול.

With this insight in mind, we can now further appreciate the subtlety of the Gra's position. When the Kohen Gadol entered the Holy of Holies to remove the כף ומחתה, his entry was not for this purpose alone, but also to take leave of the Holy of Holies at the conclusion of the day's atonements. If during the year Aaron HaKohen would enter the Holy of Holies, he would follow the prescribed order as set down in Vayikra, chapter 16 and complete all the required atonements. The atonement was complete with the שעיר לעזאזל, and there was no need for the Mussafim, which is mentioned only in Bamidbar 29:8. And so the Torah now tells us: "ובא הכהן", to indicate that now that the service has been completed, the Kohen Gadol may enter the Holy of Holies to take leave, "פרידה", and to remove the spoon and the pan of the incense.

On the day of Yom Kippur, however, in order to complete the atonement, the Mussafim offering of שעיר הנעשה בחוץ had to be sacrificed. As well as being part of the Mussaf offering, it was also part of the חובת היום. And similarly, the people's ram and that of the Kohen Gadol also are viewed as being part of the חובת היום to be offered on the outer altar, בחוץ. Thus, it was only after the Kohen Gadol completed all these services that took place with the third immersion, that he could now once more enter the Holy of Holies in order to take leave and remove the spoon and the pan which were used in the incense offering. And this required a fourth immersion, after which he put on the linen garments. This was followed by a fifth immersion and the changing into golden vestments so that he could complete the remainder of the service, which consisted of lighting the Menorah.

VII

A question remains

Yet a problem still remains, despite the Gra's ingenious resolution of the apparent contradiction between the Parasha of Acharei Mos, which requires three immersions, and the Oral Tradition, which requires five. For although he explains that the former refers exclusively to Aaron HaKohen and the order he was to follow any time he wished to enter the Holy of Holies, yet the sprinkling of the blood of the ox and the he-goat to atone for the unintentional defiling of the Temple and its utensils was required only once a year. This is explained in the Torah in ויקרא טז,לד: "אחת בשנה". Thus the Gra still does not explain why Aaron HaKohen needed to enter the Holy of Holies for this purpose each time. Therefore, how can he say that this parasha of ויקרא טז alludes to Aaron HaKohen and his entry into the Holy of Holies during the rest of the year? In fact, based on the pasuk of "אחת בשנה", it would have been forbidden for Aaron to enter for the sake of טומאת קודש וקדשיו.

We can solve this difficulty with the following insight of the ויקרא טז,א (ד"ה בזאת), משך חכמה in his commentary to (יבא). He justifies the Gra's approach that Aaron HaKohen could enter the Holy of Holies whenever he wished. For the Torah itself tells us: "כי בענן אראה אל הכפורת", "In a cloud shall I appear". This was accomplished by burning the incense. Therefore, during the forty years that Bnai Yisrael were in the desert, the cloud hovered over the Mishkan day and night, as the pasuk testifies: "כי ענן ה' על המשכן יומם ואש תהי' לילה בו" (שמות מ,לח). This means that the Kohen Gadol could enter at any time, for the cloud constituted permission, מתיר, for him to enter. Thus when the Torah says "once a year", "אחת בשנה" at the end of this parasha, this must apply to the period after Aaron was Kohen Gadol, to subsequent Kohanim Gadolim who served in the Mishkan and in the Bais HaMikdash. Thus, only the future generations of Kohanim Gadolim were restricted from entering the Holy of Holies once a year, "והיתה זאת לכם לחוקת עולם וכו' אחת בשנה". And so this particular pasuk did not apply to Aaron Hakohen at all.

The rationale for allowing Aaron to enter at all times is, according to the משך חכמה, based on the following Chazal in זבחים ו,ב, which tells us: "שני שעירי עצרת למה באין? על טומאה שאירעה בין זה לזה."

The שעיר which is brought on the Atzeres was brought for the purpose of atonement for the impurities unintentionally caused to the מקדש וקדשיו, when one did not realize that he was impure, "אין בה לא בתחילה ולא בסוף". This was a unique situation. On the other hand, the offerings of the פר and the שעיר on Yom Kippur atoned for impurities that were recognized. At some time, the person realized that he was impure. But why, then, asks the Gemara, was there need for two he-goats? Wouldn't one have sufficed to bring about atonement? The Gemara answers that after the first he-goat was offered, there arose another situation in which the person became impure, and therefore a second he-goat sacrifice was need to attain atonement for this as well. This means that if impurity is frequent, there is a need for constant atonement. The Torah tells us that during the forty years in the desert Bnai Yisrael were not allowed to eat meat that did not come from a sacrifice. This implies that meat offered as a sacrifice was eaten often. And because Bnai Yisrael frequented the Mishkan, the chances of impurity increased. Thus Aaron HaKohen must frequently enter the Holy of Holies and atone for the sin of טומאת מקדש וקדשיו.

"כל זמן שהיו ישראל במדבר הרי הן היו אסורים בבשר תאווה והיו אוכלין בשר קודש תדיר והי' מצוי טומאת מקדש וקדשיו ביוֹתר והיו צריכים לכפרה. לכן היה נכנס בכל עת בעבודת היום לכפר טומאת מקדש וקדשיו."

This explains the logic of the Gra's approach, for because of the constant need for atonement and purification of the Temple and its utensils during this forty year period in the desert, Aaron was required to enter the Holy of Holies many times.

Based on all we have outlined here, we can now appreciate why it was necessary that a prescribed order be followed, and failure to follow this would invalidate the service. For the sequence of the sacrifices which were offered followed an intricate, designated order.

1) The first step was to allow Aaron, the Kohen Gadol, to enter the Holy of Holies in order to make confession of his own sins. For if he did not atone for his own sins, how could he seek atonement for others?

2) The second stage was to purify the Bais HaMikdash and its utensils, and he then gained entry to the inner sanctum after offering the incense, etc. in the prescribed order.

3) After he purified the Bais HaMikdash, the Kohen Gadol turned his attention to the people in order to gain atonement for them.

Thus we see how a meticulously detailed order had to be carefully followed in order to accomplish what was required. If even one step was not followed in the right sequence, this would not allow the procedure to continue to the next stage, and it would invalidate the entire service.

We can now understand why the unique order of the day, חובת היום, which was prescribed for Yom Kippur and the Mussafim, were written in separate chapters of the Torah. For as the Gra understood, the order of אחרי מות was designated for Aaron HaKohen himself to follow at all times, without the need for the Mussafim, which was only called for on Yom Kippur and was therefore addressed in a separate chapter of the Torah, in Bamidbar 28:9.

The Law of Prostrating Oneself in the Avodah

I
When do we bow down?

In the Gemara in Berachos 12a, we learn:

"אמר רבה בר חיננא סבא משמיה דרב: המתפלל כשהוא כורע, כורע ב'ברוך'. וכשהוא זוקף זוקף "בשם". אמר שמואל: מאי טעמא דרב, דכתיב (תהילים קמו), ה' זוקף כפופים."

"Rabbah ben Chinenah said in the name of Rav: In prayer when one bows, he should bow at the word 'Baruch', and when returning to an upright position, he should return at the mention of the Divine Name. Said Shmuel: What is Rav's reason for this? Because it is written: 'The Lord raiseth up those who are bowed down.'"

What we see from this is that when one mentions Hashem's name, the proper manner of doing so is to straighten oneself up to an upright position. And so, the Magen Avraham asks (in סימן קיג ס"ק ה): "It would seem from what we learn in the Gemara in Yoma 66a, that during the Avodah of the Yom Kippur service in the Bais HaMikdash whenever the people heard the awesome Name uttered by the Kohen Gadol, they would kneel and prostrate themselves. And therefore we say in the Avodah [Mussaf prayers] on Yom Kippur:

"כשהיו שומעים את השם הנכבד והנורא, מפרש יוצא מפי כהן גדול... היו כורעים ומשתחוים ומודים ונופלים על פניהם ואומרים: ברוך שם כבוד מלכותו לעולם ועד."

However, according to the Gemara in Berachos 12a they should have stood erect and not bowed.

A number of answers are offered to resolve this question.

1) The Magen Avraham (ibid.) suggests a possible answer to his own question, based on something which he himself says later on (in סימן קכז סעיף קטן ה) that one is required to straighten up after bowing down only when a beracha is being recited. Thus, we bow down when we say "ברוך אתה", but we then straighten up when we mention the name of Hashem. This is based on the verse which states: "ה' זוקף כפופים". In other instances, however, where Hashem's name is mentioned not in the context of a beracha, one need not straighten up and stand upright.

2) In the sefer "באר אברהם" (חדושים על מסכת ברכות מהג'), (רבי אברהם פאסוועלער אב"ד דק"ק ווילנא), the author distinguishes between these two quotations in the Gemara in Berachos, which deal with the issue of when to bow down and when to stand up straight during prayer. If the

one engaged in prayer recites Hashem's name, then the reader is required to be in an upright position. However, the Gemara in Yoma requires those who hear the name of Hashem being recited by the Kohen Gadol to bow down, although the Kohen Gadol himself did not bow down.

3) Others maintain that the people did not bow at the moment they heard the שם המפורש, the unique Holy Name, but rather immediately afterwards. (See the commentary of the ענף יוסף in עין יעקב, in Mesechtas Berachos, ibid.)

We might suggest that there is a difference between the name of Hashem as we pronounce it and the way the Kohen Gadol pronounced the שם המפורש composed of the seventy-two letters. For when he mentioned that name he prostrated himself and accompanied his pronounciation of the name with the declaration of "ברוך שם כבוד מלכותו לעולם ועד". This is indicated in the words we say in the Avodah service: "כשהיו שומעים את השם הנכבד והנורא...ונופלים על פניהם". This "שם הנכבד", "Glorious Name", requires that one bow down when he hears it being said. And the word "ונורא", "Awesome", calls for fear and taking the precaution of not mentioning this Awesome Name outside the confines of the Bais HaMikdash, בגבולין. (See קונטרס בענין עבודת יום הכפורים, by HaRav Yosef Dov Soloveitchik. p. 31). When the regular Name of Hashem is mentioned, however, there is no need to bow down. On the contrary, in the verse of "ה' זוקף כפופים"

one is required to be in an upright position when hearing the Name of Hashem.

II

Why Moshe bowed and the Kohen Gadol did not

The Griz HaLevi explains the pasuk in Shemos 34:8 which states: "וימהר משה ויקד ארצה וישתחו". "And Moshe hurried and bowed his head to the ground and prostrated himself."

Moshe's haste to prostrate himself was due to the requirement to bow down when hearing the שם מפורש, which was uttered here by Hashem Himself, when he revealed His nature to Moshe in the statement of the Thirteen Attributes of Mercy: "ה',ה' א-ל רחום וחנון". When Moshe heard Hashem Himself speaking to him, he quickly prostrated himself as soon as he heard the Ineffable Name. This is unlike answering "Amen" *after* one hears a beracha being recited. But this distinction might seem to refute our previous contention that the people bowed down *only after* they heard the Kohen Gadol utter the Ineffable Name of Hashem.

The Gemara in Sanhedrin 111a, however, clarifies the matter by saying that the meaning of the verse "וימהר משה

"וגו' was that Moshe quickly uttered a prayer on behalf of Bnai Yisrael when he heard Hashem speaking to him.

"וימהר משה ויקוד ארצה וישתחו', מה ראה משה? ר' חנינא בן גמליאל אמר: ראה ,ארך אפים' ורבנן אמרי ,אמת' ראה."

"And Moshe made haste and bowed his head towards the earth. What did Moshe see? R' Chanina ben Gamliel said: He saw [the attribute of Hashem Who is] slow to anger. The Rabbis say: he saw [the attribute of] truth."

From this Gemara it seems that Moshe did not bow because he heard the שם מפורש, but rather because he wanted to prostrate himself in prayer to Hashem on behalf of Bnai Yisrael.

"תורת נתנאל על התורה" The קרבן נתנאל, in his sefer reconciles these two seemingly contradictory approaches by saying that indeed Moshe prayed on behalf of Bnai Yisrael, and in his prayer he uttered the Ineffable Name, the שם המפורש. This was why he hurried to prostrate himself, to conform to the halacha which requires one to bow when hearing this name of Hashem. From this it follows that one is required to bow down upon hearing the שם מפורש, not only when someone else recites it. The one who utters it is also required to prostrate himself. But if so, why did the Kohen Gadol not bow down when he recited the שם מפורש? From the description in the Mishna it would appear that the other kohanim and the people bowed down, but the Kohen Gadol himself did not when he uttered the Ineffable Name.

To resolve this difficulty we might suggest the following. The Kohen Gadol could not be permitted to bow down, even when he recited the שם מפורש, because he recited it in his confession over the פר של כהן גדול sacrifice. It was an integral part of the Avodah service, and therefore he was forbidden to bow down, for the halacha requires, based on the pasuk of "לעמוד לשרת", "that one stand and administer" during the entire Avodah service. Thus if the Kohen Gadol were to sit or even lean, he would invalidate the service. Of course, when he finds himself within the Bais HaMikdash and he hears the שם מפורש, he is obligated to prostrate himself. But he is unable to do so, for he is in the midst of his Avodah service, and if he were to bow down now he would invalidate that service. This overriding consideration helps us resolve our apparent difficulty.

III

Bowing for confession

Some maintain, however, that the word "ומודים" here in the prayer of: "כשהיו שומעים...היו כורעים ומשתחוים ומודים"

"ונופלים על פניהם וכו'" is not to be understood to mean that when they heard the שם מפורש, they bowed in deference to that name. Rather, "ומודים" alludes to וידוי, confession. When they heard the Ineffable Name, they sensed the need to confess their sins, and therefore they bowed down, which was part of the confession process. This interpretation is confirmed by a comment of Rashi's on Pirkei Avos. He tells us: "עומדים צפופים ומשתחוים רווחים". "The people stood crowded together, yet when they prostrated themselves they had ample space." This miracle took place so that when one made his confession, he would not be embarrassed that others would hear him: "שלא ישמע איש וידוי של חבירו שלא יכלם". From here we see that the purpose of prostrating themselves was to make confession. If we accept this interpretation, we would say that the שם המפורש did not call for bowing down for the purpose of giving homage to Hashem, but rather one prostrated himself because of the requirements of confession, וידוי. If this is so, then we could easily answer the earlier question of the Magen Avraham. For if one could hear the name of Hashem, even the holy שם המפורש, in an upright position, and one had to bow when making confession, then we could say that the שם המפורש here could be considered to be integral to the process of confession. Therefore, just as confession called for prostrating oneself, so too, did the שם

המפורש, for it was included in the process of confession. This adds another perspective to the issue of prostrating oneself when hearing the שם המפורש.

The Minchah Torah Reading on Yom Kippur

I

Why do we read the Torah during Minchah?

Rav Akiva Eiger, in his sefer שו"ת רעק"א, סימן כד, raises the following questions:

1) Do we read the Torah at Minchah on the day of Yom Kippur because of the sanctity of the day, קדושת היום, as we do on Shabbos?

2) Or is the Torah reading added to the Minchah service on Yom Kippur because it is a public fast day, תענית צבור, and every public fast day has a Torah reading?

There is an essential difference between these two possibilities, with the following practical consequences:

1) If the Torah reading is the result of the holiness of the day, then even if one is not fasting, he still may be called up for an aliyah to the Torah. However, if the Torah reading was added because it is a public fast day, then only one who fasting is eligible to be called up to the Torah.

2) Another difference arises regarding how we are to chant the blessing preceding the Torah reading. If the

reading was added because of the sanctity of the day, one should chant the Bircas HaTorah in the special melody used on the Days of Awe, ימים נוראים. This is the same melody as that chanted in the morning Torah reading. However, if the reading was added because of the public fast day, then no special melody need be chanted, and we should chant the beracha as we do on every other fast day.

The חלק א, סימן יד in מרחשת addresses this question of Rav Akiva Eiger and concludes that there is a difference of opinion between the Shulchan Aruch and the Rema regarding these two possibilities. In the Shulchan Aruch, the מחבר maintains (in סימן תרכב, סעיף ב) that the concluding blessing of the Haftorah at Minchah of Yom Kippur should be: "על התורה ועל העבודה ועל יום הכפורים". He therefore maintains that the reason for the additional Torah reading at Minchah is the sanctity of the day, קדושת היום. The Rema, on the other hand, believes that we should not include the phrase "על התורה ועל העבודה", and the concluding blessing should read "מגן דוד" as on any other fast day, rather than "מקדש ישראל ויום הכפורים". Thus he attributes the Minchah Torah reading to the fact that it is a fast day, and not to the holiness of the day.

The סימן תרכב in ביאור הגר"א cites the opinion of the הגהות מרדכי in this matter:

The Commentators' Machzor Companion

"אבל קריאת התורה וההפטרה ביום הכפורים במנחה אינו אלא משום התענית כמו תענית בעלמא."

Thus, according to the opinion of the הגהות מרדכי, the Torah reading at Minchah on Yom Kippur is because of the fast, even although our text does not include the phrase "קריאת התורה", but only the word "הפטרה". In other words, the statement here reads that the Minchah Haftorah of Yom Kippur is due to the fact that today is a fast day. However, we are not told the reason for the Torah reading itself.

The Sephardic Chief Rabbi of Israel, Rav Eliyahu Bakshi Doron, נ"י, attempts to explain the rationale behind the positions outlined above, namely that of the הגר"א and of the מרחשת (See "אורייתא" לימים נוראים תשמ"ז עמ' קמא ואילך).

There are two possible approaches to explain why the Torah reading is required during the Minchah service.

1) Because it is a fast day like any other fast day of the year. We know from Mesechtas Ta'anis, that on a fast day the proper procedure, סדר היום, is that there must be a Torah reading, קריאת התורה, at Minchah, and this is an integral element in the teshuvah process. This required procedure of the day is the reason for the Torah reading at Minchah time on Yom Kippur.

2) Or we might say that the Torah reading here follows the format of the סדר העבודה, the service performed in the Bais HaMikdash by the Kohen Gadol on Yom Kippur day. Just as in the סדר העבודה, the Kohen Gadol read from the Torah at the end of the Mussaf service, so too we attempt to emulate this service by an additional Torah reading in our סדר התפלות; although for reasons given by our commentators, we do not necessarily read the same Torah portions as the Kohen Gadol read in the times of the Bais HaMikdash.

Therefore, we might reiterate that according to the text of the הגו' מרדכי, only the Haftorah is dependent on today being a fast day. The source of the Torah reading, however, is the procedure which was followed in the עבודה of Yom Kippur that required the reading of the Torah at Minchah time. The Gra, on the other hand, contends that the text includes both the קריאת התורה and the Haftorah, and that the reading is due to the requirement to follow the order of the day as a fast day, סדר היום, which includes a Torah reading at Minchah. This is why on Yom Kippur we follow this סדר היום as well.

II

The Haftorah reading

Rav Yosef Dov Soloveitchik, ז"ל, (במאסף התורני "מסורה", חוברת ז) points out that this issue of whether the Torah reading is due to קדושת היום or because it is a fast day can be resolved by the mere fact that the Torah reading is accompanied by a Haftorah. Since on Yom Kippur and on a public fast day we read the Haftorah at Minchah time; whereas on Shabbos we do not, this is a clear indication that the reason for the Torah reading is because today is a fast day. However, HaRav Soloveitchik himself dismisses this "proof" by quoting the Gemara which states that in earlier times a Haftorah was read even at the Shabbos Minchah service. It was only later that this practice was discontinued, because of certain considerations. Thus we can not draw any conclusions from the fact that no Haftorah is read at the Minchah service on Shabbos.

However, he cites another proof to show that the Haftorah reading for the day of Yom Kippur is because it is a public fast day. For on both a public fast and on Yom Kippur the Haftorah is from the Prophets; whereas when there was a Haftorah reading on Shabbos, it was from the Writings. This is sufficient proof that the Minchah reading from the Torah is the result of it being a fast day rather than because of the holiness of the day.

As we have discussed elsewhere (See *The Commentators' Gift of Torah*, pp. 86-87) the reason the Minchah Haftorah reading on Shabbos was from the Writings was because, as the Maharal explains, the Writings allude to the Messianic period, as does the time of Minchah on Shabbos, according to our tradition. This is the reason we say in the Amidah prayer, "אתה אחד ושמך אחד", for this is an allusion to the time of Ultimate Redemption. Accordingly we might say that although the Torah reading at the Yom Kippur Minchah service may be due to the קדושת היום, yet the Haftorah reading was not from the Writings, because Yom Kippur does not allude to the Messianic period; but rather the idea of this day is teshuvah, which finds its theme in the Prophets, with the Maftir of Yona. Therefore the Prophets were chosen rather than the Writings.

III

Why we chant the weekday melody

It is puzzling, though, that Rav Akiva Eiger maintains that the Torah reading on Shabbos is due to the sanctity of the day, because this seems to contradict a Gemara in Bava Kama which states that the Torah reading on Shabbos was introduced by Ezra HaSofer for the purpose of "יושבי קרנות". Rashi explains this to mean that since we are required to listen to the Torah being read on Mondays and Thursdays, there may be Jews who are extremely busy on those days and thus unable to hear this reading. Therefore, on Shabbos day, when everyone is free from work, the Torah reading was established, especially at Minchah time, which was considered the most appropriate time to make up for the Kriyas HaTorah one might have missed on Monday and Thursday. This seems to indicate that the reading from the Torah at Minchah time was not due to the holiness of the day, but rather to the convenience of the hour, as alluded to in the Gemara in Bava Kama.

How we are to chant the blessings of the Torah is not necessarily determined only by whether the reading is on account of the holiness of the day, קדושת היום, or whether it is a public fast day, תענית צבור. In the sefer "בדרך עץ חיים" (ח"ב עמ' 58) we discover the following insight which Rav Yaakov Clemens, the Rav of Moscow, once told HaGaon Rav Isser Zalman Meltzer. The Midrash, cited by Rashi in Bamidbar 11:10, explains why we chant the Bircas HaTorah at the Minchah service on Yom Kippur in the normal weekday melody rather than with the special melody reserved for the High Holidays. There we read that when Bnai Yisrael heard of the restrictions concerning family relations, they wept, as the pasuk tells us: "Moshe heard the people weeping in their family groups." *Family groups* here alludes to the laws forbidding certain family members to marry each other. Thus this parasha of "עריות", which deals with forbidden family relations which troubled Bnai Yisrael to the point of tears, does not seem appropriate to chant to the Yom Tov melody, and therefore we chant the regular weekday melody when we recite the Bircas HaTorah for this parasha, even though we read it on Yom Kippur.

In the sefer (הגיוני הלכה ח״ב (מהרב יצחק מירסקי, עמ' 67, the author quotes the "ספר מנהגי בית יעקב", which presents yet another explanation as to why we chant the regular weekday melody rather than the tearful melody of Rosh Hashanah here. The reason is that if we were also to shed tears when the parasha of עריות was being read, it would appear as if we too, along with the generation in the desert, דור המדבר, also lament the prohibitions against certain family relations. To show that this is not true, we chant a melody indicating that we are reconciled to these restrictions.

Due to of all the possible considerations we have mentioned, we can now understand that the reason we chant the melody we do when we recite the Bircas HaTorah depends on factors other than whether the reading is due to the קדושת היום or the תענית צבור.

Sounding the Shofar at the end of Yom Kippur

I

To commemorate the Jubilee Year

The Shulchan Aruch mentions that it is customary to sound the shofar at the end of the Yom Kippur prayers. There are two different opinions as to how many sounds are to be blown. The טור and the מחבר believe that we are to blow the sequence of shofar blasts known as תשר"ת, which is acronym for the following sounds: תקיעה, שברים, תרועה, תקיעה. The רמ"א, on the other hand, contends that only one shofar sound is required — a תקיעה גדולה. The Sefardim follow the custom of sounding the תשר"ת, whereas the Ashkenazim make only one shofar sound, the תקיעה גדולה.

וז"ל המחבר בשו"ע או"ח סימן תרכ"ג ס"ק ו':

"בסוף הסליחות אומרים ז' פעמים, ה' הוא האלקים' ותוקעין תשר"ת (והרמ"א כתב שם), ויש אומרים שאין לתקוע רק תקיעה אחת. וכן נוהגין במדינות אלו."

Many reasons are given for sounding the shofar at this point. The טור (in סימן תרכ"ד) and the מרדכי maintain

The Commentators' Machzor Companion   437

that the shofar is sounded here as a memorial to the Jubilee year, , as the Torah commands:

"והעברת שופר תרועה בחודש השביעי" כח:ט

" Then you shall have the teruah of the shofar go forth in the seventh month, on the tenth of the month, on the Day of Atonement, you shall have shofar blasts go forth throughout your land."

The ב"ח (ibid) explains the rationale of the טור here, in the name of the "גאון", that תשר"ת is required here, because the sounding of the shofar now serves as a memorial to the shofar of the Jubilee year. At the time, תשר"ת was sounded, and therefor it is now also sounded. The ב"ח, however, contends that this is not necessarily the case. For even though we sound the shofar as a memorial to the Jubilee year, yet all that is required now is to sound the shofar once.

וז"ל הב"ח:כ"כ המרדכי בשם גאון. וכתב ראבי"ה דנראה סברת הגאון משום דדילמא שוה יובל לתקיעות ולברכות (ר"ה כו:) מיהו נ"ל דכולי האי כתקנת ר' אבהו (שם לד.) לא עשו כן ע"כ וכן אנו נוהגין לתקוע רק תקיעה אחת..."

It seems that the Ba'alei Tosafos, at the end of the second chapter of Mesechtas Megillah (מגילה כ,ב, ד"ה כל הלילה) are also of the opinion that the shofar blasts of Yom

Kippur are a memorial to the shofar blasts of the Jubilee year.

"ואחר שבירך על הספירה אומר יהי רצון שיבנה וכו' מה שאין כן בתקיעת שופר ולולב. והיינו טעמא, לפי שאין עתה אלא הזכרה לבנין בית המקדש אבל שופר ולולב יש עשייה."

"After we finish reciting the blessing over the counting of the Omer, we recite a prayer that it should be the will of Hashem to return to us the service of the Holy Temple. However, we do not do this when we sound the shofar and take the lulav..."

The question the Ba'alei Tosafos pose here is that all three of these Mitzvos — counting the omer, sounding the shofar and taking the lulav, nowadays serve as a memorial, זכר, to what was once done in the Holy Temple. If this is so, then why do we not offer the prayer for the restoration of the Temple when we do the Mitzva, as we do when we count the Omer? Thus, to which Mitzva of shofar is Tosafos referring? If it is the shofar that is sounded on Rosh Hashanah, this was a Mitzva dictated by the Torah. How, then, are we to see it as a זכר למקדש? Therefor, we must say that the shofar alluded to here by Tosafos is that shofar which is sounded on Yom Kippur as a memorial to the shofar which announced the Jubilee year. If so, then this sounding of the shofar is a memorial to the Bais

HaMikdash, and Tosafos is justified in asking why the blessing of "יהי רצון" is not said here just as it is said when we count the Omer. (See The *Commentator's Siddur,* pp. 556-563).

The שבלי ילקט takes a similar approach, in the name of Rav Hai Gaon (סימן שכב) cited in the באר היטב (op. cit. ש"ע). The הגמ״י writes as follows:

"שמי שאומר כן טועה, דאם כן לא היה לתקוע אלא ביוה"כ עצמו בשנת היובל."

"Whosoever says that the shofar is sounded at the end of the Yom Kippur service as a memorial to the sounding of the shofar in the Jubilee year is mistaken. For if this were the reason, then it should follow that we should only sound the shofar once every fifty years, on the Yom Kippur of the actual Jubilee year, and not every year on Yom Kippur."

However, the Avudraham suggests an answer to this obvious question.

"וכתב רבינו האי בתשובת שאלה מנהג כל ישראל לתקוע במוצאי יוה"כ, ולא מצאנו טעם לומר שהוא חובה, אלא דומה שהוא זכר ליובל שנאמר בו ביוהכ"פ תעבירו שופר בכל ארצכם ולפי שאינו ברוך בחשבון שנת היובל, התקינו לתקוע בכל שנה זכר ליובל..."

"Rav Hai Gaon writes in answer to the question of the source of the custom of sounding the shofar on Yom

Kippur, that although it is not obligatory, yet it is sounded today as a memorial to the Jubilee year, when the shofar was sounded. And since we are not sure when the actual year of Jubilee occurs, our Sages instituted the practice that we sound the shofar every year."

II
Other reasons for sounding the shofar

There are a number of other reasons given by different commentators for sounding the shofar at the end of Yom Kippur prayers. (See the Bais Yosef, סימן תרכד) We will present a few of them.

The Midrash (קהלת רבה, פרק ט:ז) tells us: "At the departure of Yom Kippur a heavenly voice is heard declaring: "לך אכול בשמחה לחמך ושתה בלב טוב יינך כי כבר רצה האלקים את מעשיך" — 'Go and eat your bread in joy, and drink your wine with a good heart, for your deeds have found favor with Hashem' ".

Tosafos, in Mesechtas Shabbos 114b, ד"ה ואמאי, also characterizes the end of Yom Kippur as some kind of holiday which requires a special meal.

"וכן אמר ר"י מה שתוקעים במוצאי יוה"כ אינו אלא להודיע שהוא לילה ויאכילו את בניהם שהתענו וגם להכין סעודת מוצאי יוה"כ שהיא

The Commentators' Machzor Companion

כעין יום טוב כמו שיסד הפייטן [בפזמון של מנחה ליוה"כ], אחר גמר מיצוי אכול בדצוי ורצוי".

The reason the shofar is sounded on Yom Kippur night is to make the people aware that night has fallen and therefore those children who have fasted should be fed, and also to prepare a meal on this occasion of the departure of Yom Kippur, for it is viewed as somewhat of a Yom Tov, as the poet writes: 'After the completion of an exhaustive judgment, eat your meal with joy and satisfaction.' "

Based on these sources, the Rema in סימן תרכ"ד, ס"ק ה' writes: "ואוכלים ושמחים במוצאי יה"כ דהוי קצת יום טוב". This time is viewed as a holiday to the extent that the שערי ציון tells us (in סימן תרכ"ד ס"ק טז) that we must greet one another at this time with the same greeting as on Yom Tov itself, with a "Good Yom Tov!" (יומא טבא.)

The סמ"ג (in סימן סט, ל"ת) explains the reason why the sound of the shofar is necessary here in regards to the special meal, the סעודת מצוה. For since not everyone is aware that a festive meal is now required, we sound the shofar to call to the attention of everyone in the synagogue, that they should not forget this obligation to partake of this special meal.

III

The shofar accompanies the departing Shechinah

Another reason given for sounding the shofar just before Ma'ariv is to indicate that the Divine Presence, the Shechinah, has departed. As she rises towards heaven, the congregation recites seven times: "ה' הוא האלקים" to accompany her on her journey. This concept is based on the pasuk of: "עלה אלוקים בתרועה ה' בקול שופר". The Taz (Shulchan Aruch, ibid.) tells us that the withdrawal of the Shechinah is the "preferred reason" for sounding the shofar. A similar reason is explained for this custom of sounding a long shofar blast, תקיעה גדולה, for with this sound we announce the withdrawal of the Shechinah (סילוק השכינה). This leads Rav Yaakov Emden to raise the following question in his siddur, ח"ב דף צו, ע"א — "והאמת שאיני מבין דמה עניך סילוק שכינה לכאן וכו'". "In truth, I fail to understand what the matter of the departure of the Shechinah has to do with the completion of sounding the shofar."

And he answers, based on the pasuk of "עלה אלקים בתרועה ה' בקול שופר" — As it is well known, the name of Hashem as "אלקים" denotes the God of Judgment, whereas the name of "ה'" alludes to Hashem as God of Mercy. Thus the pasuk indicates here that with the sound of the shofar Hashem gets up from the seat of Judgment, דן, and sits on the throne of mercy, רחמים.

Other commentators say that the sounding of the shofar signals the completion of this Mitzva of shofar and the requirements to now recite the pasuk of "אשרי העם יודע תרועה".

What, then, does the departure of the Shechinah, סילוק השכינה, signal for us at the end of Yom Kippur? We might suggest a homiletical explanation, based on the following insight of the Rebbe of Kotzk. Commenting on the pasuk, "Return to your tents", (Devarim 5:27) the Rebbe remarked: After Moshe admonished the nation, he reviewed the giving of the Torah on Mount Sinai. He then relates that after that great event, Hashem instructed him to command the people of Yisrael to return to their tents.

What Hashem was telling Moshe here was the following: I want to see how they will behave in their own homes. It is true that here , at the mountain which is ablaze with a Heavenly fire, their hearts are all directed towards Heaven. But go tell them, "Return, bring this burning enthusiasm back with you to your tents. Only then will the Torah achieve permanent existence." For only if we succeed in living according to the principles of the Torah in our every day lives and in the privacy of our homes, as well as in public holy places, will the Torah last forever.

This, then, is the purpose of sounding the shofar — to allude to the departure of the Shechina, and this brings this concept to the attention of those who been in a state of kedushah, immersed in a day of prayer and fasting. With the blowing of the shofar we announce that this unique God-given holy period (מקרא קודש) is over. Now comes the true test: whether or not we have absorbed this holiness and can make it a part of our every day lives. Will we be full of enthusiasm on an ordinary day as we were on Yom Kippur? If so, then we can assume that the prayers offered on this holy day were sincere and devoid of any ulterior motives, לשמה.

Although the holy presence of the Shechinah has departed, Hashem declares: "קשה עלי פרידתכם", "It is difficult for Me to part with Bnai Yisrael". And so He afforded us another opportunity at this time to find ourselves in the presence of the Shechinah, when He gave us the Mitzva of succah. This Mitzva is referred to as "צלא דמהימנותא", "in the shadow of the faith". It is perhaps for this reason that the Rema writes, at the end of Hilchos Yom Kippur:

"והמדקדקים מתחילים מיד במוצאי יה״כ בעשיית הסוכה כדי לצאת ממצוה אל מצוה."

"Those who are particular in their attitude towards doing Mitzvos begin to construct their succah immediately after the departure of Yom Kippur." In other words, they begin that very night. Perhaps this is done to show our yearning for the Shechinah. We seize upon this opportunity to be once again in the presence of the Shechinah, by preparing ourselves to be able to sit in the succah which hosts the אושפיזין, those heavenly guests who are accompanied by the Shechinah.

IV
The shofar reminds us of Moshe on Mount Sinai

Another reason given by the commentators for sounding the shofar at the end of Yom Kippur is as a memorial to the ascent and decent of Moshe Rabbenu from Mount Sinai when he received the second set of Tablets. For Moshe ascended the mountain on Rosh Chodesh Elul and descended on Yom Kippur, and he commanded that the shofar be sounded at both times. And therefore, we now sound the shofar on מוצאי יום הכפורים as a memorial to that momentous event.

Indeed, the tenth of Tishrei is the day when Bnai Yisrael received the second set of Tablets, and therefore it was established as the Day of Atonement. The Bais HaLevi concludes that Hashem originally intended to write everything on the Tablets of the Law, and this was done on the first set of Tablets. However, after the sin of the Golden Calf, Moshe was told not to write everything on the second set of Tablets, because Hashem knew that because of this sin the nations of the world would attempt to take the Torah away from Bnai Yisrael. Had they not sinned, no nation on earth, no matter how powerful, would have been able to rule over them. Thus, even the second set of Tablets could have contained the Oral Law as well, since it would have remained safely in the possession of the Jewish people. But because they were destined to go into exile, the second set of Tablets could not contain the Oral Torah.

With this in mind, the Bais HaLevi explains the Yalkut in Parashas Ki Tissa, which discusses the special radiance which shone from Moshe Rabbenu's countenance.

"מהיכן נטל משה קרני ההוד? רב יהודה בר נחמן אמר: כשמשה כתב את התורה נשתייך בקולמוס קימעא והעבירו על ראשו ומשם נעשה לו קרני ההוד."

"Where did the radiance come from? Rav Yehudah, the son of Nachman, said that when Moshe finished writing the Torah some ink was left in his pen. Moshe then took the remaining ink and rubbed it across his forehead. This is what gave him that special radiance which illuminated his countenance."

The Bais HaLevi explains that because the Oral Law was not to be written on the second set of Tablets, Moshe had a surplus of ink. It was "extra ink" which Moshe rubbed on his forehead, and this is what gave him the "קרני ההוד", those rays of glory which shone from him. (See *The Commentator's Gift of Torah*, pp.44-47.)

Homiletically, we might say that we are not to take this literally. It was not an act of magic which produced the radiant glow, the result of Moshe rubbing physical substance on his forehead. But rather we are to understand this whole process in a metaphorical sense. Since the entire Torah and its allusions were missing from the second set of Tablets, Moshe had to strain his mind to its utmost limits in order to learn and remember the Oral Law. This effort of mind and soul which he expended in toiling in Torah study is what it meant by "rubbing the ink on his forehead". When a person puts his heart and soul into studying the Torah, the results can be seen by the radiance which shines from his face. He becomes a more spiritually refined human being, and this is what is meant by the קרני ההור which illuminated Moshe's Countenance.

We sound the shofar at the departure of Yom Kippur — the anniversary of the giving of the second set of Tablets, to remind us of this lesson. For now, after all has been said and done, we have achieved atonement and we have been cleansed of our sins. What is demanded of us now is that we spiritually refine ourselves. We can accomplish this, not through prayer alone, but by concentrating, with pure heart and soul, on the study of Torah. When we do this, then we can rest assured that the efforts we have made all month will bear fruit, beginning with our prayers from the beginning of Elul, through Rosh Hashana and the Ten Days of Repentance and culminating in that special day of fasting and prayer on Yom Kippur. When we follow this with dedication to Torah study we have fulfilled what was demanded of us on these Days of Awe, and now we can look forward to a year of commitment to Hashem, His Torah and His people.